The
Magnificent
Mountain
Women

Janet Robertson

The Magnificent Mountain Women

Adventures in
the Colorado Rockies

University of Nebraska Press

Lincoln and London

Library of Congress
Cataloging-in-
Publication Data
Robertson, Janet,
1935-
The magnificent
mountain women:
adventures in the
Colorado Rockies/
Janet Robertson.
p. cm.
Bibliography: p.
Includes index.
ISBN 0-8032-3892-4.
1. Women moun-
taineers – Colorado –
Biography.
2. Women – Colorado –
Biography.
3. Rocky Mountains –
Biography.
I. Title.
GV199.9.R63 1990
796.5'22'0922 – dc20
[B] 89-14717 CIP

Endleaves:
Snowball fight
in the Indian
Peaks, then
known as
"The Arapahos."
Photo by
Ernest Greenman,
courtesy of
Baker Armstrong

To Margaret Wenzel Sponner,

an early "magnificent woman"

who loved Colorado

and found there

the same inspiration

as in the mountains

of her native Austria

Contents

*Maps
and
Illustrations*

Following page 84

Pikes Peak; Julia Archibald Holmes; Anna Dickinson; Isabella Bird; Tahosa Valley and the surrounding mountains; Boulder school teachers on a walk near Boulder; Colorado Mountain Club members on the Narrows of Longs Peak; Skiers at Breckenridge; Enos Mills and Esther Burnell; Anne Pifer; Members of the Rocky Mountain Climbers Club on Longs Peak; Ermin Sweeney Greenman; Eleanor Davis Ehrman; The Crestone Peak and Crestone Needle; Marjorie Perry; The Moffat Railroad at Rollins Pass; Harriet Vaille Bouck; Enos Mills, and several Aarapahos at Longs Peak Inn; Agnes Vaille; The Timberline Cabin on Longs Peak; Longs Peak; The rock shelter on Longs Peak built in memory of Agnes Vaille; The "Boulderfield Hotel"; Dorothy Collier; "Tiny" Collier Virginia Donaghe McClurg; Mesa Verde's Cliff Place; Doc Susie; Annie and Kitty Harbison; Katherine Garetson; Annie Shreve and Katherine Garetson; Grays Peak; Alice Eastwood; Hazel Schmoll; Ruth Ashton; Rock cabins on Trail Ridge Road; Katherine Bell; Emily Dixon Elizabeth Cowles; The Wednesday Ladies of Boulder skiing in Rocky Mountain National Park; Louise Shepherd and Jean Ruwitch; Coral Bowman; Gudrun Gaskill; Beatrice Willard; Estella Leopold; Forrest Ketchin; Elizabeth Nitze; Martha Maxwell; Helen Henderson Chain; Mount of the Holy Cross; Anne Ellis; Muriel Sibell Wolle; Belle Turnbull; Helen Rich; Alice and Helen Dickerson; Pack train in the mountains; Stanley Steamer; Helen Dowe; Muriel MacGregor

Foreword

The Magnificent Mountain Women: Adventures in the Colorado Rockies is an important historical documentation of the special and vital role women played in building a vigorous state of Colorado.

It is particularly fitting that this book be dedicated to Margaret Wenzel Sponner, the mother of Colorado House Minority Leader Ruth Wright of Boulder. Mrs. Sponner instilled in her daughter a great love and respect for Colorado's high country and a willingness to devote her time and energy to preserving our environmental heritage.

The Magnificent Mountain Women: Adventures in the Colorado Rockies will take its place among the valued histories of the state. It records a piece of history related to the efforts and accomplishments of citizens whose work and perseverance have enhanced our knowledge of and access to the high country.

Roy Romer
Governor of Colorado

Preface

The Magnificent Mountain Women: Adventure in the Colorado Rockies chronicles the exploits of several dozen women—historical and contemporary—who have sought out experiences in some of the most rugged country in America—the mountains of Colorado. The book's underlying theme is how this harsh land affected these women and how they in turn have enriched our appreciation of the mountains by their writing, their work, and their example.

Until I began my research for the book, I had assumed that, with luck, I would turn up as many as a dozen pre-1940 mountain women. Certainly the topographic maps of the Colorado Rockies gave no hint that I might find more. Most of the geographic features named for people are named for men and, in nearly all these cases, use the surname, as in Longs Peak, Joe Mills Mountain, Bierstadt Lake, Sprague Glacier, and Potts Puddle. Those features named for women—and there aren't very many—use the first name, making the identity of the honored lady ambiguous or even impossible to trace, as in Mount Silverheels (named for a legendary dancehall girl), Lake Irene, Alberta Falls, Isabelle Glacier, Mount Alice, and Mount Big Bertha. There are exceptions, but they're pitifully few. One that comes to mind is Mount Dickinson, a prominence in Rocky Mountain National Park so named under the mistaken impression that Anna Dickinson was the first woman to climb Longs Peak.

I was surprised when archives yielded over three dozen pre-1940 ladies who fit my criterion of mountain women: those who deliberately pursued mountain encounters rather than merely being passive observers forced to deal with the Colorado mountains because of circumstances beyond their control. In other words, they sought out the Colorado mountains in their own right, not just as the wives and daughters of men. Once I realized I had the makings of a full-length book, I was faced with the problem of how to refer to my subjects—Miss, Ms., or by surname. In the end I decided against all of the above, instead using my subjects' first names. Since I resuscitated many of them from obscurity and since I'm intrigued and delighted with each and every one, it felt right to address them as friends. Occasionally I refer to a subject by her full name, which is tricky if the woman had married and adopted her husband's surname. In such cases I try to use the surname appropriate to the time period.

Sadly, I was forced to omit the Native American mountain women from this book because I couldn't find detailed accounts of their lives. We don't know if they climbed mountains while searching for edible plants, for example, although it seems likely that they did. And though it also seems likely that climbing Longs Peak to trap eagles was strictly a man's pursuit, again, frustratingly, we simply don't know. Surely the Native American women who walked high ridges, exposing themselves to human enemies, grizzly bears, rockfalls, and the violent whims of weather, must have had some appalling experiences. Yet they must have had some extraordinarily beautiful ones, too. Unfortunately, we can only speculate as to what they were. The game-drive walls and arrowheads that they left behind inspire us to imagine what they saw and felt, but we'll never know for sure.

As we shall see, however, from early on, the women that we do know about took a simple, basic pleasure in Colorado's high country. They were curious about the view from the top. The first known mountain woman, Julia Archibald Holmes, who came west with a party of Kansas gold seekers, climbed Pikes Peak in 1858, thus starting a tradition of women playing in the Rockies. She also set a tradition—which wasn't broken for over a century—of women doing their serious mountain recreation *with men*. Not until the 1970s did women begin assaulting state-of-the art rock climbs manless. I have singled out only a few of Colorado's pioneer female contemporary climbers, mostly to provide a counterpoint to their predecessors. Had space permitted, I would have included others, such as the Annapurna climber Vera Komarkova, Everest expedition members Barbara

Roach and Sue Giller, and the late Katherine Freer, regarded by many as one of the finest female climbers in the world until her death on the Hummingbird Ridge of Canada's Mount Logan in 1987.

Although the recreationists dominate this book by their sheer number, in truth many Colorado mountain women had no interest whatever in hiking, climbing, or skiing. Virginia Donaghe McClurg, for example, hauled her rather large self up the steep mesas of southwest Colorado not because she enjoyed physical activity but because she was ignited by a Messianic zeal to preserve prehistoric cliff dwellings. And Susan Anderson discovered that the mountains were a refuge from the prejudice against female physicians that had confronted her in Greeley and Denver, on the plains. For Katherine Garetson also, the mountains were a refuge; they offered an opportunity to strike out on her own, to escape the role of the maiden aunt who lived with her sister's family in the city.

Perhaps the epitome of Colorado mountain women were the botanists, who regarded the outdoors as a vast laboratory. Yet, clearly their interest in the mountains was far more than professional. Alice Eastwood, Hazel Schmoll, Ruth Ashton Nelson, and Katherine Bell Hunter all went to the mountains for fun and relaxation even when they weren't collecting plants.

Most of the early mountain women depended on men to assist them. Julia Holmes, an unabashed "women's righter," would never have climbed Pikes Peak without her husband and a male guide. Isabella Bird would never have attained the summit of Longs Peak if Rocky Mountain Jim hadn't hauled her up like a "bale of goods." The plucky female home-steaders could never have passed the first legal requirement of living on their land had they not hired men to build their cabins. Despite their dependence on men, however, these same women had at least one decision to make that was theirs alone: should they wear long skirts, which were often impractical, or should they risk public censure by wearing pants?

Some, like Rose Pender, didn't attempt to go against the prevailing fashion. In 1883 she rode and hiked up Pikes Peak in a long chintz skirt and, one imagines, it didn't occur to her to wear anything else. The Harbison sisters, too, always wore skirts, though the hems dragged in the manure when they tended their dairy cows. However, other women thought it was worth a fuss to modify their attire. When Julia Holmes trekked across the prairie in 1858, she wore bloomers, the official uniform of suffragists. Furthermore, she refused to switch to a long skirt even after the only other woman in her party said that the men "talked so much" about her. In 1873 Anna Dickinson, who habitually wore skirts, purchased a pair of trousers specifically for her climb of Longs Peak, incurring the derision of a local newspaper editor. A few weeks later Isabella Bird climbed Longs Peak wearing a "Hawaiian riding costume." She was mortified—and furious—when a newspaperman from London referred to her attire as "men's habiliments."

Julia, Anna, and Isabella seemed well able to cope with insults. They, and the other subjects in this book, were confident enough to accept the consequences of their unconventional behavior and stubborn enough to meet the mountains on at least something of their own terms. Most were single, or if married were childless, at the time of their mountain encounters. Most were exceptionally well educated for their time. Most came from cities and, in many cases that we know about, were close to their fathers. Yet their shared characteristic is that they *initiated their mountain experiences* and related to the mountains in ways that should be remembered. For the sad truth is that most of the women in this book are unknown or by now forgotten. I think it is an undeserved fate for such magnificent women. It's time to set the record straight.

Acknowledgments

This book would never have been written without Ruth Wright and the Colorado Mountain Club Foundation and their encouragement in the form of a grant and kind words. *The Magnificent Mountain Women: Adventures in the Colorado Rockies* honors Ruth's mother, Margaret Wenzel Sponner, a magnificent woman in her own right, who grew up on an estate in the Austro-Hungarian Empire before the First World War. She was one of the first women to fly in an open-cockpit fighter plane, taking off from and landing in a nearby agricultural field. In addition, she took up ski touring, which was just emerging as a sport. Accompanied by her young friends, she traveled by train and primitive skis to high mountain huts.

Later, during World War I, Margaret became an X-ray technician and served in a Viennese army hospital. It was here that she met her husband, Dr. Robert Sponner, a surgeon in the Austrian Medical Corps. During the Roaring Twenties they emigrated to America, where Margaret bore two daughters. Rosemarie Sponner Sand, who lives in White Plains, New York, became a talented flier. Ruth Sponner Wright, who lives in Boulder, Colorado, became an avid skier and mountaineer, serving as a National Ski Patrolman and chair of the Boulder group of the Colorado Mountain Club. She is now in her second term as Minority Leader of the House of Representatives in the Colorado legislature, where she is a leading environmentalist.

Ruth was infinitely patient with me, for the research and writing of this book took much longer than either of us had anticipated. She heads the long list of people who have helped me. Before I undertook this project, I had assumed that most of the effort involved would be my own. By the time I finished, I realized what a naive notion that was.

Immediately it became apparent that I was absolutely dependent on librarians and photo archivists. Had it not been for them, I would have been stopped dead in my tracks before I started. They helped me locate materials and called my attention to useful sources I'd never heard of. Equally important, they threaded microfilm viewers for me (never once hinting that I was a mechanical dolt).

After perusing archives in such places as San Francisco, Hot Sulphur Springs, Leadville, and Denver, I became keenly aware of how much I owed to people I would never meet: those heirs who chose not to burn old scrapbooks, letters, and photographs but rather to donate them to the local museum or library; those volunteers (and almost without fail they were volunteers) who taped interviews of some of the subjects in this book and who made transcripts of those tapes; those photographers, amateur and professional, who understood the importance of writing down the names of their subjects, the locale, and the year in which the picture was taken.

After I'd exhausted institutional resources, I realized that the only way I was going to find out many needed details was by tracking down people who had known my subjects or who were my subjects. The ones I reached were wonderfully courteous and patient. But they offered so much more than information—often they served me hot drinks and even lunch, as well as good conversation.

Every writer dreams of quoting unpublished manuscripts. I was able to quote more than my share through the permission of the following: Eleanor Bliss, Elizabeth Dings, Laurie and Ken Houde, Elinor Eppich Kingery, General Earle Partridge, and Betty Schmutzler. In addition, many people granted me permission to quote from letters they'd written me. Others agreed to my using little-known photographs in their possession. I am grateful to them all.

Dozens of men and women read portions of the manuscript, correcting an embarrassing number of errors. (I fear that the ones remaining are my very own.) Maxine Benson and James H. Pickering offered invaluable criticisms of the entire manuscript. Kathi George, Nora Quinlan, and P. C. Gottlieb gave me encouragement during those crucial early stages when I didn't know if I would really end up with a book. Finally, my husband, David, who has led me up many a mountain, often interrupted his own work to guide me through the jungles of WordPerfect. Without his help, I never would have seen this book through to the final draft.

So, although I'm listed as the author of this book, I've been supported by a cast of hundreds.

Chronology of Colorado Mountain Women

1858	Julia Archibald Holmes climbs Pikes Peak.
1871	Addie Alexander climbs Longs Peak.
1873	Anna Dickinson climbs Longs Peak.
1873	Isabella Bird climbs Longs Peak.
1882	Virginia Donaghe becomes the first non-Indian woman to visit the ruins at Mesa Verde.
1883	Rose Pender climbs Pikes Peak.
1884	Carrie Welton dies on Longs Peak.
1887	Alice Eastwood escorts Dr. Alfred Russel Wallace up Grays Peak.
1892	Alice Eastwood and Al Wetherill collect plants in Montezuma Canyon, Utah.
1896	Kitty and Annie Harbison homestead near Grand Lake.
1906	Victoria Broughm climbs Longs Peak solo.
1906	Lucy Peabody's efforts culminate in the creation of Mesa Verde National Park.
1907	Dr. Susan Anderson (Doc Susie) arrives in Fraser.
1913	Marjorie Perry brings Carl Howelsen to Steamboat Springs.
1914	Harriet Vaille arranges for Arapaho Indians to visit the proposed Rocky Mountain National Park.
1914	Katherine Garetson files a claim on a homestead near Longs Peak Inn.
1915	The Ladies Hiking Club of Fraser is formed.
1916	Eleanor Davis is a member of the first party to climb the Crestone Peaks.
1916	Esther Burnell files a claim on a homestead near Estes Park.
1920	At about this time, Elizabeth Burnell becomes a Longs Peak guide.
1921	Hazel Schmoll becomes state botanist for Colorado.

1922   At about this time Anne and Isabel Pifer begin leading hikes for the YMCA, including climbs of Longs Peak.

1923   Eleanor Davis becomes the first Colorado female member of the American Alpine Club.

1925   Agnes Vaille is a member of the first party to climb the East Face of Longs Peak in winter but dies in the attempt.

1928   Marjorie Perry makes her last four-hundred-mile ride from Denver to Steamboat Springs and back.

1931   Dorothy Collier is a member of the first party to climb the East Face of Longs Peak at night.

1933   Ruth Ashton's book *Plants of Rocky Mountain National Park*, the first description of plants in the park, is published by the U.S. government.

1941   Betsy Cowles makes first ascents on a trip she organized to climb the Santa Marta Range in Colombia.

1946   Marianne Stevenson Magnuson and Betty Wollsey ski on Gannett Peak, becoming the first people to ski on glaciers in the Wind River Range of Wyoming.

1950   Betsy Cowles is a member of the first party of Westerners to reconnoiter Mount Everest from the Nepalese approach.

1955   Ruth Ewald becomes Rocky Mountain National Park's first female naturalist in uniform.

1956   Dr. Susan Anderson stops practicing medicine in Fraser.

1957   Inestine Roberts climbs Pikes Peak for the last time, at age eighty-seven.

1971   Katherine Bell and Emily Dixon spend the winter living above timberline in Rocky Mountain National Park, doing botanical research.

1972   The Wednesday (née Thursday) Ladies hiking and skiing group of Boulder is formed.

1975   Molly Higgins, Stephanie Atwood, and Laurie Manson become the first all-women team to climb the Diamond of Longs Peak.

1980   Jean Ruwitch and Louise Shepherd become the first all-women team to make a free climb of the Diamond of Longs Peak.

1981   Coral Bowman founds Great Herizons, the first technical climbing school for women in Colorado, if not in the United States.

1983   Coral Bowman portrays Isabella Bird in filmed climbing sequences on Longs Peak.

1988   Gudy Gaskill culminates fifteen years of effort with the dedication of the 470-mile-long Colorado Trail.

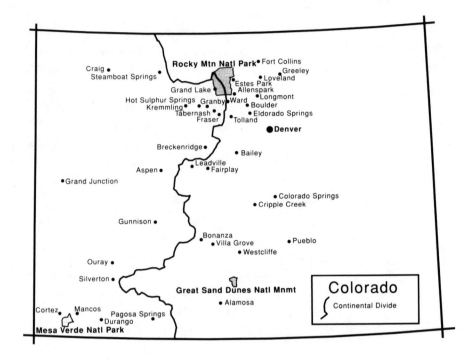

Craig •
Steamboat Springs •

Rocky Mtn Natl Park • Fort Collins
• Greeley
• Loveland
Grand Lake • Estes Park
• Allenspark
Hot Sulphur Springs • • Longmont
Kremmling • Granby • Ward • Boulder
Tabernash • • Eldorado Springs
Fraser • Tolland

● **Denver**

Breckenridge •
• Bailey
• Leadville
Aspen • • Fairplay

• Grand Junction

• Colorado Springs
• Cripple Creek

Gunnison •

Bonanza •
• Villa Grove
• Westcliffe
• Pueblo

Ouray •

Silverton •

Great Sand Dunes Natl Mnmt
• Alamosa

Cortez • Mancos •
Pagosa Springs •
• Durango
Mesa Verde Natl Park

Colorado

Continental Divide

Colorado map by David Robertson.

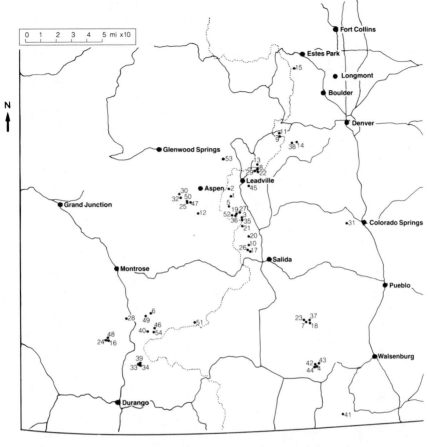

1 Mount Elbert	19 Mount Belford	37 Humboldt Peak
2 Mount Massive	20 Mount Princeton	38 Mount Bierstadt
3 Mount Harvard	21 Mount Yale	39 Sunlight Peak
4 Blanca Peak	22 Mount Bross	40 Handies Peak
5 La Plata Peak	23 Kit Carson Peak	41 Culebra Peak
6 Uncompahgre Peak	24 El Diente Peak	42 Ellingwood Peak
7 Crestone Peak	25 Maroon Peak	43 Mount Lindsey
8 Mount Lincoln	26 Tabeguache Mountain	44 Little Bear Peak
9 Grays Peak	27 Mount Oxford	45 Mount Sherman
10 Mount Antero	28 Mount Sneffels	46 Redcloud Peak
11 Torreys Peak	29 Mount Democrat	47 Pyramid Peak
12 Castle Peak	30 Capitol Peak	48 Wilson Peak
13 Quandary Peak	31 Pikes Peak	49 Wetterhorn Peak
14 Mount Evans	32 Snowmass Mountain	50 North Maroon Peak
15 Longs Peak	33 Mount Eolus	51 San Luis Peak
16 Mount Wilson	34 Windom Peak	52 Huron Peak
17 Mount Shavano	35 Mount Columbia	53 Mount of the Holy Cross
18 Crestone Needle	36 Missouri Mountain	54 Sunshine Peak

Colorado's fourteeners—peaks above 14,000 feet.

1

The First Female Mountain Climbers, 1858–1906

It is ironic that Colorado, which contains some of America's most challenging mountains, remained unknown to sports enthusiasts from the rest of the country for so many years. However, it is not surprising that women outdoor recreationists of the 1800s and early 1900s, except for cyclists, were few and far between in Colorado; they hardly existed elsewhere—in the United States or Europe.

For more than a century after the sport of mountaineering was born (generally regarded as occurring in 1786, when Europe's highest mountain, Mont Blanc, was first conquered), getting to the top of difficult peaks was almost exclusively a male pastime. Early on, the British dominated the climbing world, although they largely ignored their home terrain and instead concentrated on the Continent, hiring local guides. In 1857 the world's premiere organization for mountain climbers was founded, with headquarters in London. It was called the Alpine Club—not the *British Alpine Club*—and was for men only. However, the Alpine Club's misogyny was not justified, at least on the basis of ability. During the 1800s a handful of women, moneyed and often titled, did in fact make respectable ascents in the Alps, especially during winter months. (Typically they climbed in skirts, but the more daring switched to riding breeches after they'd passed the last chalets.) The first American female climber of note was Meta Brevoort, who scaled the heights in the 1870s, accompanied by her nephew and a guide.

Early mountaineering in both the Alps and the Colorado Rockies shared one trait: the object was simply to reach the top by the easiest route possible. In 1806 Zebulon Pike attempted to climb the mountain that now bears his name, thus becoming the first person known to have tried to scale any Colorado peak. However, he misjudged the distance to its approach and gave up, commenting with a pronouncement typical of thwarted mountaineers that he didn't believe any human being "could have ascended its pinacal."[1] He was wrong. In 1820 members of a government exploration party headed by Major Stephen Long found the ascent of Pikes Peak to be relatively easy. Their achievement was touted as the first successful ascent by white men of a major mountain in the American West. No more recorded ascents took place until 1858, when two separate parties of gold seekers from Lawrence, Kansas, made the summit. The second included a woman, Julia Archibald Holmes.

JULIA ARCHIBALD HOLMES

It is unlikely that Julia Archibald Holmes was aware of the female mountain climbers in Europe, but whether or not they served as an example to her is academic; her climb was extraordinary. She was living in an era when women were physically—and psychologically—restricted by long skirts and corsets. As one physician lamented in 1889, "The active sports that make the brothers healthy and strong are not permitted the sisters, and yet without good reason."[2] However, Julia rejected the socially acceptable fashions of her time. She wore bloomers. And as we shall see, many other mountain-climbing females in Colorado who followed her dared to break the female dress code as well.

When Julia made her memorable ascent, she was a twenty-year-old bride who came from strong-minded stock. Born in Noel, Nova Scotia, on February 15, 1838, she was the second of eight children. By the age of ten, she had moved with her family to Worcester, Massachusetts. However, her father, John Archibald, was such a staunch opponent of slavery that a few years later he took his family to Kansas to help make it a Free State. Her mother, Jane, supported women's rights; she was a friend of the suffragist Susan B. Anthony, whose brothers were pioneers in Kansas. The Archibald house in Lawrence was a frequent gathering place for abolitionist meetings and was part of the Underground Railroad, which hid runaway slaves.

In 1857 Julia married James Holmes, a New Yorker turned Kansan. He was one of John Brown's men and a hero in some of the violent skirmishes between Free Staters and proslavery Missourians. For a few months the young couple lived on the Neosho River near Emporia. However, in the spring of 1858, when they heard that a group from Lawrence was going to look for gold near Pikes Peak, they decided to go too. The Holmeses and Julia's eighteen-year-old brother, Albert, joined a wagon train of several dozen people. For the trip, Julia donned an "American Costume," or bloomers, the official uniform of suffragists in the 1850s. Her full attire consisted of a calico dress that reached a little below her knees, calico pants, Indian moccasins, and a hat. Julia commented, "However much it lacked in taste, I found it gave me freedom to roam at pleasure in search of flowers and other curiosities, while the cattle continued their slow and measured pace."[3]

There was one other woman on the trip, who confined herself to the hot covered wagon, criticizing Julia for not wearing a dress. Julia pitied her and rejoiced that she was "independent of such [conventional] views of propriety, and felt that I possessed an ownership in all that was good or beautiful in nature, and an interest in any curiosities we might find on the journey as much as if I had been one of the favored lords of creation."

"I commenced the journey," Julia wrote, "with a firm determination to learn to walk. At first I could not walk over three or four miles without feeling quite weary, but by persevering and walking as far as I could every day, my capacity increased gradually, and in the course of a few weeks I could walk ten miles in the most sultry weather without being exhausted. Believing, as I do, in the right of woman to equal privileges with man, I think that when it is in our power we should, in order to promote our own independence, at least, be willing to share the hardships which commonly fall to the lot of man." Accordingly, Julia requested that she be allowed to help guard the camp at night on her husband's watch. The guard master, a "gentleman formerly from Virginia," turned her down. "He believes that woman is an angel (without any sense,)" Julia commented, "needing the legislation of her brothers to keep her in her place; that restraint removed, she would immediately usurp his position, and then not only be no longer an angel but unwomanly."

Julia wrote that the "waving prairie . . . with the blue sky overhead, [and] the endless variety of flowers underfoot" made her heart "leap for joy." On July 4, the party had its first glimpse of Pikes Peak. "As all expected to find precious treasure near this wonderful Peak, it is not strange that our eyes were often strained by gazing on it," Julia recorded. "The summit appeared majestic in the distance, crowned with glistening white." Four days later, the party camped by the Boiling-Spring River (Fountain Creek) near present-day Colorado Springs, seventy miles south of Denver and as close to the mountains as possible. They remained there for a month. Very likely the "disgusting inactivity and monotony of camp life" inspired Julia to attempt a climb of Pikes Peak.

On July 9 three men left the Lawrence party for what turned out to be a successful climb of Pikes Peak. A few weeks later, one man of that party, J. C. Miller, agreed to accompany James and Julia Holmes and George Peck to the top of the mountain. Miller later wrote that Mrs. Holmes showed her good sense in wearing bloomers for the climb, since there was no trail and the route went through rocks and brush.

On August 1, after an early breakfast, the Holmes party set out. Considering that they were carrying six days' worth of provisions, their packs were light; Julia's weighed seventeen pounds and James's thirty-five. Between them they carried nineteen pounds of bread, six quilts, clothing, one pound of hog meat, three fourths of a pound of coffee, one pound of sugar, a tin plate, a knife, a fork, a half-gallon canteen, a half-gallon tin pan, a tin pint cup, writing materials, and a volume of Emerson's *Essays*.

It was rough going. They misjudged the route and struggled up—and around—steep slopes. Their throats became parched because they'd neglected to fill their canteens. Finally, spying a stream at the bottom of a deep canyon, they descended and set up camp. Julia wrote in her journal:

It is now ten o'clock in the evening, and I am reclining before some blazing pine logs beside a torrent in a mountain canyon several hundred feet deep. The straight, slender, tapering pines that stand around so beautiful in their death, smooth, white and sound, having been stripped of their bark by fire, calmly point to a sky more serene, and to stars far brighter than usual. The trees and the sky almost seem to strive together in preserving a deeper silence. But there is music from the foaming stream, sounds from a dozen little cascades near and far blend together—a thundering sound, a rushing sound, a rippling sound, and tinkling sounds there are; and a thousand shades of sound to fill up between them. The burning pine crackles and snaps, showering sparks, cinders and even coals around and all over the sheet I am writing on, as if to mock the tame thoughts they light me to write.

The following morning they climbed up in a snow squall to a high camp, which they named Snowdell. For several days they camped there, exploring country so rugged that at one point they took off their moccasins so that they could use the toes and balls of their feet "in clinging to the asperities of the sidling rock." Julia made light of the hardships.

We have given this name to a little nook we are making our home in for a few days. It is situated about four or five rods above the highest spring which gushes from the side of the Peak. On the cold moss overhung by two huge rocks, forming a right angle, we have made a nest of spruce twigs. Some smaller rocks form, with the larger ones just mentioned, a trough about three feet wide, and ten feet long. At the outlet of this narrow space we have built a chimney. When we lie down the fire is burning but a yard from our feet, while we can stretch our hands over the smaller rocks into a large bank of snow. This we call our home. . . . The beauty of this great picture is beyond my powers of description. Down at the base of the mountain the corral of fifteen wagons, and as many tents, scattered around it, form a white speck, which we can occasionally distinguish.

Early on the morning of August 5, the party left Snowdell to try for the summit, taking with them only "writing materials and Emerson." They deviated from the most direct route to push large boulders off the edge of what they had named Amphitheater Canyon, listening to the "crashing, thundering sound from the hidden depths below, which seemed to continue until lost in the distant lower region." Soon they tired of the sport and continued up the rocks, some so steep that they "found much difficulty in clambering up them." Julia discovered "a green tuft about the size of a teacup from which sprung dozens of tiny blue flowers most bewitchingly beautiful." Almost certainly, these were alpine forget-me-nots.

They reached the top, which offered a less extensive view than they had hoped for because of clouds and snow flurries. Although Julia wrote that they were now nearly 14,000 feet above sea level, they were in fact at an elevation of 14,110 feet. The members of the party left their names on a large rock and then wrote letters to friends, "using a broad flat rock for a writing desk." As a final gesture before starting down, Julia read aloud some lines from Emerson's poem "Friendship":

A ruddy drop of manly blood,
    The surging sea outweighs;
The world uncertain comes and goes
    The looser rooted stays.

By the time they reached Snowdell, it was snowing hard. They retrieved their packs and set up a comfortable camp much farther down. The next day they arrived at the Lawrence camp. Julia was obviously proud of having climbed Pikes Peak, for she wrote her mother:

I have accomplished the task which I marked out for myself and now I feel amply repaid for all my toil and fatigue. Nearly every one tried to discourage me from attempting it, but I believed that I should succeed; and now, here I am, and I feel that I would not have missed this glorious sight for anything at all. In all probability I am the first woman who has ever stood upon the summit of this mountain and gazed upon this wondrous scene, which my eyes now behold.[4]

A few days later the Lawrence party split up, some members returning to Kansas while others remained in what became Colorado. The Holmes party made its way to Taos, New Mexico, eventually continuing south to Santa Fe. James Holmes succeeded Miguel Otero as secretary of the Territory of New Mexico. Julia, who was proficient in Spanish, served as a correspondent for the *New York Tribune*.

She gave birth to four children, only two of whom survived to adulthood. In 1870 the Holmes family moved to Washington, D.C., and shortly afterward Julia divorced James. She remained in Washington, where local newspapers referred to her as a poet. Following her mother's example, she became active in the women's suffrage movement. Julia held several government jobs and for several years was chief of the Division of Spanish Correspondence in the Bureau of Education. She died in January 1887. Apparently, Pikes Peak was the only mountain Julia Archibald Holmes ever climbed, but it was enough to earn her a place in Colorado's record books. Thirteen years passed before any other woman was known to have climbed a Colorado mountain—Longs Peak.

Longs Peak, named for Major Stephen Long, was a much tougher climb than Pikes. After an unsuccessful attempt of Longs in 1864, William Byers, the mountain-climbing editor of the *Rocky Mountain News*, wrote that its elusive summit "still towered hundreds of feet above our heads presenting sheer precipitous sides, and a smooth rounded summit upon which it looked as though a man must be tied to remain, if ever by any miracle he could reach it."[5] In 1868 a party that included William Byers did in fact reach the top. Three years later Addie Alexander became the first female known to have stood on Longs' flat summit, which is about the size of a football field.

ADDIE ALEXANDER

Unlike Julia Holmes, Addie Alexander left no written account of her ascent. As a result, for more than a century the feat has been buried in old newspaper accounts. In 1914 Enos Mills, who worked tirelessly for the establishment of Rocky Mountain National Park, further muddled Addie's role: he proposed, successfully, that a mountain in the future park be named Mount Dickinson to honor Longs Peak's supposed first lady. Enos had the right idea, but the wrong woman.

Anna Dickinson was definitely not the first woman to climb Longs Peak, as evidenced by the August 26, 1871, issue of the *Boulder County News*, which stated, "Al Dunbar from Estes Park, last week piloted a party to the summit of Long's Peak, among whom were Misses Alexander and Goss of St. Louis, the first ladies who ever made the ascension."⁶ Two years later a Mr. Painter of the *Greeley* [Colorado] *Sun*, describing his climb of Longs Peak, noted that there were four piles of rocks left by previous climbers as monuments to their "ascensions." Then, under the heading "Well-Muscled Females," he wrote, "The names of two ladies—Addie Alexander and Henrietta Goss—are recorded in one of the monuments as having ascended, but parties who have every opportunity of knowing state emphatically that only one of them accomplished the feat, while the other gave up in despair within a few hundred feet of the summit."⁷

Although Painter did not mention which of the two ladies did make the top, an anonymous reporter for the *Rocky Mountain News* also wrote a story about Mr. Painter's climb, stating: "There are also the records of two ladies, only one of whom—Addie Alexander—made the summit. Henrietta Goss' name is on the summit, but she failed to reach the top when only a few hundred feet from the desired goal. Both these women deserve praise for their muscle and their perseverance."⁸

These newspaper accounts are virtually all that is known about Addie Alexander. It seems possible that she and Henrietta Goss came to Colorado as part of the St. Louis–Western Colony, near Greeley, a town fifty-five miles north of Denver, formed in 1871, but this is only speculation. Perhaps she wouldn't have sunk into such obscurity had not one of the most famous women in America, Anna Dickinson, ascended Longs Peak two years later, in 1873, accompanied by the Hayden survey and a deluge of publicity. Ironically, we now know that Anna was not even the second woman to climb Longs. A few weeks after Addie Alexander's climb, the *Boulder County News* reported that a Miss Bartlett had made the top.

ANNA DICKINSON

It does seem appropriate, however, that a Colorado mountain is named for Anna Dickinson, even though its gentle, lackluster summit falls far short of conveying her character. In the summer of 1873, when Anna Dickinson arrived for her third visit to Colorado, one newspaper called her "the spice, the pepper and the brains of the woman's movement." Another commented, "It is Anna's misfortune to have been born pretty and fascinating and all that, just as everybody must admit it is Susan B. Anthony's misfortune to have been born minus either of the above faults."[9]

Anna Dickinson was thirty years old and a gifted, opinionated speaker known as the "Queen of the Lyceum." However, during the presidential election of 1872 she had committed a political gaffe; she had attacked the leader of her own party, President Ulysses S. Grant, and had instead supported Horace Greeley, publisher and editor of the *New York Tribune*. After Greeley lost the election, Anna's marketability withered. To add to her troubles, the popularity of lectures as entertainment began waning. She became depressed.

When an old beau, Ralph Meeker, invited her out to Colorado, she eagerly scraped together money for the trip, although she regarded Ralph's ardor as "amusing" and once referred to his "queer, enthusiastic" presence. On August 16, 1873, Anna, properly chaperoned by her brother, John, a clergyman, arrived in Denver. For the next three weeks, she rode mules or horses to the summits of some of Colorado's fourteen-thousand-foot mountains (known as "fourteeners"): Pikes Peak, Mount Lincoln, Grays Peak, and Mount Elbert. It is likely that she was the first woman to stand on top of Mount Elbert, now recognized as Colorado's tallest (14,433 feet). Later she wrote about the "not commonplace delight" of rolling big boulders off the top and watching them fall. Apparently, in Anna's view it made little difference whether an ascent was achieved by the sweat of her own efforts or those of a horse. She is reputed to have boasted to a friend that she believed she had been on top of more of America's great mountains than any other woman alive.[10]

When she wasn't climbing Colorado fourteeners, Anna gave lectures.

The *Rocky Mountain News* reported that the "largest audience that ever graced the Governor's Guard Hall" heard her speak and that the "vast audience seemed spellbound by the eloquence of the fluent lady." In her speech, "What's to Hinder?" Anna said: "Women are the chief obstacles to themselves. She seldom looks to the future. She lets that take care of itself. But if her determination is different, if she thinks like a man and acts like a man regarding her daily labor, her remuneration and success will be the same as the man's."[11]

A few days later, Anna met the famous Hayden survey party for a prearranged climb of Longs Peak. (The Hayden survey, officially known as the United States Geological and Geographical Survey of the Territories, was a forerunner of the United States Geological Survey. It was directed by F. V. Hayden from 1867 to 1879.) The climbing party included William Byers, editor of the *Rocky Mountain News*, who, it will be recalled, had been a member of Major John Wesley Powell's party that in 1868 made the first known ascent of Longs Peak. Anna hoped that the publicity resulting from the climb would revive her faltering career. By the same token, as James T. Gardiner of the survey wrote, "She [Anna] has pledged herself as an advocate of our cause and she is no mean power to enlist."[12]

On September 12 Anna's party rode horseback from Estes Park, a large park-like area in the mountains sixty-five miles northwest of Denver, to a camp near what is now known as Jims Grove, arriving six hours late because the guide, Griff Evans, missed the trail. The next morning the cooks arose at 4 A.M. to prepare a "marvelous breakfast" for the climbers, who left at six. Half the party walked and half rode horses as far as what we today call the Boulderfield. The day was sharply clear and the temperature "agreeable." Four to six inches of new snow covered the rocks, but it must not have hindered the party very much, for one account noted that some members made the ascent in considerably less than three hours. It also mentioned that Miss Dickinson took three and a half hours, "or counting from the upper camping place which is the usual point of departure, just three hours and ten minutes."[13]

Anna and her companions followed the Keyhole route (named after a distinctive rock formation), which is commonly used today. The view from the summit was far-reaching, "except toward the southeast where it was cut off by smoke from forest fires near Gold Hill." Anna wore trousers for the climb, a scandalous detail reported in the *Boulder County News*, which wrote, "Anna Dickinson purchased a pair of those things at Longmont for the purpose of riding up Longs Peak which allow a lady to ride on both sides of a horse at once."[14] A week later, the *News* reported additional juicy details about Anna's climb of Longs: she had split open her trousers while sliding down the snow.

Were you ever a boy?, and did you ever slide down hill and burst open your unpeakabouts where the burst forced you to know what a cold and cheerless thing is snow? If you never was a boy and never did such a thing then you are to be commiserated for being a woman *not* like Anna Dickinson. She enjoyed this peculiar and interesting experience the other day when she ascended Long's Peak in a singular and sensible costume. But please don't tell anybody about it.[15]

Today we can only speculate about what Anna and her companions talked about as they sat around their campfire, but some historians believe that they named two nearby mountains, Mount Lady Washington and Mount Meeker. Certainly Anna was attracted to the Mount Washington in New Hampshire, for she ascended it at least twenty-eight times, although only ten of those times were "foot expeditions." It seems reasonable to suppose that the gentlemen in the party might have invented the name "Lady Washington" as a way to honor her. And it also seems probable that Anna, William Byers, and Ralph Meeker might have suggested naming the massive Mount Meeker, several hundred feet lower than Longs, to immortalize Ralph's father, Nathan, who had founded the agricultural-colony town of Greeley on the Colorado plains. (William Byers had helped Nathan Meeker, agricultural editor of the *New York Tribune*, select the townsite in 1869.) We don't know very much of what Anna actually thought about her climb of Longs Peak because she hardly mentioned it when she wrote her book *A Ragged Register* several years later. However, it seems entirely possible that Jim Nugent, a local "character," accompanied Anna and the Hayden survey on their climb of Longs Peak, for on September 26, the *Boulder County News* said, "'Mountain Jim' has furnished us with an account of life in Estes Park and an ascent of Long's Peak with Anna Dickinson and party which shall have our attention next week." The account never appeared in the newspaper. On October 17, the *News* reported that Mountain Jim was talking of writing a book. Neither the article nor material for the proposed book has survived, if, indeed, either was ever written.

Anna Dickinson's ascents of Colorado fourteeners symbolized the literal and figurative high points of her long life. After her trip to Colorado, she was forced to acknowledge that her real talent, public speaking, was no longer in demand, and she took up writing plays and acting. Most critics panned her efforts. Although she had many suitors, she spurned them all and chose to remain single. Sometimes her behavior was so erratic that friends feared she was insane. During Anna's declining years, she lived with her longtime friends Sally and George Ackley in upper New York State. A recluse, she died on October 22, 1932, at the age of ninety.

ISABELLA BIRD

A few weeks after Anna Dickinson climbed Longs Peak in 1873, the English writer Isabella Bird arrived in Estes Park. She had come to Greeley by train on September 10 and was immediately taken with Longs Peak's "glorious solitude."[16] For two weeks she tried to locate someone to take her up the canyon to Estes Park, without success. By September 26 she gave up and began her journey back to England, first spending the night in the village of "Longmount" on the plains, near the stage stop. She confided her disappointment to the proprietor of the boardinghouse in which she was staying, who told her it would be a shame for her not to see Estes because it was "the most beautiful scenery in Colorado." A short time later, two young men, S. S. (Sylvester Spelman) Downer and Platt Rogers (a future Boulder judge and future mayor of Denver, respectively), arrived at the boardinghouse and, in chatting with the proprietor, mentioned that they were riding up to Estes Park the next morning. He told them about Isabella, who had retired for the night, and strongly urged them to take her along. The young men didn't know how to refuse. Many years later, Platt wrote:

We were not at all partial to such an arrangement as we were traveling light and free and the presence of a woman would naturally operate as a restraint upon our movements. However, we could not refuse, and we consoled ourselves with the hope that she would prove young, beautiful, and vivacious. Our hopes were dispelled when, in the morning, Miss Bird appeared, wearing bloomers, riding cowboy fashion, with a face and figure not corresponding to our ideals.[17]

The ride took ten hours. S. S. apparently couldn't stand the slow pace and galloped on ahead while the "town bred youth," Platt, stayed behind with Isabella, who was obviously delighted by the ride. When they were in the lower part of Muggins Gulch (which Isabella called "M'Ginns"), the verdant valley of the present-day Meadowdale Ranch, they went over to a "rude black log cabin" that was covered with pelts and surrounded by antlers and the offal of wild animals. Isabella knew that it belonged to the "notorious . . . desperado" Rocky Mountain Jim but wrote that she "longed to speak to someone who loved the mountains."

Mountain Jim emerged from the cabin. Isabella noted his ragged clothes, the two sides of his face—one "repulsive," the other that "might have been modeled in marble"—and "the tawny hair in thin uncared-for curls." She wrote, "I almost repented of having sought his acquaintance." But then, on realizing there was a lady present, he "raised his cap, showing as he did so a magnificently-formed brow and head, and in a cultured tone of voice asked if there were anything he could do for me?"

Isabella requested water, which Jim brought "in a battered tin, gracefully apologizing for not having anything more presentable." They then entered into a conversation, and Isabella "forgot both his reputation and appearance, for his manner was that of a chivalrous gentleman, his accent refined, and his language easy and elegant. I inquired about some beavers' paws which were drying, and in a moment they hung on the horn of my saddle." As she rode away, Jim remarked that he could tell that she was a compatriot of his (Jim claimed to have been born of Irish parents in Canada) and that he hoped she would "allow him the pleasure of calling on her."

Four miles later, in a meadow now covered by Lake Estes, Isabella and Platt came to a tidy ranch with milk cows and a freshly butchered steer. The owner was the same Griff Evans who had guided Anna Dickinson up Longs Peak. He was a Welshman who lived in the park during the warmest months, ranching and renting out four small log cabins to tourists. Isabella took one for eight dollars a week, which included the "unlimited use of a horse, when one can be caught." Every night, a family of skunks that lived underneath the cabin awakened Isabella when they sharpened their claws on the floorboards. She sometimes heard wolves and mountain lions as she walked from the main cabin to her own. Ecstatically, she wrote her sister, Henrietta: "I have found far more than I ever dared to hope for."

Isabella was nearly forty-two years old, having been born in Borough-bridge, Yorkshire, on October 15, 1831. For much of her life she had suffered from chronic back problems that frequently brought on a "spinal prostration" so severe that she was forced to stay in bed until noon.[18] When she was twenty-three years old, the family physician, alarmed by her general poor health, complete with insomnia and low spirits, had urged her to take a sea voyage. Isabella had sailed to Canada and the eastern United States and had come back amazingly revitalized. She had then published a book about her travels, titled *The Englishwoman in America*. Isabella had discovered that her maladies vanished—or at least lessened—when she traveled. She visited North America twice more before embarking on an eighteen-month trip to Australia, New Zealand, Hawaii (then known as the Sandwich Islands), and finally Colorado. This was her only trip to the American West.

By the time she reached Estes Park, Isabella was obsessed with climbing Longs Peak, although early October was a marginal time of year for a safe ascent. Griff Evans kept "throwing cold water" on the project, but after the weather became more settled, he began encouraging her to go, even if she got no farther than timberline. He then went down to Denver, leaving Rocky Mountain Jim as the only possible guide. Platt Rogers later wrote: "Although it was very late in the season, she wanted to climb Long's Peak. . . . Now the only guides to the peak in those days were Griff and Jim and each held in contempt and derision the trail used by the other in making the ascent. Miss Bird wanted Jim, and Mr. Downer was finally persuaded to ride over to Muggins gulch, see him and make the necessary arrangement."

The party took steaks, freshly baked bread, tea, sugar, and butter. Isabella tied "three pair" of camping blankets and a quilt behind her saddle. Since her own boots were badly worn, she also took along a pair of Griff Evans's, which she intended to wear for the climb. They set out on their horses. At first, Isabella was very conscious of the contrast between the "awful looking ruffian" and his "exquisitely beautiful Arab mare," which "he fretted . . . incessantly to make her display herself."

However, Jim's "grace of manner" soon made her forget his appearance. They talked for more than three hours as they rode up to timberline. There they set up camp in a grove of "beautiful silver spruce" close to where Anna Dickinson had camped with the Hayden survey. Longs Peak turned red with the afterglow of the sun, and "before it faded a big half-moon hung out of the heavens, shining through the silver blue foliage of the pines on the frigid background of snow, and turning the whole into fairyland."

Jim built a large fire, and after supper they sang songs. "Then," wrote Isabella, "'Jim' recited a very clever poem of his own composition and told some fearful Indian stories." She found him to be "very agreeable as a man of culture as well as a child of nature. . . . He was very courteous and even kind to me, which was fortunate, as the young men had little idea of showing even ordinary civilities."

Griff Evans had warned the young men to keep their whiskey flasks away from Jim. Of the campfire camaraderie, Platt wrote:

Jim was resourceful, romantic, and reminiscent. His adventure with the bear in Middle Park . . . was elaborated for Miss Bird's benefit and all the doggerel which he had composed in the loneliness of Muggins gulch was recited by him. The principal theme of his poems was himself, varied by references to a fair maiden, of whom he seemed to be enamored and who we afterwards learned, was Griff Evans's daughter.

Jim commanded his dog, Ring, "Go to that lady and don't leave her again tonight." At 12 degrees Fahrenheit, it's unlikely that three blankets kept Isabella warm, even with Ring at her back, but she wrote no complaints. The wolves howled and the wind blew. Isabella was too excited to sleep but noted that "the notorious desperado" slept "as quietly as innocence sleeps."

They were up before the sun rose. The sunrise was so spectacular that Jim took off his hat and exclaimed, "I believe there is a God!" By seven the party was off to the "Lava Beds," which today we call, more accurately, the Boulderfield. While the men walked, Isabella rode her horse. When the way became too rough, she dismounted and quickly discovered that Griff Evans's boots were so much too large for her that she had "no foothold." By miraculous good luck, she discovered a pair of small overshoes behind a rock, probably abandoned by Anna Dickinson, who, like Isabella, was five feet tall. They fit.

After the Keyhole, which Isabella called "The Notch," the party found it hard going. The loose snow encountered by the Hayden party on September 13 had turned to ice and had been augmented by subsequent snows. Isabella slipped on the rocks and became terrified. She said she wanted to go back to the Keyhole, knowing that her "incompetence would detain the party." One of the "youths said almost plainly that a woman was a dangerous encumbrance," but Jim replied that if he "were not to take a lady up he would not go up at all." Neither side yielded. So S. S. and Platt proceeded to contour over to the steep gully now called the Trough and to scramble up it, while Isabella and Jim descended—and then ascended—two thousand feet toward the spectacular Glacier Gorge to avoid the ice.

The young men probably had to wait several hours for their guide. Platt wrote: "When they finally came up with us she was so fagged that she was unable to make her way unaided up the last slope to the peak. By alternately pulling and pushing her and stimulating her with snow soaked with Jamaica ginger, we got her to the top."

Isabella later wrote that despite reaching the top of Longs, she was "humiliated" by her success and that Jim had dragged her up with his muscles "like a bale of goods." "You know I have no head and no ankles," she confided to her sister, " . . . had I known that the ascent was a real mountaineering feat I should not have felt the slightest ambition to perform it." On the way down each party retraced its ascent steps. Isabella said that after S. S. and Platt went their separate way, Jim lost all his brusqueness and "was gentle and considerate beyond anything." She was sure that he was "grievously disappointed" in her lack of strength and courage.

Platt and S. S. again had to wait several hours for Isabella and Jim. They were reunited at the Keyhole at six, just as the sun was setting. By now, if Isabella's account is to be believed, she had climbed or been hauled up some seven thousand vertical feet. In fact, though, this was probably not the case. Even seasoned mountain climbers have a hard time judging vertical distance, especially above timberline, where there are no trees for reference points. It would be strange if Isabella had not misjudged the number of vertical feet she and Jim had descended and ascended to avoid the ice, simply because of her inexperience. Moreover, the stupendous amount of energy she expended during her climb could also have caused her to exaggerate distances. Isabella Bird was no shining example of cardiovascular fitness; she was overweight and flabby from riding horses rather than walking. Still, she probably gained a total of at least five thousand vertical feet, which is comparable to what hikers today gain when they leave from the Longs Peak Campground. Moreover, Isabella gained all her elevation above eleven thousand feet. All things considered, her feat was rather amazing, and it wiped her out. She was so stiff and weak that the men hoisted her up onto her horse. Once back at camp, they lifted her off and "laid [her] on the ground wrapped up in blankets," a procedure that Isabella described as "a humiliating termination of a great exploit." She fell into a merciful sleep but awakened with "icy cold" feet. Jim was also awake, and they talked. He then told her of "a great sorrow which had led him on a lawless and desperate life," and wept. Isabella wondered if "it was semi-conscious acting" or if, indeed, the silence and beauty of the place had profoundly touched "his dark soul."

A week later, when Isabella recalled her climb of Longs Peak, she spoke of the "perfect beauty and extraordinary sublimity" of the experience and said that no one had ever made a more successful ascent of the peak. Perhaps her climb was made sweeter by the fact that new snow fell on the summit, ending the climbing season for eight months. Life at Griff Evans's ranch settled into pleasant routines. Isabella, accompanied by Mountain Jim or fellow ranch guests, explored the country on horseback. She rode astride, rather than sidesaddle. Isabella was a skilled horsewoman, having been taught by her father. After Griff Evans observed her helping round up cattle, he told her she "was as much use as another man" and offered her a job as cook for the winter. She turned him down, commenting that riding after cattle suited her better and that she didn't like making bread.

In October Isabella temporarily left Estes Park to take a six-hundred-mile sight-seeing trip on her Indian pony, Birdy. Usually she wore her "Hawaiian costume" while riding astride Birdy; it consisted of full Turkish trousers worn under a skirt that reached to her ankles. However, when she came to the outskirts of Colorado Springs, she "got off, put on a long skirt, and rode sidewise, though the settlement scarcely looked like a place where any deference to prejudices was necessary."

In late November a financial panic swept the country, closing the banks. Isabella returned to Estes Park, where she could live without cash. Obviously, though, it was preference as well as expedience that inspired her return, for when she was down on the plains, looking west, she wrote, "Long's Peak rises in purple gloom, and I long for the cool air and unfettered life of the solitary blue hollow at its base."

During her sojourn in Colorado, Isabella wrote long letters to her sister, Henrietta, which appeared in the *Leisure Hour* several years later. In 1879 the letters formed the basis for a book, *A Lady's Life in the Rocky Mountains*, published by John Murray in London. It was a great hit in England, then in France, and finally in the United States, where reprints continue to sell well today. Although it was written over a century ago, *A Lady's Life in the Rocky Mountains* retains a remarkable freshness, for Isabella was an accurate observer (having been taught to be so by her father), as well as a candid one. Her book even mellowed Platt Rogers's evaluation of her, forty years after he and S. S. had so reluctantly accompanied her to Estes Park and Longs Peak. He later wrote, "Her physical unattractiveness, which so influenced us when we first met her, was really more than compensated for by a fluent and graphic pen, which made the mountains as romantic and beautiful as doubtless were her own thoughts."

A Lady's Life in the Rocky Mountains is, however, an edited version of the letters Isabella wrote her sister and, as such, presents a less-than-frank picture of her relationship with Rocky Mountain Jim. It does give a few hints, as when Isabella refers to Jim's "black moods" and when she writes that the sordid details of Jim's life came "between me and the sunshine sometimes." But Isabella definitely did not tell all to her reading public.

For example, Isabella wrote to Henrietta—but failed to make mention in her book—of Jim's being "attached" to her and of her opinion that he was "a man whom any woman might love but who no sane woman would marry."[19] Nor did she mention in her book that when she said her final farewell to Jim, each promised that whoever died first would appear before the other. (The following summer, according to Isabella's official biographer, a vision of Jim dressed as a trapper did appear before Isabella when she was vacationing in Switzerland; she later determined that it occurred at the exact moment he died from a gunshot wound inflicted by Griff Evans.)

In 1880, shortly after Henrietta died, Isabella accepted the marriage proposal of the family physician, Dr. John Bishop. After his death five years later, she began traveling "compulsively," to Tibet, China, Japan, Korea, India, Turkey, Persia, and Morocco. In July 1892 she was made a fellow of the Royal Geographical Society, the first woman to be so honored. She wrote thirteen books, several of which are currently in print. In 1904, she died in Edinburgh, Scotland.

Thanks to *A Lady's Life in the Rocky Mountains*, Jims Grove in Rocky Mountain National Park was so named. There is no natural feature in Colorado named for Isabella, however.

ROSE PENDER

Ten years after Anna Dickinson and Isabella Bird climbed Longs Peak, another Englishwoman, Rose Pender, and her husband toured the American West, partly to inspect a Wyoming cattle ranch in which they'd invested. Along the way, Rose climbed Pikes Peak by a route far less demanding than that taken by Julia Archibald Holmes. Yet one has to give Rose Pender her due, for she did it in a proper lady's style—wearing a skirt.

Rose Pender and her husband, James, arrived in Colorado Springs in mid-May 1883. She had no desire to climb Pikes Peak, thinking it looked "so cold and so terribly high up." But another English couple staying at the same hotel persuaded her to join them and give it a try, accompanied by her husband, his business associate "Mr. B.," two Americans, and several guides. Rose later recalled:

Shortly after 5 o'clock we were up and preparing for the expedition. I wore a short striped skirt of chintz, and my Norfolk jacket over a flannel shirt. My boots, an old pair of patent leather ones, worn for comfort in our long railway journeys, were extremely unfit for rough walking. In a very broad-brimmed hat and my thick veil, I fancy I looked the British tourist, as depicted by *Punch*, to the life. Mr. B.—— would insist on wearing a Scotch cap, in spite of our remonstrances. As the glare of the sun on the snow would be great, and good head-covering indispensable, J—— [James] took the precaution of carrying a large silk bandanna; he had climbed Swiss mountains before, and knew what to expect. Oh, I must not forget my umbrella, a faithful companion, from which I never separated.[20]

The party's route was considerably easier than Julia Holmes's had been in 1858, for the United States Signal Service, later to become the United States Weather Bureau, had built a weather station on top of Pikes Peak in 1873, complete with a trail leading to it. So the party rode horses (except for Rose, who chose a "nice little black mule") up a "lovely" path that wound its way up the lower reaches of Pikes Peak through forests of pine. By the time the party had reached the snow line at about 11,500 feet, the other English couple had lost all enthusiasm for going any farther. So had the guides, who tried to dissuade the others from continuing, saying the snow was too deep. But Rose and her husband, the Americans, Mr. B., and a Brazilian insisted on continuing, now on foot. As Rose later wrote:

Some breakfast had been sent from the hotel, and this was then spread out. I declined to partake, feeling that I should require all my breath and agility if I was ever to reach the Observatory, but I wrapped up a biscuit and a piece of cheese and pocketed them, and secured a small flask of brandy.

Seeing we were determined, the guides then proceeded to fasten gunny-sacks to our feet. . . . Our first climb was very severe and nearly stopped our breath; but after a bit we got better, and went along at a good pace, till we reached the last crown of the Peak. The snow was very deep and not hard, and often I slipped through up to my waist, struggling out as best I could. The sun was scorching, and I felt grateful for my thick veil and the handkerchief round my neck. The umbrella had to be closed, as it was impossible to scramble along holding it up.

Near the top, first one of the guides and then the Brazilian became so weak that they had to sit down. Rose revived them both with her brandy and food, and on they went. "When not more than a quarter of a mile from the longed-for top," Rose wrote, "I began to feel 'done.'"

My breath came in sobs—my feet felt like iron, and a terrible pain at my chest warned me to persevere all I knew. The telegraph wires now showed us the route, the poles sunken half-way in the snow. I resolved to go from one to another without stopping. Alas! I had to stop twice, and now the guide and the Brazilian collared me, passed me, and, to my bitter mortification, reached the door of the Observatory quite ten yards ahead! It was no use, I could get on no faster.

Rose was faint, extremely tired, and "nearly blind with a terrible head-ache." Yet she described the view as "wonderful" and marveled at the clarity of the air, which enabled her to see "150 miles over the Rockies." "No words," she wrote, "can give the least idea of the glory of it all." The party then descended and returned to their hotel. Rose took a hot bath, changed into fresh clothes, and took her place at the dining room table as though she had "done nothing out of the way." Her companions, however, were not so lucky, especially Mr. B., who "suffered terribly from sun-scorching."

His face and neck were severely blistered, and he was burnt a real scarlet; glycerine and rose-water gave him a little relief, but it was many days before he recovered from the effects of the sun and snow combined. The poor guide was snow-blind for some days, and the two Americans went about wearing dark glasses, and declared themselves quite knocked up. Thanks to the precaution of wearing a thick veil and neckerchief, I did not suffer in the least; indeed I enjoyed the whole thing thoroughly, and like to shut my eyes now to recall the grand view and the marvelous coulouring.

In 1888, after James Pender was knighted, his wife became Lady Rose. (James's father, John, was associated with the laying of the trans-Atlantic cable and the telegraph line that connected England and its eastern colonies.) James died at the age of eighty; Rose outlived him by eleven years.

CAROLINE JOSEPHINE WELTON

In climbing Pikes Peak, Rose Pender had found in herself an unexpected determination to reach the summit, a trait necessary for all mountain climbers. Caroline Josephine Welton possessed it to excess. In 1884, one year after Rose's visit to Colorado, Caroline arrived in Colorado Springs. Carrie, as she was called, was the only child of a wealthy businessman from Waterbury, Connecticut. After her father's death, she and her mother quarreled and went to court to determine the division of the inheritance. Apparently Carrie received a large settlement, for she soon took off, well fortified with gold and silver certificates. After giving $250,000 to the New York Humane Society, she headed west, booked a room at the luxurious Antlers Hotel in Colorado Springs, and climbed Pikes Peak. It was then that she probably had her first glimpse of Longs Peak to the north, easily visible on a clear day. Even viewed from 100 miles away, Longs is an impressive, regal mountain; Carrie decided to climb it.

At the foot of Longs, she rented a tourist cabin owned by Parson Elkanah Lamb, a United Brethren minister, and his son, Carlyle, both of whom were mountain guides. Carrie, whom Elkanah described as a "young lady of intellectual culture and a passionate and true lover of nature," arranged for Carlyle to take her up Longs.[21] On the appointed morning, September 23, 1884, she donned a "gentleman's suit underneath a lady's garb" and a yellow silk mask to protect her face from the sun. The clear morning skies boded well, and the pair started out with high hopes. By the time they reached the Keyhole, however, it was obvious that a storm was in the making. The wind had picked up and clouds hovered over the top of the peak.

Carlyle suggested they call it quits, pointing out that even if they made it, they wouldn't be able to see anything from the summit. Carrie would not be dissuaded, however, saying she never undertook anything she didn't intend to finish. So they pressed on against the rising gusts. They reached the top at three in the afternoon, which is considered imprudently late to start back down even today, when the route is considerably better defined than it was in 1884. Carrie's strength was nearly depleted, and she depended heavily on Carlyle's strong arms to help her descend the smooth rock slabs, now known as the Home Stretch, and to negotiate the vertigo-inducing ledges, today called the Narrows. As the last light pinked distant peaks, the evening air began to chill. Darkness came on, slowing their progress still further; at midnight they reached the Keyhole, where Carrie collapsed. Carlyle gave her all the clothes he could spare and half-carried her down to a sheltered rock. All the while the wind roared with no hint of letting up.

Carlyle was nearly spent, but by going very slowly he managed to make his way down the mountain to the family cabin far below in what is now called Tahosa Valley. He roused his father, and the two set out. Elkanah described the scene in his autobiography:

At timberline the wind was so furious that sometimes we were compelled to double over and touch the ground to keep a secure foothold. By strenuous exertions, I passed on, leaving my son and the pony in the rear to follow as best they could, my son having been up all night was almost completely exhausted. About a mile across Boulderfield, I came in sight of the tragic spot where Carrie J. Welton lay at rest, having died alone amid the revelry and dismal dirge, and which was yet holding high carnival over her body by blowing every section of her garments in its unrelenting fury, seemingly sporting with its victim in demonical triumph. She still wore the yellow mask.

After the Lambs took Carrie's body down to their ranch, they tele-graphed Carrie's relatives; a cousin came out from the East. Elkanah then sent his family and Carlyle down to Fort Collins, on the plains thirty miles west of Greeley, for the winter. He remained behind, alone, building two more cabins "to accommodate increasing travel." He often thought about Carrie's death. The first night after his family had left, he glanced up at the window of his bedroom, and there, "seemingly as natural as life," stood Carrie J. Welton, looking toward his bed. "Now," Elkanah wrote, "I am not superstitious and I do not believe in ghosts, spooks, or hobgoblins, but this ghostly appearance in the solitude of my lonely situation was the severest test of my mental equilibrium and courage ever before experienced in my life." It took more than Carrie Welton's ghost to daunt the parson, how-ever. "One thing is certain," he wrote. "I did not yield to the situation. I stayed with it to a finish. . . . I stayed six weeks—forty two days alone except once a week visiting the post office for my mail." Carrie Welton's death on Longs Peak was the first on record.

By the late 1880s at least a hundred people were attempting to climb Longs every year, although many got no farther than the Keyhole. The approach to the base of the mountain was much easier than it had been in 1873, when Anna Dickinson and Isabella Bird had made their climbs, for the Lambs had built a crude road past Lily Lake to their cabins and a trail on the lower part of Longs. Elkanah was getting up in years, although in 1900 he was still fit enough to accompany his wife, Jane, when she climbed Longs Peak to celebrate her seventieth birthday. However, the next year he sold his Longs Peak guest ranch to a nephew, Enos Mills, who renamed it Longs Peak Inn.

VICTORIA BROUGHM

One day in 1906, Victoria Broughm from Michigan, who was a guest at Longs Peak Inn, expressed an interest in climbing Longs Peak, solo. Enos Mills required her first to prove that she was competent, by climbing a lesser peak. She did. "There was nothing for me to do," he later wrote, "but to allow her to climb Long's Peak alone."[22] While she was preparing to set out on a cool September morning, Enos decided to send his collie, Scotch, along with her because "he knew the trail well and would, of course, lead her the right way, providing she lost the trail." Enos commanded Scotch, "Go with this young lady, take good care of her, and stay with her till she returns."

Victoria rode a horse to the Boulderfield, tied him up, and, with the dog, continued on foot. Though clouds were collecting, she, like Carrie Welton, ignored them. Shortly after she reached the summit, a storm engulfed her. Visibility shrank. In making her way down the Trough, Victoria missed the cairns—piles of rocks—that marked the route's right-angle turn toward the Keyhole. She continued down into the deep and rugged Glacier Gorge. As Enos wrote:

At once [Scotch] came forward, and took the lead with an alert, aggressive air. The way in which he did this should have suggested to the young lady that he knew what he was about but she did not appreciate this fact. She thought he had become weary and wanted to run away from her so she called him back. . . . Once more he started off in the right direction, and this time she scolded him and reminded him that his master had told him to not desert her. Scotch dropped his ears and sheepishly fell in behind her and followed meekly along. He had obeyed orders.

Finally Victoria realized she was lost. Shivering, she hugged Scotch and settled down for the night. Enos Mills had given his word to Victoria that he himself wouldn't search for her if she failed to return, so he stayed behind and sent out a search party of men. Hundred-mile-an hour winds turned them back near treeline. At midnight a second party went out, consisting of Carl Pilz; Enos's brother, Joe; and William S. Cooper, who many years later played a large part in establishing Alaska's Glacier Bay National Monument. Just below timberline, they encountered the same winds that had turned the first party back, but after tying up the horses, they kept on. As the men gained altitude, the gales increased, so that by the time they reached the Keyhole, the wind was "like a fire hose," hurling them back when they attempted to crawl through, single file. They put their arms around each other. "Even so," Joe Mills wrote, "we were blown back like so much chaff."[23]

After shivering the night through, they tried again at dawn and managed to break through. Cooper and Pilz decided to go up, searching the Trough, whereas Joe Mills decided to go down. Since it was obvious the wind would drown out their shouts, the men arranged a visual signal and separated. A short time later Joe spied, in a small patch of sand, a human footprint with a dog's print on top. He "wigwagged" to his companions to come down and hurried on, calling out, "Scotch! Scotch!"—although he thought his voice wouldn't carry. Suddenly he saw the dog standing on top of a great boulder. Instinctively he speeded up, but then considering what he might find, he hesitated. Finally, Joe started to crawl under the rock—and met "Miss Broughm" coming out.

She was very cold and her lips were blue and cracked. She explained that she had hugged Scotch all night and had never given up or lost courage. Victoria even managed a "brave if twisted smile." At first her legs were so numb that she was unable to walk by herself, but with the men supporting her, she slowly started down. After a few miles the feeling came back in her legs, and the party was able to make good time. By late morning they reached the inn, whereupon Victoria retired to her room. Several hours later, in a scene reminiscent of Rose Pender after her climb of Pikes Peak, she reappeared for "luncheon," looking quite like her old self.

Though Victoria Broughm's climb was not an untarnished success, she was the first woman known to tackle a major Colorado peak solo, or, perhaps one should say, with the aid of a dog.

2

Outdoor
Sportswomen,
1915–1935

Beginning in 1915, and for the next ten years or so, exploding numbers of Colorado female recreationists met the mountains far more on their own terms than their predecessors had. All were benefiting from a subtle change in Americans' attitudes toward outdoorswomen, exemplified by the founding of the Appalachian Mountain Club (the AMC). From its beginning in 1876, one of the AMC's unstated aims was "the training of both men and women to climb and to walk easily distances of a considerable number of miles at a stretch—an accomplishment that the Americans, especially American women, rarely possess."[1]

Although only 10 percent of the AMC's founding members were women, for the next thirty years women joined the club in droves, comprising 30 to 40 percent of the annual new membership. The early AMC was for Bostonians, but it served as an example for everyone: the Sierra Club was formed in California in 1892, the Mazamas of Portland, Oregon, in 1895, the Seattle Mountaineers in 1907, and the Colorado Mountain Club (CMC) in 1912. All these organizations welcomed both sexes and surely exerted a definite, though immeasurable, influence on attitudes toward outdoor women. (Incidentally, author Francis Keenlyside speculates that the increased number of proficient female climbers in the Alps during the 1920s was due to the Groupe de Haute Montagne's admittance of men and women equally on climbing qualifications.)

In addition, the mushrooming Colorado mountain towns, which often made their own rules, were fertile ground for new ideas about the so-called weaker sex. Women in Colorado mining towns had taken up skiing at least as early as the 1880s, just as the men had. (Scandinavian immigrants had introduced the sport to Americans in California goldfields and in northern states such as Minnesota.) Unlike some of the Colorado men—such as Father Dyer, the itinerant Methodist preacher and mail carrier who skied from town to town—Colorado women hadn't ventured far from civilization. Yet they must have enjoyed schussing down open slopes near town, for many group portraits survive, showing them bundled in heavy coats and skirts down to their ankles and standing on skis.

In August 1915 the Ladies Hiking Club was organized in the railroad town of Fraser, Colorado, in the mountains west of Denver. The members met twice a week and hiked from three to eight miles. Apparently the club didn't last long, but the fact that it existed at all is a striking anomaly in Colorado's history. For the next sixty years no comparable group existed.

To be sure, there was no dearth of men who were condescending toward outdoor women in Colorado, such as the acting superintendent of Rocky Mountain National Park who wrote in 1920: "The CMC has requested a ski course at Fern Lake, sufficiently slow to permit its use by ladies and by amateurs, it being felt that the present course is a little too steep for timid runners."[2]

But as we shall see, other men—like Albert Ellingwood, James Grafton Rogers, Carl Blaurock, and Jack Moomaw—accepted the fact that women could be competent, and encouraged them. Enos Mills, especially, championed women. He stated that the most "nimble and sure-footed climber" he ever guided to the top of Longs Peak was Miss Elsie Bowmen of New York, although "for good nature, lung capacity, endurance, alertness and skill as a climber," Miss Gladys Wells of Florida stood "pre-eminent." But he deplored "lady mountaineers" who climbed in long skirts, which he felt impeded the wearer and were dangerous to everyone in the party. Rather, Enos advocated "a divided skirt of bloomers."[3]

ELIZABETH AND ESTHER BURNELL

Enos Mills, a self-taught nature lover and an admirer of John Muir, was also an innkeeper, a nationally known lecturer and writer, and a staunch supporter of the creation of Rocky Mountain National Park. After the park's formal dedication in the fall of 1915, Enos gave a speech in Cleveland, Ohio, during which he invited members of the audience to visit the nature study center he ran at Longs Peak Inn. Two members of his audience, Elizabeth and Esther Burnell, were intrigued and took him up on his invitation the following summer.

The sisters were "congenial" and had "fine features."[4] Elizabeth, who at twenty-seven years was two years older than Esther, had a master's degree from the University of Michigan in physics and mathematics; she was head of the mathematics and physics department of Lake Erie College in Ohio. Esther, a graduate of the Pratt Art Institute in Brooklyn, had worked as a consulting decorator for the Sherwin Williams Paint Company until job stress forced her to take some time off. Once at Longs Peak Inn, she extended her vacation by assisting Enos on a book he was writing. She began going into the mountains to observe nature, sometimes at night, by herself. Enos offered her a job as a secretary, but she turned him down, having made up her mind to file a claim on a homestead. Esther invited an artist friend, a former classmate from New York, to join her, but the friend declined quite firmly. So Esther homesteaded alone.

After drawing her own plans for the cabin, she assisted in its construction, shingled the roof, and designed and built some of the furniture. The cabin, which Esther named Keewaydin, was on the edge of Horseshoe Park near "MacGregor Pass," apparently the local name for a low point between Castle Mountain and MacGregor Mountain, now part of Rocky Mountain National Park. It had a good view of the Fall River valley and was about a mile from two summer resorts, Horseshoe Inn and Fall River Lodge, both accessible by road. In winter the road was probably closed by snowdrifts, but this would have been irrelevant to Esther, since she had no car.

Once a week or so, wearing knickerbockers, she walked four miles east into Estes Park to pick up mail and buy provisions. Whenever she came to town, she usually let her friends the Bonds know that she was all right, since they worried about her. Esther had other homesteading neighbors, some as close as two miles away, so she was not completely isolated. She put a feeding table for birds outside one window. Mountain sheep and deer used a game trail that ran next to her cabin. Although most of her 120 acres was forested and steep, she managed to turn several acres into a garden that included potatoes.

Esther explored the country around her, frequently camping out overnight. On Christmas Day she and another woman, whose homestead was fifteen or so miles from Keewaydin, walked to a midway point and cooked "a merry campfire lunch among the pines" (see "Katherine Garetson" in chapter 4). In late spring she snowshoed thirty miles across the Continental Divide to Grand Lake by the North Inlet route, spent the night with her friends the Cairns, and snowshoed back the next day by what is today called the Ute Trail. The local residents thought she had done a remarkable thing, especially for a woman.

Although Enos was often away from Colorado during the winter attending conferences and lecturing, he occasionally stopped by Keewaydin on his horse, Cricket. On one such visit he agreed to read some stories Esther had written, and she offered to do typing for him. Thus began a lively exchange of manuscripts.

After Esther's first homesteading season, Elizabeth joined her for a second summer at Longs Peak Inn. The sisters explored the nearby trails and sometimes slept out at night. Elizabeth began arranging wildflower exhibits so that guests at the inn could learn the common names. That same summer, 1917, the Rocky Mountain National Park administration trained female nature guides "in flowers, birds, animals and trees . . . first aid work," and "knowledge of the country." Their operations were limited to "one-day trips below timberline and to sections they are familiar with," unless accompanied by a first-class guide. In 1918 permits were issued to four such nature guides, including the Burnell sisters. Elizabeth took a sabbatical from her position at Lake Erie College so that she could join Esther at her homestead for the year. That summer, on August 12, 1918, Esther Burnell and Enos Mills were married quietly in the little Enos Mills homestead cabin across the road from Longs Peak Inn. The balding Enos was forty-eight, nearly twenty years older than his slim, "very good-looking" bride. On April 27, 1919, their daughter, Enda, was born.[5]

A few years later Esther's homestead cabin, which she had never proved up on, was burned to the ground by "a fire of unknown origin."[6] On September 21, 1922, Enos Mills died at his home from an infected tooth, and Esther took over Longs Peak Inn, running it for over twenty years. With the help of "Aunt Bessie," she raised her daughter. In 1964 Esther Burnell Mills died in Denver.

In the 1920s Elizabeth Burnell, influenced by Enos Mills, gave up teaching math and became the supervisor of nature study for the Los Angeles City Schools, a job she held for nine years. She was coauthor of the *Field Book of Birds of Southwest United States.* During her summers, from 1917 to 1930, she led nature walks and conducted overnights for guests of Longs Peak Inn. She also guided parties up Longs Peak, the first woman to do so. By her estimate she made over fifty ascents, for many years the women's record. In 1932 Elizabeth married a mining engineer, Dr. Norman E. Smith. She died in Englewood, Colorado, in 1960.

ANNE AND ISABEL PIFER

A few years after Elizabeth Burnell began guiding parties up Longs Peak, two other female guides came to know the mountain. However, they used a route that most of today's hikers and climbers wouldn't consider taking, one that begins and ends at the grounds of the Western Conference of the Young Men's Christian Association near Estes Park.

When Anne Pifer was nineteen and her sister, Isabel, was seventeen, they visited the YMCA in Estes Park for the first time. The year was 1920; the Y was eleven years old and a far cry from the bustling community of several thousand that it is today during its peak season. The Pifers lived in a housekeeping cabin without electricity or running water, which Anne and Isabel came to "love."[7] They also took to their beautiful surroundings and began learning the trails from other Y guests and from maps and ranger hikes. A few summers later the "Pifer Girls" began acting as guides for Y members. They received no pay for their guiding, although grateful "clients" often bought them special dinners. But Anne and Isabel took their jobs quite seriously, making sure that all members of a party had cut their toenails because "it makes all the difference when you go down, down, down" and urging them to "get into training."

Instead of knapsacks, the Y hikers used bandannas to hold their sandwiches, raisins, and fruit, rolling them up in a cotton shirt and a wool shirt tied around the waist. No one carried water; they filled their folding cups directly from the streams. On every hike, Anne and Isabel wore the same costume—men's corduroy pants, an undershirt, a middy blouse, clean socks, and boots that laced up nearly to their knees. Sixty years later Anne was astonished to see that hikers "[didn't] want to look the same Monday that they looked last Thursday!"

When guiding, Isabel and Anne tried to imitate Enos Mills. They emphasized that making the summit was secondary to having a "perfectly beautiful nature experience," and they had their clients sit still for several minutes so that the hikers could hear the gentle sounds of the wilderness such as the dull roar of a distant waterfall or the rustling of a bird hidden in leaves. But the Pifer sisters added a "spiritual" dimension to the nature experience, which they regarded as the most important part of climbing a mountain.

For four summers they led Y hikes, the most ambitious of which was up Longs Peak. It was such a demanding undertaking that Anne and Isabel assembled their party on the Y grounds at three or four in the morning. Then, in complete darkness, they set out, stumbling up the Wind River Trail for several miles until they reached Highway 7. By now, the sun would be flushing Longs Peak in alpenglow. Often, as they filed past Longs Peak Inn Enos Mills would be standing on the steps, greeting the party with, "Look while you're hiking," or simply, "Enjoy." As the route steepened, the sisters would lead group singing to help everyone stride with a good rhythm. Although Anne and Isabel regarded achieving the summit as a somewhat incidental part of the mountain outing, the entire party usually did reach the top. On the way back, in the early evening, the weary Y hikers would stop to rehydrate at the Wigwam, a tearoom on the Wind River Trail. Finally, at 7 or 8 P.M., they would drag into the Y's Administration Building, where they'd stashed Turkish towels the night before. They would then walk (or hobble) to one of the twelve tubs of hot water on the Y grounds. The bath was well earned; they'd hiked approximately twenty-six miles and gained sixty-two hundred feet in elevation. (In contrast, today's Longs Peakers gain only forty-eight hundred feet in elevation and hike a mere sixteen miles.)

The Pifer sisters climbed many peaks besides Longs, often on their own. Despite encounters with a mother bear and her two cubs and with a mountain lion that stalked them, their "wonderful mother" never suggested that they stop their "cockeyed" adventures. In 1923 they took a break from college and spent a winter in Estes Park teaching school. That year, the Estes Park Chamber of Commerce hired a Swiss ski instructor to give lessons. The Woman's Ski Club chose black and blue as their colors. Eagerly, the Pifer sisters joined the other townspeople who had decided to learn how to ski. Since there were no tows, "just about everybody" herringboned up the slopes and had a go at turning and stopping on the way down. Beginners practiced on the slopes around town; more advanced skiers headed for the declared ski area just below Old Man Mountain. Park ranger Jack Moomaw introduced the Pifer girls to skijoring and to snow baths.

After their year in Estes Park, Anne did graduate work in religious studies, married, and raised a family. Isabel "had a fabulous career" as an educator in Israel, Beirut, and India. Recently the YMCA "hikemasters," now professionally run, reenacted an "Anne [Pifer] Austill 1920 Trip" up Longs Peak. Late in the evening the party dragged into the Y grounds, exhausted. "We made it," they told Anne, "and we were glad to do it in your honor . . . but once is enough!"

ELEANOR DAVIS EHRMAN

Eleanor Davis, unlike the mountain women who preceded her, was a trained athlete. She became acquainted with Colorado in 1911 on a family vacation that was inspired by neighbors' enthusiastic reports of the area and also by Isabella Bird's book, *A Lady's Life in the Rocky Mountains*. The Davises took a Stanley Steamer from Lyons up the North St. Vrain road, which they found terrifying, through Estes Park to Steads, a guest ranch in Moraine Park that has since been razed. Like the Pifer sisters, Eleanor and her sisters immediately fell into the local routines. They hiked during the day and danced during the night. Toward the end of their stay they hired a Swiss guide, who operated out of Longs Peak Inn, to take them up Longs. There they met Enos Mills, "a rather odd looking fellow—kind of bald," who immediately introduced them to "his dear little squirrels and chipmunks."[8] Eleanor climbed Longs Peak wearing a long skirt.

Eleanor and her sister Sarah then moved to Colorado Springs. After a year, Sarah reluctantly returned to a teaching job at Wellesley while Eleanor stayed on and became a teacher in the Department of Physical Education at Colorado College (CC), a job for which she was well qualified. She was in her late twenties, having been born in September 1885 in Greenfield, Massachusetts, the fourth of seven children. Because her father was a commander in the navy, the family had lived in places like Hawaii and Paris. Eleanor's family encouraged outdoor exercise and independence. From childhood on, she'd canoed and hiked, frequently climbing Mount Monadnock. Once, as a teenager, she and a sister had driven a buckboard and horse, alone, up to Maine for a two-week trip. Their father's only stipulation had been that the girls carry a pistol underneath the seat cushion, although neither knew how to use it.

Eleanor had graduated from the Boston Normal School of Gymnastics, which was later absorbed by Wellesley. The school emphasized a Swiss-style course of physical education but also included a psychology class at Harvard and chemistry and physics classes at M I T. Although Eleanor hadn't learned ballet because her dance instructor thought it harmed one's back and feet, she received instruction in modern dance, gymnastics, hockey, tennis, swimming, canoeing, and horseback riding. After graduating, she taught physical education for six years in the southern and eastern United States.

At C C she made friends with a group who hiked constantly, since almost no one owned a car. With a map by Manly Ormes, a Colorado Springs librarian and hiker, they investigated the local trails and charged cross-country through the brush. Sometimes Eleanor and the other young faculty members chaperoned fraternity parties at cabins in the nearby mountains and at the Bruin Inn, a log-cabin steak house in Cheyenne Canyon. Since the inn was a forty-minute hike from the streetcar line, C C faculty and students often ran at breakneck speed down the path from the inn, barely in time to catch the ten o'clock streetcar, the last one, back to town. The dean of women was a popular guest on these outings "because if she was there and we were late, it was her fault, not ours."[9]

In 1914, a year after Eleanor began teaching at C C, a young political science instructor named Albert Ellingwood arrived—or rather, returned. After attending high school and college in Colorado Springs, where he had acquired a taste for mountain climbing, he'd been awarded a Rhodes scholarship and for three years had studied in England. While there, Albert became active in the Oxford University Mountaineering Club and took holidays in English climbing centers and in Switzerland. Along the way he learned how to use ropes, pitons, and ice axes. By this time British mountaineers, who had earlier climbed almost exclusively on European snow and ice, had finally turned their attention to the rock faces on their own island.

Albert met Eleanor and, perhaps after playing tennis with her, recognized her exceptional coordination. He offered to instruct her in climbing techniques, and she eagerly took him up on it. He first taught Eleanor how to tie the special knots used on the climbing rope and then how to make "the calls," a formalized set of terms that inform climbers roped together what each is doing, even though they can't see each other. Albert didn't teach rappelling (descending by sliding on rope) to her and his other climbing friends until later. Eleanor recalls that although they thought rappelling was fun, they thought it was "sort of silly, too." (It should be pointed out that Albert and Eleanor were not the first Coloradans to take ropes on their climbs; members of the Boulder-based Rocky Mountain Climbers Club began carrying ropes while ascending the exposed [long and steep] Flatirons shortly after 1900, although they didn't always uncoil them while on the rock!)

Gradually, as Eleanor caught on, she and Albert became a frequent team; Albert always led and Eleanor was always second. This arrangement illustrates perhaps better than anything else the confidence that Albert had in Eleanor's climbing ability, for it is the second person on the rope who must catch the leader, should he fall. Eleanor was five feet two and usually weighed 115 pounds, although once, after a long, hard trip, she dropped to 85; it seems doubtful that she could have caught Albert on a big fall. They used static belays, which put an intolerable strain on the ropes and have long since been replaced by dynamic belays, and Manila ropes, which were pathetically weak and have long since been replaced by nylon ropes. Fortunately, the issue of stopping a fall was academic. Robert Ormes, who later wrote the classic *Guide to the Colorado Mountains*, said of Albert Ellingwood, "Of course he didn't fall."[10]

After Eleanor moved to Colorado she adopted the outdoor attire favored by the local outdoor women: jeans and slacks. She also paid a dressmaker to convert one of her skirts into a pair of knickerbockers for riding and climbing. Puttees and Boy Scout shoes completed her outfit. Typically, she camped out with army blankets rolled up in a tarp, although on their trip to the Crestones the party took tents to accommodate Mrs. Ellingwood and Eleanor's sister Sarah. Their standard food was rice, canned soup, raisins, nuts, chocolates, cereal, and cocoa—never tea or coffee, because Albert didn't drink either one. Bob Ormes climbed and hiked with Eleanor several times. He enjoyed her company and recalls that "she was not inclined to ramble on and on about how beautiful the scenery was," since she thought it "took away" from the experience. He calls Eleanor "a little wren of a type, very tough and strong and not disturbed by altitude," and a "damn good climber and nervy."[11]

In July 1916 Albert organized a party to make an assault on the last unclimbed fourteeners in Colorado, and of course he invited Eleanor. He described the Crestones as "exhilarating" and wrote, "No other mountains in our state are quite so picture-bookish, quite so like the idealized representations of what mountains ought to be."[12] The eight climbers set out from Colorado Springs "in high spirits." Eleanor's sister Sarah took most of the party's gear by train on a spur railroad that ran three times a week from Villa Grove to the town of Crestone on the edge of the San Luis Valley, roughly two hundred miles southwest of Denver. There she met the rest of the party, who had walked for several days to save train fare because, as Eleanor explains, "We didn't have so much cash in those days."[13] At Crestone they hired burros to take the loads to Willow Creek, where they camped on a ridge that Albert thought was one of the prettiest campsites he had seen in Colorado. The next morning they made a first ascent of Kit Carson Mountain, whose only difficulty lay in the final southwest arete (steep rock ridge) some three hundred feet below the top.

Two days later "the more energetic of the party," which meant Albert, Eleanor, Joe Deutschbein, and Bee Rogers, moved camp to Spanish Creek, intending to "make a test of the unclimbability of the Crestones." On July 24 they knocked off the first one, Crestone Peak. Although they roped up midway, Albert's nearly unerring sense of the route made it appear fairly straightforward. However, the jagged, exposed ridge between Crestone Peak and Crestone Needle appeared to be quite another matter. Bee Rogers and Joe Deutschbein decided to return to camp. Albert and Eleanor continued. Albert described the climb:

The ups and downs we had to follow to the Needle's base were easy enough, but rather tantalizing, for the many loose-rock gullies were a bore after the firm-set buttresses of the peak. The west face of the Needle brought us compensations, however, for it is a steep wall, inclined well toward the vertical and studded generously with small stones that are as firmly fixed in their places as if they had roots ten feet long. The climbing on this stretch of some two hundred feet is thoroughly enjoyable.

For the third time in a week they found no trace of humans on the summit and decided that, once again, they'd made a first ascent. Later, Albert wrote that the "prolonged virginity" of the Crestones was "not due to any inherent difficulty or inhospitality, but only to the lack of a not too faint-hearted wooer." Eleanor recalls the climbs up Crestone Peak and the

Needle as being rather exciting, even though the rock was firm and the handholds were reliably solid. In August 1924, eight years after they first climbed the Crestones, Albert and Eleanor returned, along with Marion (Mickey) Warner and Steve Hart. By this time Eleanor was an extremely experienced climber. The year before she'd been the first woman to climb the Grand Teton, in Wyoming, and as a result had become the first Colorado female to become a member of the largely eastern and largely male American Alpine Club.

The day's challenge for Steve, Mickey, Albert, and Eleanor was to be the eastern arete of Crestone Needle, on which the party hoped to find a "plausible course . . . that led errantly by crack and ledge, up cliffs and ribs of rock that looked appallingly abrupt." After three hours and fifteen hundred feet of "careful climbing," just as the party reached a critical face, a sudden storm loosed a layer of hailstones that lodged in cracks and slicked up the rock. The group pressed on. Several times the route seemed to dead-end, but each time Albert found an alternative. Bit by bit, they ascended the face. It took four hours to climb the last four hundred vertical feet, but finally, at 5:25, they made the top. The route, which came to be known as Ellingwood's Arete, established a new standard for Colorado rock-climbing in much the same way that Alexander's Chimney, on the East Face of Longs Peak, would a few years later.[14]

Eleanor regards the Crestones as the highlight of a climbing career that included a second ascent of Mount Wilbur, in Glacier National Park, and early ascents in the Wind River Mountains of Wyoming. She has other favorites, such as Pyramid and Capitol (both fourteeners), and feels affection for fourteeners Sierra Blanca and Holy Cross, saying she came to regard them as "her" mountains. Eleanor climbed Sierra Blanca from three different sides; on one of those climbs she encountered a sheepherder, who asked her party to "look over and see the ocean for me" when they reached the top. She climbed Holy Cross by three different routes, too, including the steep, snowy "stem" of the cross, accompanied by a young climber, Polly Bouck. All told, Eleanor climbed about thirty of what were then recognized as fourteeners, many while she was on Colorado Mountain Club outings, and she would have climbed more if she hadn't been out of the state for several summers teaching. She would also have garnered an impressive first ascent in the Tetons if Albert Ellingwood hadn't been a "late-riser." Bob Ormes, who was just a "young kid" at the time, recalls that

Albert's party started climbing Mount Owen, which had never been climbed, so late that they would have had to stay out all night if they'd been successful. Despite his disappointment, however, Bob feels indebted to Albert "for attacking cliffs and peaks by their difficult routes, and for exploring them in general."[15]

During Eleanor's climbing heyday, merely reaching the mountains was complicated. Trails were scarce. "You saw your peak and you went to it," Eleanor explains. "You just took the most direct route." Until she bought a car in 1918 or so, Eleanor and her friends rode trains or hired a local man with a truck. They camped out in mine tunnels, on ranch porches, or on open ground. Once, Eleanor used her packhorse's saddle for a pillow while sleeping out, unprotected, in a hard rainstorm near Aspen.

Often, when she wasn't climbing, Eleanor roamed Colorado by herself or with Colorado College students. She usually stayed the night at ranches, where she was warmly received. However, once, she and a student had a quite different experience while hiking in the Tarryall Mountains near Colorado Springs. Before setting out, Eleanor had asked a ranger if he thought she and the girl should make housing arrangements ahead of time, but he had assured her that everyone was so nice and friendly at the ranches that they wouldn't have any trouble finding places to spend the night. So, late in the afternoon of the first day out, they knocked on the door of what seemed to be a likely ranch. A woman came to the door, and Eleanor asked if they could spend the night. The woman stared at Eleanor and her companion, who were both wearing knickerbockers, and announced that she wouldn't think of taking in women who were dressed like men. Disappointed, Eleanor then asked her where the next ranch house was. "It won't do you any good," the woman answered, "because I'm on a party line and I'm going to phone everyone on it about some women dressed in trousers." Eleanor and the girl slept in a haystack and went home the next day.

From 1914 to 1930 Eleanor was a physical education instructor at CC, and for ten of those years she was head of the department. At age forty-five she married George Ehrman, a widower with three children, and gave up teaching and rock-climbing. Today she lives in Colorado Springs, and although she walks with a cane because of an old accident on ice, Eleanor has the figure and alertness of the athletic centenarian that she is. When asked recently if she had ever been scared while climbing, she replied no, that she had always "had a good head" and that heights had never bothered her. She recalled that from early on she'd had a kinesthetic sense, which, as she put it, "You either have . . . or you don't."

MARJORIE PERRY

Eleanor Davis Ehrman was never a skier, and Marjorie Perry was never a mountain climber. So, although both women were members of the Colorado Mountain Club at the same time, they knew each other only casually. However, Marjorie did for skiing what Eleanor did for technical climbing: she showed that a woman could hold her own in a sport dominated by men.

Like many of Colorado's mountain women, Marjorie was not a native, having been born in Chicago on November 15, 1882. In 1887 she and her family had moved to the dry climate of Denver to benefit her asthmatic mother. Her father, Sam, a self-made man, prospered in Colorado. Before long he owned a coal mine at Oak Creek, near Steamboat Springs, on the Western Slope. (In Colorado, "West Slope" and "East Slope" refer to the western and eastern sides of the Continental Divide.) Although the Perry family lived mainly in Denver, Sam spent so much time at Oak Creek that he came to know its surrounding country extremely well, as did his two daughters. Marjorie often accompanied him on his twice-yearly hunting trips; Charlotte disliked hunting.

Marjorie paid tribute to her mother by saying that she "always understood," but it was clearly Marjorie's father, Sam, who most influenced her.[16] Unhesitatingly, she followed him into the mountains, usually on horseback. He taught her how to ride in the backcountry, how to camp out and to care for the horses, how to read the weather signs and to track game. Marjorie grew up feeling utterly at home in country without trails and came to love animals, domestic as well as wild. During Theodore Roosevelt's presidency she trained a pair of orphaned bear cubs. One cub became so rambunctious that she gave him to the zoo, but the more docile one became a pet whom Marjorie's mother often featured as a live Teddy bear at her garden parties on the grounds of the family home at 1140 Grant Street.

A few years after Marjorie graduated from Smith College in 1905, Sam Perry became involved with railroads and gave Marjorie free passes. She rode the Moffat Railroad so frequently that she became well acquainted with most of the firemen and engineers and their familes who lived in the towns along the way. On February 12, 1913, when she was on her way to

Steamboat Springs, two hundred miles northwest of Denver, the train stopped in Hot Sulphur Springs. Marjorie got off to chitchat with some friends, who insisted she stay for their ski carnival to watch the Norwegian Carl Howelsen ski jump. (Carl had Americanized his name from the original Karl Hovelsen.)

Marjorie was impressed, and after meeting Carl she persuaded him to go with her to Steamboat Springs, saying he'd find a bigger jumping hill and more snow there than in Hot Sulphur. She was right. Carl cut a few trees and built a little jumping course on the side of Woodchuck Hill, where the Alpine campus of Colorado Mountain College is now. When he tried it out, the townspeople cheered. At the end of the weekend he had to go back to his job in Denver, but the following autumn he returned to Steamboat and purchased some land in Strawberry Park. That year, 1914, he instigated Steamboat's first Winter Ski Carnival, held on February 12 and 13. Carl helped lay out a course for the ten-mile cross-country race, which he won, and put up the platform for the big jump competition, which he also won. Marjorie Perry took second place in the "Ladies' Race, Free-for-All," and won a silver fruit spoon valued at six dollars.

Fortunately for Colorado and American skiing fans, Carl Howelsen called Steamboat Springs home for eight years. Ten years earlier, in Norway, he had won first prize for the fifty-kilometer cross-country race and the Prince Regent's Cup, first prize for the combined races and His Majesty King Oscar's Cup, and finally, the highest award of all, the Holmenkollen Gold Medal. Shortly after this triumph, however, Norway's economy had become so bleak that Carl had emigrated to the United States. After "ski sailing" for Barnum and Bailey, he became a bricklayer in Denver and discovered the superb snow in Colorado mountains.

At the time Carl came to Steamboat the locals were using homemade skis to get around. But Carl demonstrated that skiing could be more than transportation; it could also be an incredibly graceful, exhilarating sport. He constructed a ski jump on a hill later named for him, which launched many world-record jumps, and taught the local residents what he knew about skiing. "Every skier who took classes [from him]," Marjorie said, "had his technique."[17] After ski lessons the children, some only three years old, would go home and practice on the wooden roofs of their houses, which were laden with snow.

In 1921 Carl left Steamboat Springs for what he thought would be a two-month trip to Norway for his parents' fiftieth wedding anniversary. But he married his sister's beautiful sister-in-law and never returned. His influence remained, however; Steamboat Springs has nurtured more Olympic skiers than any other town in the United States—and all because Marjorie Perry persuaded him in 1913 to go to Steamboat Springs, where they had "real" snow.

In 1914 Marjorie Perry's sister, Charlotte, and Portia Mansfield, both Smith graduates, founded the Perry-Mansfield Camp for Girls and School of Theatre and Dance, a few miles out of Steamboat Springs. During the summer Marjorie ran the camp. She spent the winters in Denver leading an active social life, which included "wonderful times" with an innocent group known as the "Shack Crowd." Parties were held in a primitive cabin accessible from the Moffat Railroad between Tunnel Two and Tunnel Three, near Rollinsville, thirty miles west of Denver. Marjorie was the first female member of the Shack Crowd, but later some of her female friends became regulars too.

She spent part of every winter skiing in Steamboat Springs, at Grand Lake, on CMC outings at Fern Lake in Rocky Mountain National Park, and, at least once, on the grounds of the State Capitol Building in Denver. At first Marjorie donned the traditional long skirt. However, sometime before 1920 she persuaded her father to buy her an imported red ski outfit, displayed in the window of a local department store. Very likely, Marjorie was the first Colorado woman to wear an "official" ski suit.

During the summer of 1924 Marjorie met Eleanor Bliss, who became her good friend and for several years her riding assistant at the Perry-Mansfield Camp. (Eventually, Marjorie severed her tie with the camp after she and Charlotte quarreled.) During the thirteen years that Marjorie managed Perry-Mansfield's riding department, every spring she rode her own horse two hundred miles from Denver across the mountains to Steamboat Springs. In the fall she reversed the trip. Since horse trailers hadn't yet been invented, it was the only way she could have her own mount for the summer. It was also the perfect excuse for an adventure. In 1926 Eleanor Bliss accompanied her.

The women set out from Steamboat on October 3. Eleanor carried a nightgown, extra socks and underwear, a toothbrush, a comb, a nail file, toothpaste, cold cream, Ungentine and Analgesique, a tiny bottle of iodine, heavy gloves, sweaters, windbreakers, slickers, lunch, and little bags of nuts, raisins, and cheese. She rode a "green-broke" colt, named Secret because she and Marjorie hadn't told their parents about him, while Marjorie rode Tony, a reliable nineteen-year-old who'd made the trip before.[18] As was her custom, Marjorie mailed oats for the horses to the ranches along the way. The first night out, she and Eleanor stayed at Sam Perry's mine, the Moffat Coal Company, just north of Oak Creek. The second day they rode up Morrison Creek to the last ranch below Gore Pass, known as the Hall Place, whose walls were insulated with newspapers. Since Mr. Hall was away, Mrs. Hall insisted that Eleanor and Marjorie sleep in the one and only bed while she slept on the couch.

During the night Marjorie developed a toothache. However, she and Eleanor set out early the next morning, accompanied by Mrs. Hall, who, "in her split overalls, little hat and pasty powdered face," jogged behind them up to the Divide. Then, after a "fond farewell," Marjorie and Eleanor rode on the Gore Pass road until they came to the Pinney Ranch, where they stopped for lunch. By this time Marjorie's toothache was so painful that she could eat only bread and milk. Oddly, Eleanor also developed a toothache in the identical tooth. So, after reaching Kremmling, on the Colorado River, the women left their horses at a livery, took the night train to Denver, saw the dentist, and returned twenty-four hours later. Although they felt considerably better, they had lost an entire day; Marjorie was worried that they'd be caught in what she called the "equinoctial storm."

Marjorie's route had always followed Highway 40, which was a dirt road in those days, climbing east to Hot Sulphur Springs and then over Berthoud Pass. However, for several years she'd toyed with the idea of going over Jones Pass, to the south of Berthoud. Until her 1926 trip she hadn't been able to persuade anyone to try it with her; she was pleased that Eleanor was game. But while Marjorie and Eleanor slept in Kremmling, the weather turned, casting doubt on their plan of trying Jones Pass. Great masses of dark clouds hung down, parting occasionally to reveal snow up high. Marjorie was fearful that the storm had finally come. So after an early lunch at the Buckhorn Lodge on the Colorado River, run by a Brit who broke broncos on an English saddle, she phoned several nearby ranchers to get their opinions. They all agreed that if it didn't storm, she wouldn't have any problems, since there was a good government trail on the west side of Jones Pass and an old wagon road, used for hauling ore, on the east side. But it seemed chancy, and the wife of the Buckhorn proprietor, Mrs.

Messiter, insisted on giving Marjorie two woolen mufflers "to help out over the pass." Eleanor and Marjorie then rode south on the road up the Williams Fork, slipping into their usual routine of walking their horses for three miles, trotting for one, walking for three, and so on. At 3:30 it began to rain, and the women put on their slickers. Finally they reached the last ranch on the road, owned by the Taussigs.

By morning, three inches of snow had accumulated and it was still snowing hard. The Taussigs tried to talk Marjorie and Eleanor out of going over Jones Pass, saying they should retrace their steps to the Buckhorn and then go over Berthoud. But Eleanor protested that it would add two days to the trip and that with some of the phone lines down she wouldn't be able to notify her New York relatives of the delay. Couldn't someone take them to the top of Jones Pass and then point out the road on the other side? Finally, Warren Taussig agreed to do it, but "not for less than $15.00."

By ten o'clock, he was ready to go and they started out. Warren rode ahead on a horse that was "barefoot," so the snow didn't cling to his hooves. The women followed. They tried to keep up, but their horses, which were shod, kept picking up snow; it would build up under one hoof, then under another, like stilts, until it fell off. Secret slipped badly three or four times. Once Tony fell down on his side but was able to scramble up quickly. "Warren led the way over fields of fluffy down," Eleanor wrote, "[and] through willows bowed to the ground in graceful curves and between rows of pines and spruce which dropped their heavy burdens of snow as we passed. The world was wonderfully pure and still. . . . All the way along I kept thinking that I hoped heaven looked like that; it was overwhelmingly peaceful and unbelievably beautiful."

After lunch in a deserted miner's cabin, they continued climbing. Above timberline, the wind blew mercilessly. The horses' eyes and nostrils began icing up. In order to breathe, the women leaned down and put their faces on the lee side of their horses' necks. They didn't try to talk because it was obvious the wind would snatch their words. Somehow they reached Jones Pass, only to find that a great snowdrift blocked the way down. Warren dismounted, tied the reins together, put them around his own neck, and plunged into the drift, "pinwheeling his arms so that he became a human snowplow." His horse followed, compacting the snow so that Marjorie and Eleanor went through a "sort of tunnel," twenty feet long, that ended at the edge of a steep snowfield. Warren then tied his reins around the horse's saddle and shouted to the women to "do what I do." He sat down, slid fifty feet, landed on a shelf, and whistled to his horse. The horse then sat on his rear and slid down the snowbank too. Marjorie and Eleanor followed and somehow persuaded their horses to do the same. By now the women's feet were numb and they were glad to walk, leading their mounts. Repeatedly, they lost the trail, but finally they reached the trees and, at 4:30, the bottom of Berthoud Pass, which converged with the Jones Pass route. Eight miles later they ended their forty-two-mile ride in the safety of Glen Arbor Lodge. The next day they rode in to Denver.

A few years later Marjorie bought a pickup and converted her mother's old electric chassis into a horse trailer, ending the need for her epic trips across the Divide. However, shortly before February 26, 1928, she made a memorable skiing trip with Elinor Eppich Kingery, whom she called her "Winter Elinor, . . . [a] pal, a good skier for those days, a girl who was free and fearless."[19] (Marjorie called Eleanor Bliss her "Summer Eleanor.") The trip occurred when the women were coming back from the Winter Ski Carnival at Steamboat Springs, which Marjorie attended every year, and were riding one of the last trains to cross the notorious Rollins Pass, roughly forty-five miles west of Denver. (A week later the newly opened Moffat Tunnel replaced the Rollins Pass route.) Elinor and Marjorie were wearing ski clothes, for Marjorie was hoping that the train would be delayed. At 9 A.M., the train chugged to the top of Rollins Pass and stopped at the collection of snowsheds and buildings known as Corona. By now the train was several hours late. Passengers were ordered out to eat breakfast in the little lunchroom, and much to her delight, Marjorie overheard the conductor telling a waitress that they were going to stay for at least a couple of hours.

So after breakfast, she and Elinor retrieved their skis from the baggage car, despite the protests of the conductor, who thought their plan of skiing sixteen miles down the other side to Tolland was sheer madness. The brakeman, who was standing nearby, whispered: "We aren't going to start down 'til the snow plow and the train from Denver come up. Here's a fuzee. You light this and put it in the track no matter where you are and the train will stop for you." Two other passengers, women from Boston, agreed to look after their luggage, and Marjorie and Elinor set off.

It was a glorious sunny day but the wind was terrific and that's what I was counting on, for it was at our back. Out of the shed in the bright light, we looked at the top and considered going over instead of following the track. It could not have been much more than 12,000 feet as the sheds were 11,666. I had no fear of getting lost for, as they say now, the visibility was perfect. But Elinor was hesitant because she had never seen the other side of the 'Hump'.

The tracks were cleared, but between them was a packed ski trail and we slid easily into motion as we hit it. Around the grade we spun—not too fast—just moving along friskily. The hillside was very steep as we wound around the mountain, hardly daring to look at the bottom of the draw, thousands of feet below. I knew about the trestle where a deep crevasse cut into the sidehill but I had always seen it from the cozy coach where getting over it was not my responsibility. We were suddenly scared but now the rugged hillside was impossible to scale. Elinor had those horrible ski bindings that wrapped around and around, so she left her skis on. I took mine off, crawled on my hands and knees as she hung onto me. Without that fierce wind it wouldn't have been so bad, but it was a long way down! Thank goodness, it was only about 200 feet long and then we went gaily on. There were short snow sheds where our voices echoed and soon a long one, half a mile, perhaps. Elinor was chatting gaily (usually she's rather quiet), but she was happy and excited, and I was frantic for I knew a lot that she didn't know. When I told her to keep quiet, she asked why.

"I want to hear the snow plow if and when it's coming up the hill," I explained.

We were travelling thru a narrow cut of snowshed and the only way we could get out of the track was to climb an icy support to get up under the roof. I figured she could push me up and then I could pull her up with her skis on, but I wanted all the time possible. This was something I hadn't counted on but there was no turning back. At last we came out into the open, the hillside was not so steep and we could see where the track made a switchback. Right there we left our beaten track and went down a snow field, reaching the side of the track again just as the rotary plow chugged up the hill past us. With horror Elinor watched those grinding metals turn and throw the snow high over the bank. It would make pulp of anything in its path. When it had passed she shuddered and only said, "Why didn't you shut me up sooner?"

Far below we saw the little train waiting at Dixie Lake [today's Jenny Lake] and knew that we had plenty of time to reach our goal with all the hazards behind us. Back in the track again, we lifted our poles and, blown by the wind, in no time were standing on a bank beside the train, higher than the car windows. My savage conductor was startled as he turned the switch and saw us.

"How far is it to Antelope?" I yelled above the wind. His answer was a command to get on that train in a hurry but we only laughed at him and repeated the question. He opened up a tirade on the man that let me leave his train and what my father would say if he knew it and how no human being could do such a thing and live thru it, and then he told me to get on down in the timber and wait for the train at the section house. He roared so loudly that passengers began to stick their heads out of the windows, trying to see what was attached to the feet they could not see. I told him it wouldn't hurt him to tell me how far it was to Antelope as long as we were going to our death anyway. As his train moved off, the conductor called, "Nine miles—but don't you go there!"

The grade was still 8% [more likely, 5%] and we knew we had a clear track so we just set sail and went. As we sped along past the section house, the little man with a broom opened his mouth but no sound came forth, he was so astonished. Occasionally we had to brake with our poles for the wind seemed stronger and we felt as if we were flying as the big pine trees sped by. Twice our track turned into the wind and for a short time we had to push, but on we went and Antelope, only an uninhabited flag station, was soon behind us. Around another bend we could see three long switchbacks thru the open timber and tiny Tolland far below. We left the track and went straight down the hill, making big curves, with the perfect powdered snow swirling in the air. After crossing the track we went on again straight down. No need to fall—the world was ours and we could make our own trail. I didn't used to be such a dumb skier in that kind of snow.

We made for Ladora, another flag stop, because by then we could see that the Tolland flats were icy and blown bare. No need to spoil such a perfect day, so we waited at Ladora. In about half an hour along came the train and we flagged it without the fuzee, which I kept for future emergencies. I have it yet! Quite a reception we had, especially by the Bostonians, who fell on our necks and fed us dates from a friend in Africa and all sorts of delicacies. They were practically hysterical because, while watching from the back platform, they had lost our tracks when we cut down the first snow field, and they knew we were dead.

In 1936, after her parents died, Marjorie bought ten acres in Littleton, a suburb of Denver, eventually increasing the acreage to two hundred. The Highline Canal flowed through her property, lined with huge old cottonwoods. Marjorie put in a pond, built a house, and raised cows, sheep, chickens, horses, and vegetables. She hired a caretaker, who lived in his own quarters, and a cook, who lived in the main house with her. In the spring of 1948 Eleanor Bliss moved to Colorado and lived with Marjorie. The women divided their time between Eleanor's house in Steamboat and Marjorie's farm at 4646 Belleview Avenue in Littleton.

Although Marjorie took trips to Hawaii, Mexico, and London, she much preferred driving through the mountains of Colorado. She loved her farm. Once, to the amusement of her relatives, she drove to the fancy wedding of Ruth Boettcher Humphrey and David Robinson Crocker Brown in a 1920 Dodge pickup, slightly muddy. It was so disreputable among the Cadillacs and Mercedes that the young attendant very nearly refused to park it. But for Marjorie it was simple expedience; her Franklin was being worked on and her modern pickup was being used on the farm.

After attending the first Steamboat Springs Winter Ski Carnival in 1914, Marjorie made all of the next fifty-five carnivals but one, missing that one because of a broken knee suffered when her horse slipped on ice. At the age of eighty-six she hung up her skis for good, ending more than sixty years of skiing. The next year, on August 4, 1969, she died in Denver.

HARRIET VAILLE BOUCK

Elinor Eppich Kingery was a close friend of Marjorie Perry's and, as we shall see, of Agnes Vaille's. For all these women, the Colorado Mountain Club provided a way to meet mountain-loving companions and to explore the state's nearly inaccessible backcountry. For Agnes Vaille's sister, Harriet, it offered a way to become involved in the hottest conservation issue of the state, the campaign to create Rocky Mountain National Park.

Bob Marshall of the U.S. Geological Survey convinced the CMC's first president, James Grafton Rogers, that Congress would be more likely to appropriate money to create a national park if the map of the proposed region were filled with named features rather than blanks. Accordingly, James Rogers appointed Harriet Vaille to chair a nomenclature committee of the Colorado Mountain Club for the purpose of researching appropriate names.

Harriet's father, F. O. Vaille, was the founder and president of Denver's first telephone company. Harriet was one of the first Denver women to own and drive a car and was well educated, having attended Bryn Mawr and graduated from the Boston Normal School of Gymnastics. She joined the CMC within a year after its founding in 1912, as did her younger sister Agnes.

As a first step to researching Colorado names, Harriet formed the Colorado Reading Party. At about the same time, she was appointed secretary of the Colorado Geographic Board, which consisted of such influential members as Mrs. William Byers, Governor Elias Ammons, Enos Mills, and Ellsworth Bethel, a high school teacher who was active with the Colorado State Museum. Harriet's initial approach to ferreting out Indian names was to go to the nearest center of Indian information, the Newberry Library in Chicago. She didn't have much success. Finally, she and other members of the Colorado Reading Party decided that it made sense to arrange for some of the old Indians who had lived in the area of the proposed national park to come back to Estes Park and recall the names they knew for the land. The logistics for putting this plan into effect were not obvious. However, the party followed the advice of Dr. Livingston Farrand, then president of the University of Colorado, who suggested they seek out old Northern Arapaho men on the Wind River Reservation in Wyoming, some five hundred miles north. Harriet Vaille persuaded a friend, Edna Hendrie, to accompany her there.

The women made their way to the reservation by train and wagon, carrying a letter of introduction from the commissioner of Indian Affairs that requested the superintendent of the reservation help them in every way possible. "Arapaho police were sent to every corner of the reservation to round up old Arapahos who knew our mountains," Harriet later recalled. "Five or six were found and interviewed and a competent younger Arapaho, Tom Crispin, was engaged to act as interpreter."[20]

Harriet and Edna selected seventy-three-year-old Gun Griswold, whose "only luggage was an eaglefeather fan," and sixty-three-year-old Sherman Sage, the reservation's chief-of-police "with an excellent sense of humor," and, of course, Tom Crispin.[21] Then the women returned to Colorado, where Harriet collected money for the Indians' trip, as much from her father as from the Colorado Mountain Club and the Colonial Dames combined. Harriet arranged for her cousin Oliver Toll, a college student, to conduct the two-week pack trip through the proposed national park. It was unthinkable that she should go herself, since "young ladies just did not do that."[22] She and Edna enlisted family automobiles to meet the Arapahos at the Longmont train station. The Hendrie chauffeur drove one car, and Harriet's father drove the other. After spending the night at Longs Peak Inn, the Arapaho entourage took a sight-seeing trip to the end of the partially completed Fall River Road. The following day Shep Husted, Oliver Toll, and the Arapahos began their trip, hoping to see as many high-country vistas as possible.

Shep Husted of Estes Park guided the party. Oliver Toll meticulously recorded the Arapahos' comments and attempted to convey the pronunciation of their words for geographic features. As a result of the trip, a few names were indeed added to the map of what became Rocky Mountain National Park—names such as Big Meadow, Tonahutu Creek, Lumpy Ridge, and Never Summer Range. In addition, the trip yielded the only oral history of the area from the Indians' viewpoint, so we now know that the Indians climbed Longs Peak to trap eagles long before the white man's supposed first ascent in 1868.

After the pack trip with the Arapahos, Denver newspapers published accounts of the project, and Harriet lectured at the Denver Public Library. She became so fascinated with Indian culture that she decided to attend the University of Chicago to take classes from a well-known professor. However, her mother had a stroke, which forced Harriet to stay in Denver to take care of her. On a Colorado Mountain Club trip, Harriet met Francis Eugene Bouck, an attorney whose wife had died, leaving him with two daughters, Polly, eleven, and Constance, fifteen. A romance blossomed, and in 1917, when Harriet was thirty-seven, they were married.

A short time later, after Eugene was elected district judge, the family moved to Leadville, 110 miles southwest of Denver and nearly two miles above sea level. It was not an easy place to live, even for a housewife accustomed to hard work. Harriet rose to the occasion. She applied paint and "sunny color schemes" to her home, a "very undistinguished old frame house" with no heat upstairs, and made it "as comfortable and homey as it could be, in its drafty way." Harriet's own daughter, born when Harriet was forty-one and named after Harriet, remembers her mother "bringing up hods of coal from the basement and having to get up early in the morning to light the fires."[23]

Harriet was "joyously welcomed" by her young stepdaughters, especially Polly, who was only ten months old when her mother died. Polly remembers:

Mother had had little experience with children, aside from brief visits with her sister Edith's children . . . and the groups of little girls in the gym classes she gave at Neighborhood House [a settlement house.] She had, however, a natural attraction to and for children and some of her ideas were ahead of her time. She believed in allowing a small girl plenty of freedom for tomboy-play as well as for all girlish games like "playing house" and "dressing up." Accordingly, she clad me for school in pretty but simple and hardy cotton crepe dresses with bloomers to match, and the following summer I had a boyish haircut and bib overalls.

I recall a warm day when one of Denver's fine cloudbursts came down. I can still feel the ecstasy of being allowed to run out and get drenched, then come in laughing and shivering to strip and be given a rubdown.[24]

Harriet joined the D.A.R. and P.E.O. chapters in Leadville and hiked with her family in the nearby mountains, some of the most spectacular in the state, including Colorado's highest, Mount Elbert. Polly fondly recalls that often the family sat around the "old stove in the living room, feet up on its nickel-plated flange, alternately reading aloud the classics from which Constance and I had to distill 'blue book' reports for English class." If a good rainbow or "one of Leadville's incomparable sunsets" appeared, the family would bound up from the table and run down the board sidewalk for a good view.[25]

In 1933 Eugene Bouck was appointed to the Colorado Supreme Court, and the family moved to Denver. Harriet died in 1962.

AGNES VAILLE

Harriet Vaille's sister, Agnes, was ten years younger than she and several inches taller. Like Harriet, Agnes was well educated, having graduated from Smith College. Consistently, Agnes was described as a "restful person and gentle and quiet," even-tempered and not critical of others. She was a good pianist and one of the state's earliest female technical climbers. Carl Blaurock, a friend and one of Colorado's extraordinary early climbers, called her "a strong, husky woman, just crazy about climbing." She took a lot of trips with the Colorado Mountain Club and served as its Outing Chairman. Agnes wrote her checks, "Pay to the order of the Colorado Mountain Club—Myself."[26]

Polly Bouck spent a year in Denver living with her Grandfather Vaille and Aunt Agnes while attending the Anna Wolcott School for Young Ladies, named for her great-aunt. Polly recalls that her Aunt Agnes was "at ease with everyone . . . friendly, but not what you'd call gregarious. . . . She had a nice sense of humor and a special kind of buoyancy. Her mouth turned up at the corners naturally and her personality went along with it.

The bookplate someone designed for her carried the motto, 'Laeta sorte mea' ('Happy in my lot'), which Mother said surely described Agnes."[27] When Polly was sixteen, Agnes gave her a pair of skis, her first.

Elinor Eppich Kingery was Agnes's good friend. On one occasion the two set out to climb Mount Yale but became lost and had to spend the night out. It was in May, and cold, so they built a fire. Elinor went to sleep. When she awakened, she realized that Agnes was behind her, keeping her warm while Agnes herself froze.

When World War I broke out, Agnes was among the first to volunteer to help overseas with the Red Cross. The work was demanding and the hours were long; she wrote home that for the first time in her life she "had enough to do." A few years after Agnes returned to Denver, for two summers she attended the National School for Commercial and Trade Executives, held at Northwestern University in Chicago. When the Denver Chamber of Commerce reorganized in 1924, she was hired to be its secretary. As it was later reported in a newspaper article, "She . . . decided to carve a career for herself in the business world. In this she was successful and often was paid the tribute by businessmen with whom she came in contact that she had 'the brains of a man.'"[28]

Like Marjorie Perry, Agnes owned a little skiing cottage on Rilliet Hill, at the base of Lookout Mountain. She went on at least one CMC winter outing to Fern Lake, and in 1923 she made, solo, the first known ascent of James Peak in winter. Her sleeping bag, which she designed herself, weighed "only seven pounds, marvelously light for those days. It was down-filled, covered with aeroplane cloth and lined with cotton crepe."[29] By 1924 Agnes had become a competent enough rock-climber to make a first ascent of the Bishop, a 120-foot rock formation in Platte Canyon near the town of Buffalo. Her climbing companions were Stephen Hart and Albert Ellingwood, who had both climbed with Eleanor Davis Ehrman. Their route, a chimney, or crack wide enough for a climber, that occasionally penetrated thirty feet into the rock, took five hours to go up and three to come down.

Sometime in the early 1920s Agnes Vaille met Walter Kiener, a Swiss five years her junior. His father was a "rough and brutal" man, but his mother had instilled in him a love of science and the arts, and he had learned French, German, and English.[30] While in his twenties he had emigrated to the United States, eventually drifting to Denver where he "secured work at his trade" as a butcher. He joined the Colorado Mountain Club there and met Agnes.

In the early fall of 1924 he, Agnes, Herman Buhl, and Buhl's wife, Elmira, climbed to the top of Mount Evans, a beautiful fourteener west of Denver. Herman was German and a former member of the Swiss Alpine Club. Elmira was the first woman to have climbed the East Face of Longs Peak, on September 10, 1922. As the four were resting, they looked north and beheld the "grand appearance of Longs." Agnes and Walter "resolved to climb its east face in the near future." Neither Agnes nor Walter had climbed the East Face before, and certainly Agnes had never made a technical climb approaching its length—sixteen hundred feet. Still, given her abilities, making such a climb in October didn't seem especially foolhardy or unreasonable. Besides, as Elinor Eppich Kingery has pointed out, there was another factor: Agnes Vaille regarded Walter Kiener as the leader of the trip, since she thought he had had experience on snow and ice and with winter climbing in Switzerland. For ten years Agnes had been steeped in the Colorado Mountain Club's cardinal rule, "Let the leader lead." "Agnes was gentle . . . she was a stickler for following a course agreed on," Elinor wrote. "Given a leader, nothing but complete physical exhaustion could have persuaded Agnes to object or to renege on the leader's course."[31]

Much of the following information about the Walter Kiener–Agnes Vaille climb of the East Face comes from a previously unpublished thirteen-page typed manuscript. Although Charles Edwin Hewes, one of the owners of the Hewes-Kirkwood Inn a mile west of Longs Peak Inn, was the author, he apparently attempted to act only as a scribe for Walter Kiener. The manuscript is in the first person, as though Walter were the narrator. Undoubtedly, it is not a totally authentic account of the climb. Charlie Hewes tended to romanticize women and the mountains in flowery language, as his self-published books of poetry illustrate. He was a good friend of Walter Kiener's and may well have bent some facts in Kiener's favor; he may also have forgotten parts of the conversation that the manuscript is based on. Finally, Walter Kiener may have unconsciously changed some details in attempting to assuage his guilt. Nevertheless, the Hewes-Kiener manuscript is the only extant written account that comes close to being Kiener's version of what happened on the ill-fated climb of the East Face. It is quoted extensively in the following pages, having been edited for spelling and grammar. The account begins:

With the reputation that Agnes enjoyed in the Colo. Mt. Club as the equal of any member, man or woman, for daring, endurance, and other qualifications of an able mountain climber, and my own experience in both Switzerland and America, we felt that we could make a successful winter climb. . . . [T]he previous ascents had been made in late summer and early fall when the face of the mountain was about as dry and free from ice and snow as it ever gets.

In light of this mention of a winter ascent, it is puzzling why Walter and Agnes made an attempt in October; perhaps it was a scouting trip for a subsequent climb. At any rate, they made a first attempt in October. When they were well into the climb, Walter dropped his ice axe.

Calling to Agnes, I told her the situation and that we must return. Having a very precarious footing on the steeply inclined wall, I succeeded in finally lodging my partner in a place where she could hold on; then, for the second time in my life (the first time, in a tight place in Switzerland), I loosened the rope from my body so that in case I slipped and fell she would not be dragged down. On account of the long time we had been employed in cutting steps in the ice, darkness had come on. I soon realized that I was in a difficult situation. Soon, however, my body was wriggling over the edge of the wall, with fingers clinging to the slight indentations in the rocks and with my feet finally finding the niches previously cut in the ice. I made my way down to safety and we returned to camp.

In November they decided to make a second attempt. Agnes phoned Carl Blaurock, asking to borrow his ice axe. He was horrified to hear that she was going to try the climb in a season when storms could come up quickly and temperatures plunge dangerously without warning. Carl tried to talk her and Walter out of the attempt, but when his efforts failed, he offered to come along since he knew the way. The party set out but made errors in choosing the route, and at 5 P.M., just fifty feet below the summit ridge, they decided to turn around. In darkness, they made a painstakingly slow descent, arriving so late in Denver that they barely had enough time to clean up and dress for the Monday workday. Carl Blaurock said he wouldn't try the East Face again in winter but would be happy to accompany Agnes and Walter in the spring. "I tried to talk them into waiting," he later wrote, "but no, they wouldn't."[32]

A month later Agnes and Walter tried again and were turned back by bad weather. By now Agnes's friends and relatives regarded her desire to climb the East Face in winter as an "obsession."[33] The Hewes-Kiener account continues:

At this juncture a sort of disagreeable, unhealthy situation developed in our East Face efforts. Agnes became the object of considerable adverse criticism on the part of those who tried to dissuade her from any further attempts to climb the East Face. Members of her family, fellow Mountain Club members, friends and others contributed to this—and with the highest motives, believing that the climb was too dangerous—until they became a unit in asserting that it was impossible to ascend the East Face of Longs Peak in winter. In opposition to this was Agnes and myself, both of us believing that it could be accomplished. Thus a regrettable but definite challenge arose in the matter which we proposed to meet. Although I moved in almost wholly different strata of society from hers and therefore was not subjected to this criticism as she was, I, too, endeavored to dissuade her from going again, stating that when the talk quieted down we could slip up to the peak and make the ascent almost before anyone knew we were going. To these remarks, however, she was not favorable.

Agnes sent out her Christmas greetings, postcards with a photograph—undoubtedly taken by her—of mountains, with the message: "I hope that this Christmas day will be full of joy for you, and that the coming year will be brimming over with opportunity, achievement and happiness. These mountains are sending you this message, too!"[34]

On Saturday, January 10, 1925, Walter, Agnes, and Elinor Eppich (Kingery) set out from Denver for the fourth attempt on the East Face. Since Agnes had to work at the Chamber of Commerce half-days on Saturday, they didn't leave Denver until one in the afternoon. Agnes drove her Dodge, unintentionally doing a few 360s on the ice as they headed out of town. Elinor had agreed to come along only on the condition that Agnes not try to persuade her to do the actual climb. "She was always a person of her word," Elinor recalled, "and did not in fact so much as suggest that I try to climb with them."[35]

Agnes drove her car until snowdrifts on the road forced her to stop. According to the Hewes-Kiener manuscript, after she parked, a mile below Baldpate Inn, the party skied several miles to Longs Peak Inn, arriving at 8 P.M. But Elinor recalls that they managed to drive within a mile or so of Longs Peak Inn and that they then drained the car's radiator because temperatures were expected to plunge. They soon skied by a pond where men were cutting ice and chatted with the young caretaker of Longs Peak Inn, Herbert Sortland. Although the Hewes-Kiener manuscript says they arrived at Timberline Cabin long *after* midnight, Elinor is quite sure in her account that it was earlier. They found that snow had drifted in through the cracks, but after lighting a fire in the little stove, they warmed up enough to sleep at least occasionally.

Concerning the hours before the climb, the written accounts of Hewes-Kiener and Elinor Eppich Kingery agree on one point: in the morning the wind was blowing so hard that attempting the ascent seemed out of the question. But then the accounts disagree. The Hewes-Kiener account reads:

After eating breakfast and joking and visiting awhile, Elinor gave a sudden exclamation and told us to look out of the window at the peak, for as if by magic the wind had ceased and the appearance of the mountain was so magnificent that every drop of blood in my body anticipated its conquest with the girls equally enthusiastic. The storm over and the sky clear, we said goodbye to Elinor who returned down the trail to Longs Peak Inn where she was to wait until we came back.

In contrast, Elinor recalled:

The next morning the sun was shining but it was very cold and the wind was cruel. I asked Agnes something about their going and she said, "I don't think we'll go." I went outside for a few minutes to go to the john and when I came back, here were Walter Kiener and Agnes, all ready to take off.

I believe it was at this time that Walter Kiener made the attempt to persuade me to go with them, although I did not have proper climbing shoes with me nor other necessary equipment—which he knew because I told him. It must certainly have been at this time.

It is these few minutes, and because I know from these two incidents that the final decision to make the climb on that day was not Agnes's, and that the judgment of Walter Kiener was not necessarily infallible or even good (*nobody* goes on a climb like that in ski shoes, without crampons or ice axe or even proper gloves), that I have resented so and fought against, the general assumption of the world, or practically everyone who has heard the story, that it was all Agnes's stubbornness and poor judgment that were responsible for the whole tragedy.

That simply is not so.

The Hewes-Kiener manuscript continues:

Although we made a late start, I felt that we could attain our object if we could maintain a reasonably rapid speed. Reaching the glacier, we climbed to Broadway and traversed that ledge to its junction with the Notch Couloir, the gully which descends from under the great notch of the peak on the east side. The day remained calm and beautiful but the couloir was filled with snow and ice and we spent about four hours in cutting our steps up its steep incline. Then another two hours was occupied in getting from the top of the couloir north on the face of the mountain to a point that had been selected from which we could finish the climb up through the little notch to the summit.

It was four o'clock in the afternoon and the darkness had set in, and although I felt strong and fit for the remainder of the ascent, I was greatly perturbed and grieved to note that my companion's strength was about spent. For some time I had noticed that she was far from being in the wonderful form and endurance that she was noted for and for the past two hours she had been almost helpless; and often as we paused she complained and apologized for being such a burden on my hands.

Although I had long since abandoned all hopes of rapid ascent, I tried not to betray it, encouraging her all I could. But it was soon evident that she was helpless to proceed and for close to twelve hours I had to cut the steps alone, handle the rope, and pull, lift and assist her until we finally reached the summit about 4 A.M.

This last twelve hours of the climb was made in complete darkness and the way was exceedingly tantalizing, for the face of the mountain at this point is a series of projections, like great steps, at this time of year being covered by a blanket of snow and ice. One step would be on the sheer rock face just under a thin covering of ice, and at the next we would sink to our waists in snow. Thus every step we advanced became an effort of dogged labor.

We lost our two lanterns on this slope and here I took the only thermometer reading of the trip—14 degrees below zero. We found it fairly quiet on the summit and Agnes suggested that we register as proof we had made the ascent. But, anxious to get off the mountain on account of her exhausted condition and fearing a now gusty wind would bring in something stronger, I said jokingly, "What's the use? Of course it would be proof that we reached the summit, but by which side and that's the point. Let's go on." By this time the summit began to be enveloped in clouds; we lost our way and wandered off toward the northwest, when a fortunate opening in the clouds occurred just at day break and I got our location exactly, seeing Mount Lady Washington to the east, the Boulderfield below me and our route down the north face.

My joy and exultation in this observation was suddenly dispelled, however, when the light of the dawn revealed the features of my brave companion, for they were those of one who was doomed; the most appalling lines of suffering and anguish—pained, haggard and deep drawn—had developed in the countenance of that heroic woman. Her eyes were fearfully bloodshot and she now talked in tones that seemed supernatural. I did my best to conceal my own intense agitation and despair. Even as far advanced as she must have been into the spirit, kept still on the earth by her dauntless will and courage, she read my glance . . .

The apologies she sought to make for being in such a condition were heartbreaking, but I passed them over by asking as gently as I could if she felt that she could go on; she nodded in the affirmative . . . and we started down a north face near Chasm View, for the Boulderfield below. Reaching the point where a large rock jams the long lateral crack where the cable is now, I tried to get her to go around instead of over it. She was probably too far gone to heed the suggestion; she went over the top of it and slipped, as I had feared she would, fell and skidded a long ways down over the smooth, snowy slope and lay there until I could descend.

It was broad daylight now with the wind steadily rising from the west and as the sun rose over the distant plains we discussed the situation. She was so weak that she could not hold onto me. I was so far gone that my knees shook and I fairly tottered. All the time she was insisting, in that supernatural voice that smote and terrified me, that a half hour's sleep would restore her. I assisted her to some rocks that seemed to offer protection from the wind. I put her knapsack under her head as a pillow and placed her ice axe in her hand, for she seemed to cling to it as a treasured thing. Then with all the speed at my command I started across the Boulderfield for help.

It was not long before I was brought up quick by two or three terrible falls made between the great boulders which were covered with the treacherous snows. As I lay recovering in one place, I wept at my miserable weakness and helplessness and debated as to whether I ought to return and die with her or push on for blankets, restoratives and aid and bring her off the Boulderfield.

Walter decided to push on and at 1 P.M. reached Timberline Cabin, where he found that the ice-cutters from Longs Peak Inn had formed a rescue party. Walter and three others started back up to Agnes. By now "the wind had risen to a terrible gale and it was intensely cold," so two turned back, including Herbert Sortland, the young caretaker from the inn. No one dreamed that it was the last time he would be seen alive.
The Hewes-Kiener account continues:

When Christen and I [reached] Agnes, she was dead and frozen. During my absence she had partially risen, turned over and was lying face downward, still clutching her ice axe. The gale was raging in unabated fury, driving the cold against our bodies without cessation or mercy. There was nothing to do but return, for we could not carry the body. . . . We would do well if we got back alive ourselves.

They descended in a whiteout, knowing only that they wanted to go downwind. By this time Walter Kiener was a "wreck," having been without real sleep for two nights. His feet were frozen and felt like "stilts," making it nearly impossible for him to balance on the snow-covered boulders. His hands too were "gone," the fingers frozen so thoroughly that they "rattled like icicles" whenever his gloves fell off. Walter made it to Timberline Cabin only because of Christen's assistance.

Elinor's manuscript tells how, after Agnes and Walter set off for the East Face, she went down to Longs Peak Inn to await their return. During the night she listened for their voices, which never came. At the break of day she decided to go back up to Timberline Cabin to wait for them. The ice-cutters were at the inn; Elinor tried to persuade them to go with her, but they didn't want to.

I promised them day wages (though I really had no money, I knew I could get it someplace) but that had no effect, and when all else failed, I cried. This was the only time in my life that I deliberately turned on the tears. But goodness knows I certainly had something to cry about and that persuaded them. They insisted on telephoning to Mrs. Mills, who I believe was in the Village [Estes Park] before they went, and she suggested taking hot coffee, which was a good idea. They were not too well equipped, and I gave them everything I had to help them keep warm— woolen socks to tie over their ears, a leather coat for Herb Sortland, who wanted to go also. . . . I called Agnes's cousin, Roger Toll, who was Superintendent of the Rocky Mountain National Park. . . . I know I was instructed to stay at the Inn and very promptly the Park Service people and many friends of Agnes came to help.

Roger Toll wrote an official report of the tragedy, without first inter-viewing Elinor Eppich (Kingery), and his account has served as the refer-ence for subsequent articles on the subject. Many years after Agnes's death, Elinor wrote her account of the events leading up to Agnes Vaille's climb of the East Face, as Elinor personally knew them. She especially wanted to correct the record about "those details which disturbed me so much in the official report because things hadn't happened that way. I suppose [Roger Toll's] concern—his business as Superintendent of the Park—was with the rescue operation, which he certainly knew better than I, rather than with what preceded it."

Agnes's sleeping bag, crampons, ice axe, and scrapbooks were given to Polly Bouck, at the time a student at Vassar. The next summer she and Bill Ervin, her aunt's "closest man friend," retraced the Kiener-Vaille route up the East Face.[36] Agnes's father arranged for a stone shelter to be erected near the Keyhole. Completed in 1927, it commemorated Agnes and Herbert Sortland, the young member of the rescue party who had turned back, lost his way, and perished near Longs Peak Inn. Mr. Vaille paid for all of Walter Kiener's hospital and doctor bills. Walter lost most of his toes, part of one foot, and many of his fingers. He was forced to give up butchering. Sometime after the tragedy, Walter told Elinor that his friends thought he should sue Agnes's family for damages on account of the trip. She replied: "'Wasn't this just as much your trip as hers? Didn't you want to go, too?' And he agreed that it was so."

For five summers Walter was a fireguard on top of Twin Sisters, which flanks the east side of Tahosa Valley and looks across to Longs, on the west side of the valley. Eventually, with the Vailles' generous financial support, Walter earned a PH.D. in botany. He worked for the Nebraska Game, Forestation and Parks Commission and taught at the University of Nebraska. He died in 1959, when he was sixty-five.

DOROTHY AND "TINY" COLLIER

The Agnes Vaille tragedy sent shock waves through the close-knit community of Colorado mountaineers. But it also, inadvertently, created a summer home for Dorothy Collier and her daughter. Because of the accident, Roger Toll directed park ranger Jack Moomaw to install two sections of steel cable on the steep section of Longs Peak approximately where Agnes had fallen. The dilapidated Timberline Cabin was officially closed, and a primitive hotel was constructed in the Boulderfield, managed during its nine-year existence (1927–35) by Bob and Dorothy Collier and open from June until Labor Day. The job suited Bob Collier perfectly.

As a kid he'd "cut his teeth on the Rockies," staying at a family cabin on the MacGregor Ranch just outside Estes Park.[37] After graduating from college, he'd become a chemistry teacher at South High School in Denver. One summer, a fifteen-year-old minister's daughter, Dorothy Dean, visited his sisters. Bob fell in love with her, and nearly two years later, in 1920, they were married. He introduced his young wife to "hiking, skiing, bonfire cooking, donkey packing, rappelling, ski jumping, etc." On January 6, 1921, their only child, Dorothy Ellen ("Tiny"), was born. Bob and Dorothy promptly took their infant daughter camping on a Colorado Mountain Club outing, in a laundry basket. When Tiny was a year and a half old, Bob carried her on his back in an old knapsack in which he had "cut holes for two fat little legs to stick out."

Although Dorothy's heart was damaged by rheumatic fever after her pregnancy, she apparently tolerated the thirteen-thousand-foot elevation of the "Boulderfield Hotel" quite well and enjoyed living in her stark surroundings. The Boulderfield was enclosed by treeless mountains: Storm Peak, Mount Lady Washington, and, of course, Longs Peak, which dominated the scene and intimidated nervous tourists who had not yet climbed it. Although the earlier name for the area, the Lava Beds, was geologically incorrect, it did convey the right feeling of sterility. A close look revealed tiny brilliant flowers and a few animals and birds, but the overwhelming impression was that nothing but rock and snow and weather could possibly grow there. The Boulderfield Hotel consisted of an eighteen-foot-square room, plus a loft that served as a kitchen, a dining room, and sleeping quarters for twelve guests in addition to the Colliers and Longs Peak guides. Nearby was a second structure, eighty-five feet long, that contained a latrine, a stable, and a tack room. Both buildings were built of native rocks. Extra guests either were squeezed into the hotel, sometimes doubling its intended capacity, or were put up in the tack room. A phone line connected the hotel to Estes Park.

Dorothy and Bob were the operation's chefs. They cooked on the wood and coal range, which also heated their water; in addition, they used a three-burner gasoline stove and, for baking, a stove-top oven. It was challenging to cook at the cabin's high altitudes because water boiled at such a low temperature and the leavening in cakes and muffins behaved unpredictably. But after the first year it became routine. A former guide, Melvin Wickens, recalls that there was usually a great pot of barley soup simmering on the stove, supplemented occasionally with canned soups for "gourmets." Bob Collier made au gratin potatoes, which he called "cheesical," and put leftover corn in his pancakes; "hobnailing" meant studding a baked ham with cloves.[38] Bob and Dorothy were usually not in residence simultaneously. Often, one would manage the hotel while the other would be in town shopping for groceries, picking up guides at the bus station, conducting business, or giving lantern-slide shows at local resorts. During the summers of 1929, 1930 and 1931, Tiny attended the nearby Cheley Camp for a few weeks, and her mother, Dorothy, worked there as a counselor. In 1932 and 1933, Bob ran tours to the Chicago World's Fair.

The first summer "on the field,", as Tiny refers to it, she was six years old. Bob made her a bed in one of the seat-high storage boxes along the wall of the hotel, at the head of the built-in bunk. One of her jobs was to fetch whatever her mother wanted from their "icebox," a twenty-gallon soup kettle buried in a snowbank about a quarter of a mile away. "That first summer, Daddy let me go with a party to climb the peak," Tiny recalls. "He had to boost me a bit on one part of the Cable—but otherwise I think I kept up or ahead of everybody." The next year, when she was seven, Tiny walked eight miles cross-country, by herself, down from the Boulderfield to the base camp of supplies, which was in a cabin called Graystone, on the lower slopes of Twin Sisters. "You really can't get lost when you are surrounded by tall mountains to use for orientation," she explained many years later.

Tiny loved living at the cabin. She had good times with her father, a scientist who always answered her questions "very satisfactorily." Sometimes the two of them hiked above the hotel to Chasm View, which overlooks Chasm Lake, at the base of the East Face. Peering over the side, Bob would then tell her about the effect of the sun's heating up the water, creating clouds that swirled around them. "The teapot's boiling," he would say, describing how, when the clouds soared as high as Longs Peak, they clashed with the cold prevailing winds from the west, causing snow.

Tiny recalls that "only nice people" visited them at the Boulderfield Hotel.

Seven miles of steep mountain trail effectively separated the men from the boys. The cabin was in a slight depression about three quarters of a mile from the edge of the Boulderfield and when climbers followed the trail diagonally across the edge, they were silhouetted against the sky line. As soon as I saw them, I would run very fast and meet them more than halfway to the cabin. Then with breathless cajolery, I could usually get to ride one of the horses the last half mile to the cabin.

When Tiny was fourteen she spent the entire summer at the Boulder-field. One of the guides, Eddie Watson, promised he'd take her up the East Face if she could get from base camp to the cabin in one hour and forty-five minutes. "I really ran—it took me one hour and 53 minutes," Tiny remembers. "He didn't make the offer again and I think he was thankful I didn't make it. He said, 'Mr. Bob would kill me if we tried to climb it.'"

Dorothy Collier had so much work to do at the Boulderfield Hotel that she didn't have as much time to climb Longs as her daughter or husband did. However, she was the only female member of the first party to make a night ascent of the East Face, late in August 1931. To practice for the climb, Dorothy circumnavigated the rock hotel, hanging onto its slight projections without touching the ground. On the day of the climb Everett Long, who guided during the summers of 1931 and 1932, chopped steps up Mills Glacier, at the base of the East Face. Then, in the evening, the party set out. It consisted of Ev; his brother Carleton, who was also a guide; Melvin Wickens, who had been a guide during 1929 and 1930; and Dorothy. They descended into the cirque of Longs via the Camel, a route that leads directly down from Mount Lady Washington to the base of the East Face. The stars gave off so much light that they didn't have to use flashlights, although they carried them. Everett recalls that Dorothy was a robust and skilled climber. The climb took six or seven hours, "portal to portal." Many years later, when Tiny told her mother that she had been brave to do what she had, Dorothy replied that she hadn't been brave at all—she had been "scared to death!"

One stormy night, while Dorothy was hanging a pair of crampons onto a tie rod, a huge clap of thunder rent the air and Dorothy fell to the floor as if dead. Everyone in the hotel rushed round her and lifted her to a bunk bed. She was paralyzed from the waist down. One of the tourists, a doctor, discovered a small mark on her hip, the only telltale sign that she'd been struck by lightning. The next morning the guides and some of the tourists improvised a litter. Six men carried her down the trail to a waiting ambulance, which took her to a Denver hospital. In time, she fully recovered.

The year 1935 marked the end of the Boulderfield Hotel, that "clean, happy place," as Tiny describes it. The walls and roof had deteriorated so badly that the Park Service ordered the building blown up. That fall Dorothy left Bob, whom she later divorced. Dorothy died in 1961. Tiny married George Bullivant and lives in Durham, New York.

By the 1930s Longs Peak had passed through the stages described by the famous English climber Albert Frederick Mummery. After first being called "an inaccessible peak," it had become "the most difficult climb" in the area, and finally the peak was "an easy day for a lady." In general, Colorado climbing was following the same patterns seen in the Alps. After Colorado's highest peaks had been climbed by their easiest routes, climbers pioneered hard routes up nonvirginal mountains, and sometimes climbed solo or in winter.

For the most part, Colorado mountaineers continued to be insulated from the mainstream. Put another way, one might say that European mountaineers and members of the American Alpine Club (who for all practical purposes were also European mountaineers) were stuck in a rut and hadn't yet recognized the superb climbing possibilities of the American West. It would fall to Elizabeth Strong Cowles Partridge (see chapter 6) to embrace the mountain worlds of Colorado, Wyoming, Europe, and beyond and to share her love of the world's high places with the climbers of her adopted state.

3

The
Women's
Park:
Virginia
Donaghe
McClurg
And
Lucy
Peabody

Virginia Donaghe McClurg and Lucy Peabody are unique among the women described in this book in that they accomplished what they did only because they had the backing of hundreds of well-organized, motivated women in Colorado. Virginia is also unique because, unlike Colorado's other mountain women, she was corpulent, wore feathered hats and rouge, and "plastered on" lipstick.[1] Bob Ormes's mother, and no doubt others, found the woman amusing but admired her, too.

Virginia Donaghe came to Colorado Springs "seeking health" in 1877, four years after Anna Dickinson and Isabella Bird climbed Longs Peak. Apparently she had no interest whatever in mountains. Already a well-known writer, she took some classes at Colorado College, and in 1879 she opened a "select school" for young women, located at the corner of Platte and Nevada avenues. Almost certainly her impeccable lineage helped attract students; she was descended from colonial and state governors, the founders of Harvard and Yale universities, and the founder of the town of Hartford, Connecticut. In addition, she was related to John Eliot, whose translation of the Bible into an "Indian tongue" was one of the first books published in America, and from Thomas Stanton, "Gentleman, Indian Interpreter for all the colonies." Her father was a physician and surgeon who had been in charge of a hospital for wounded Union soldiers at Shiloh. Virginia had been raised in New York City and educated at an academy in Staunton, Virginia.

In the late summer of 1882 she accepted an assignment from the *New York Daily Graphic* to write a story about "buried cities and lost homes." After taking a train to Durango, in southwest Colorado, Virginia discovered that the local Indian-white relations were nearly boiling over. Two cowboys had shot and killed several innocent Utes who were hunting, with the agent's permission, off the reservation, and the rest of the tribe had then countered by shooting an innocent settler and destroying his home and cattle.

Because the situation was so tense, U.S. troops escorted Virginia to see a cliff dwelling, Sandal House, on the Mancos River, as well as the watch-tower in Navajo Cañon and some other minor prehistoric cliff dwellings. Thus Virginia became the first white woman to visit the Mesa Verde area. Apparently the ruins cast a powerful spell on her, for in 1886 she returned with her own expedition, which consisted of a guide, a photographer, a chaperon-housekeeper, and horses for riding and for packing supplies. After Indians drove the party away from the Mancos River, the group set up camp for three weeks in Cliff Cañon. There the party stumbled onto ruins, which they named the Three Tiered House and Echo Cliff House. Their most important discovery, or so they thought at the time, was an extensive pueblo ruin—covered with a smooth rose-colored stucco—in which they found a loom. Virginia and her companions dubbed the ruins Brownstone Front. According to some reports, the name was later changed to Balcony House, but Benjamin Alfred Wetherill (known as Al) described the two as separate sites. In fact, S. E. Osborn, a prospector, was apparently the first white man to discover Balcony House, in 1884. He described it quite fully to the Wetherills and told them how to find it. (The Wetherills, a family of literate Quakers, had homesteaded on the Mancos River in 1880; the five Wetherill "boys" and their brother-in-law, Charles Mason, would become entwined in the early explorations and archeology of the area.) Osborn also wrote about his discovery in the *Rico Times*, a newspaper published in a little town several hundred miles from Colorado Springs.

Despite its lack of true "firsts," Virginia's venture was audacious. At the time it took place—1886—few white men, let alone women, had laid eyes on the inner recesses of Mesa Verde, which, it would turn out, contained the most remarkable of the ancient dwellings. (The Ute Indians were well aware of the ruins and had been for centuries.) The most accessible ruins of the area, those of Mancos Canyon, had been photographed for the first time in 1874, only a dozen years before Virginia's exploration, by William Henry Jackson of the Hayden survey. And although members of the Wetherill family had begun to learn Mesa Verde's secrets shortly after they had homesteaded on the Mancos in 1880, their spectacular discovery of the Cliff Palace was not made until 1889. Finally, Virginia's exploration predated the visits made by Frederick Chapin, a Bostonian, in 1889 and 1890, which would result in the first book about Mesa Verde, *The Land of the Cliff Dwellers*. (Earlier, Chapin had written a book about his mountaineering experiences in Colorado; see page 144.)

Virginia published sketches made during her 1886 trip and then began giving public lectures on the cliff dwellings of Mesa Verde. In 1889 she married Gilbert McClurg, a lecturer, writer, and publicist, and they honeymooned in Paris. (They had one son, Dudley Boyleston.) Virginia closed her school and increased her speaking engagements on the subject of cliff dwellings. For example, in 1893 she gave one speech at the Columbian Exposition in Chicago, two lectures in the Woman's Building, and yet another at the International Woman's Reception hosted by Susan B. Anthony and May Wright Sewall.

In 1894 she taught a short course, "The Prehistoric West," in St. John's Cathedral in Denver. At the conclusion of Virginia's fourth and final lecture, Mrs. Frederick J. Bancroft circulated a petition asking that Mesa Verde be set aside as a national park. Scores of people signed it. Next the petition made the rounds in Colorado Springs, collecting many more names, including those of the president of the University of Chicago, visiting in Colorado, and General William Jackson Palmer, a Colorado Springs visionary who promoted the Denver and Rio Grande Railroad. Senator Edward Wolcott of Colorado then presented the petition to Congress, where it fizzled and died.

However, the petition marked the beginning of a long, drawn-out effort to make Mesa Verde a national park. For the next twelve years Virginia McClurg devoted her enormous energies and influence to the cause, believing it was the only way to protect the ruins not only from the "gnawing tooth of time" but also from the "ravages of ignorant treasure-seekers and the iconoclastic relic-hunters."[2] When the drive finally reached its climax, however, Virginia McClurg completely bungled her position. In a complicated series of developments, today impossible to unravel completely because a fire destroyed some of Mesa Verde's early records, it was Lucy

Peabody, not Virginia McClurg, who emerged as the heroine of Mesa Verde National Park.

In 1897 there was no hint of this turn of events. Virginia McClurg was very much in command of the movement to preserve Mesa Verde as a national park. She easily persuaded the Colorado State Federation of Women's Clubs to appoint a standing committee to "investigate and promote the cause of the Colorado cliff dwellings." Predictably, Virginia was selected to head it. At the time there were over five thousand federated-club women in Colorado. Virginia's view was that these women, "as a rule, are of the wealthy class and must have some outlet for suppressed zeal and such an opportunity as this will give them the opportunity desired."[3]

In 1900 the standing committee of the federation became autonomous, incorporating as the Colorado Cliff Dwellings Association. Its motto was "Dux Femina Facti," which roughly translated into "Feminine leadership has accomplished it." In addition to Virginia, there were nineteen charter members of the association from all parts of the state: Mrs. Jesse Gale of Greeley; Mrs. J. D. Whitemore, Mrs. George Summer, Mrs. W. S. (Lucy) Peabody, Mrs. John McNeil, Mrs. Henry Van Kleeck, and Miss Minnie Reynolds of Denver; Mrs. William F. Slocum, Mrs. C. A. Eldridge, and Mrs. H. C. Lowe of Colorado Springs; Mrs. Mahlon Thatcher (a relative of Lucy Peabody's), Mrs. Thomas Addison Lewis, and Mrs. John J. Burns of Pueblo; Mrs. Edward G. Stoeber and Mrs. B. Austen Taft of Silverton; Mrs. Gordon Kimball of Ouray; Mrs. J. Kellog Scoville and Mrs. Boyle of Durango; and Mrs. C. B. Rich of Grand Junction. The *Denver Times* noted, "Just what the organization will do was not definitely stated, but the ultimate purpose is to have the tract of land known as the cliff dwellings set aside by the government as a national park."[4] Lucy Peabody was elected vice-regent and Virginia McClurg was elected regent, although she sometimes referred to herself as the "regent general."

Also in 1900, having been appointed the U.S. delegate to the Ethnological Congress of the Park Exposition held in Paris, Virginia delivered her cliff dwelling lecture in French, illustrated by lantern slides. The president of France received her at the Palace Élysée and presented her with the Gold Palm, or more correctly, with the Order of "Officier de l'Instruction Publique." Clearly Virginia relished the honor, for on at least one occasion she signed herself as "Regent of the Colorado Cliff Dwellings Association, Corresponding Member of the Brooklyn Institute, Officier de l'Instruction Publique."

One of the association's first tasks was to secure a lease with the Weemi-nuche Utes, whose land included Mesa Verde, to buy time while negotiating for the permanent protection of the ruins. Such a lease would protect Mesa Verde's valuable relics from the likes of the Swedish anthropologist Gustaf Nordenskjöld, who had visited Mesa Verde in 1891 and shipped six hundred of its most outstanding artifacts back to Sweden. He had then publicized his deeds in a book, thus outraging many Americans. But securing a lease with the Utes was complicated. The association had a hard time figuring out which of the Ute chiefs and subchiefs had the authority to approve such an agreement; the group was also hard pressed to draw up the documents in a language that was satisfactory to the bureaucrats in Washington. Simply communicating with the Utes was difficult. Virginia made at least one 450-mile trip to Navajo Springs with an amended lease, only to find that the necessary signators were away.

She undertook the journey a second time—and it was no easy trip across the mountains from Colorado Springs to the southwest corner of the state by train and wagon—to confer with Chiefs Ignacio and Acawitz. It was probably on this occasion that she found Ignacio ailing and offered him two mustard plasters, "sharp and to the point." "Then his pallor was so apparent under the bronze that I followed them with a glass of cherry bounce, which I indicated to him was of my own make," she wrote. "Under the revivifying influence of cherry bounce, the treaty proceeded."[5] The final treaty with the Utes, signed in 1901, gave the Colorado Cliff Dwellings Association water rights and permission to build and improve roads, to collect tolls for the roads, and to put up a rest house, etc. The treaty ran for ten years and cost three hundred dollars annually, a sum that was at least partially raised by soliciting twenty-five cents from each member of the Colorado State Federation of Women's Clubs. With the lease secured, the association plunged ahead.

Virginia McClurg and Mrs. Eldridge personally inspected three different routes proposed for the first wagon road through Mesa Verde, and selected one. The association paid to have the road built and also paid for an accurate map of the area to be made. Although the association's main source of income was donations, it once held a rummage sale in Pueblo and made $288, which in those days was enough money to build seven miles of new wagon road. One of its members, Mrs. John Hays Hammond, donated money to develop a spring at the Spruce Tree House, a godsend in such hot, arid country.

In 1901 the Colorado Cliff Dwellings Association took advantage of the fact that the American Association for the Advancement of Science was holding a meeting in Denver. Cliff Dwellings Association members persuaded the Denver and Rio Grande Railroad to reduce rates for a specially arranged trip to view the ruins in Mesa Verde. Members also picked up the entire tab for Dr. Jesse Walter Fewkes, from the Bureau of Ethnology, and his wife. A group of distinguished anthropologists and Cliff Dwellings Association women took the train to Durango and then rode wagons up Mancos Canyon, to the end of the road. After dinner they gathered around a campfire; each lady gave a required short speech by way of introducing herself to the scientists. The next day the party took horses down into the canyons to view the ruins. A *Denver Republican* reporter described the trip.

Then the horses were left and the party began a free-for-all scramble up the trackless side of the canon that must have made the angels weep. There were triumphant ascents to purer airs and broader views and ignominious and ungraceful tumbles to far lower levels. There were bruises, tearing of clothes and scratching of hands and faces. Cries of despair from the weaker sex, fagged and exhausted upon some isolated spur of rock, were drowned by the exultant though breathless whoops of the masculine contingent looking down in dizzy triumph from above.

Finally when it was all over and the victors stood and gazed proudly from the level mesa while the vanquished and dying of feminine vexation wept upon the rocks in the bed of the canon, a solemn vow was taken that never should the names of those who failed be divulged.[6]

The endeavor was a rousing success, for it impressed the very important Dr. Fewkes. "Mrs. Fewkes' dainty little sunbonnet quivered in exhaustion and Dr. Fewkes limp shirt sleeves betrayed his exertion," Virginia wrote. Scarcely had they gained breathing space on the height when Dr. Fewkes, fresh from the Arizona ruins with the Hemenway expedition, pronounced: "These cliff dwellings of Mesa Verde seem to be the most spectacular and representative area of cliff dwellings known."[7]

Also in 1901 Virginia's husband, Gilbert, who was director of Colorado's Quarto-Centennial Jubilee of statehood, invited Theodore Roosevelt, then vice-president, to be the honored guest at the celebration. He accepted. Members of the Cliff Dwellings Association made sure that Roosevelt inspected the parade float they had built, and they presented him with a "special souvenir," a prehistoric Indian bowl whose motifs—a five-pointed flower and heavy black bands—could be construed (with a good imagination) as representing a star and stripes. The bowl came complete with a Virginia McClurg poem, "Stars and Stripes of the Cliff Dwellers," which began:

Long ere the Genoese traversed
the sea,
On arid plateaux dwelt
a peaceful race
Whose castled cliffs rose from the
cañon's base
To unscaled heights of sunrise
mystery.

The vice-president wrote a gracious thank-you note. After he became president in 1901, Roosevelt proved to be an invaluable ally of the association. As Virginia put it, "The regent general was received personally by President Roosevelt every year to 'tell what Colorado is now doing about the ruins.'" She always had new activities to report, for Virginia was indefatigable in publicizing Mesa Verde to gain support for its protection. She gave directions to, and even planned the itineraries of, tourists who stopped in Colorado Springs on their way to the ruins. Frequently she opened her house at 619 Cascade Avenue for teas or "evening entertainments" to show local groups her collection of rare prehistoric and modern Indian crafts, which she kept in "the Indian room."[8]

When Senator Thomas Patterson of Colorado returned, covered with white alkaline dust, from a three-day overland trip to inspect the ruins, it was Virginia who awaited him on a hill outside the town of Cortez. She offered him juicy red peaches from the Animas Valley, one for each hand, and asked him if Mesa Verde was worthwhile. He replied that half the interest and beauty of the Mesa had never been told to him before and said that he believed one day it would be considered Colorado's greatest treasure. He later wrote Virginia, "Your zeal and enthusiasm did more to arouse a militant sentiment in behalf of the preservation of the ruins than anything else."[9]

Virginia became a popular national speaker. She spoke about cliff dwellings at the International Congress of Americanists at their New York meeting; the New York City chapter of the D.A.R.; several women's clubs in

New Jersey and Washington, D.C.; the First Congregational Church in St. Paul, Minnesota; the Chicago Medical Society; the Universities of Chicago, Michigan, and Wisconsin; the Board of Public Instruction of New York City; and the St. Louis Exposition, among other places. So great was Virginia's enthusiasm for cliff dwellers and dwellings that she even worked them into a poem, titled "Ode to Irrigation," which won a fifty-dollar prize in a contest sponsored by the National Irrigation Congress. (Virginia used her pen name, "Desire Stanton," when the poem was published as a song in 1903.) The ode was set to music and sung twice daily for two weeks by the Salt Lake Tabernacle Choir in Madison Square Garden. All sixteen hundred attending members of the Congress joined in the chorus: "The waste reclaims the ribboned rills, by toil and patience won—Land of the wise, peaceful people, long passed to their homes in the sun."[10]

As regent of the Colorado Cliff Dwellings Association, Virginia McClurg dominated the early movement to save the Mesa Verde ruins. However, during this time Lucy Peabody was certainly not a passive member of the association. In 1900, for example, she headed a committee and submitted an official report about the restoration and preservation of Indian ruins. As vice-regent of the association, she was second only to Virginia.

One wonders if Virginia was friends with Lucy Peabody or if she was jealous of her. For Lucy almost certainly knew more about prehistoric Indian ruins than Virginia did. Although Lucy had been born in Cincinnati in 1864 and was partially educated there, she had later moved to Washington, D.C., where she went to school and eventually became a secretarial assistant in the Bureau of Ethnology. Through her researches at the bureau, she had met and fallen in love with William Sloane Peabody, twenty-five years her senior, who was the executive officer of the U.S. Geological Survey. They were married in 1895. After Major Peabody retired, he and Lucy moved to Denver, where they lived at 1430 Corona Street. (William's brother, James, was the governor of Colorado from 1902 to 1904.) Lucy Peabody became influential in state politics, successfully pushing for child labor laws, a "traveling library bill," and the recognition of Lincoln's birthday as a state holiday.

There is no way to determine when Lucy and Virginia had their falling-out. We do have some hints that by 1904 at least some members of the Colorado Cliff Dwellings Association were disgruntled about what they regarded as the association board's high-handed ways. Virginia tried to mollify this unhappy segment in her annual report.

There are those among you who feel, and very naturally so, that you should be taken further into the councils of the Board of Trustees. It is not practicable that certain matters we have to do with should be discussed at Women's Clubs, or heralded in newspapers. Why? Because the political aspects of Mesa Verde involve differing interests, jealousies, party machinery, etc. . . .

A chance rumor, a misstated fact, may injure our cause in Washington, or set the Ute Indian reservation all agog. A Trustee, as his or her name implies, is a person to be trusted, and we beg, having put us in this position of trust, that you will give us as much confidence as you can, until the day when all things are made plain, and the harvest bread will be none the less sweet that it was baked in the dark. We want in the Cliff Dwellings Association women who join to their good works a large measure of faith.[11]

By late 1905 the Peabody-McClurg feud had burst into flame. Virginia McClurg, in a complete turnabout, had abandoned the position she'd espoused for so many years—that Mesa Verde should become a national park. Instead, she was now proposing that Mesa Verde become a Colorado state park, administered by the Colorado Cliff Dwellings Association. U.S. Congressman Franklin E. Brooks from Colorado backed Virginia's new position.

Meanwhile, Lucy Peabody staunchly maintained her original position that Mesa Verde would best be served as a national park under the aegis of the federal government. However, in a comedy of errors, the bill she was backing, the Hogg Bill, proposed boundaries that had inadvertently been drawn up so that all the major ruins were excluded from the park. Lucy's advocates were the U.S. Congressman from Colorado, Herschel Millard Hogg, and Senator Thomas Patterson of Colorado. As historian Patricia Hoben points out, Virginia may well have capitulated primarily because of the absurdity of the Hogg Bill.

The difference of opinion between Lucy and Virginia forced the other members of the Colorado Cliff Dwellings Association to choose up sides. By this time, although the association's largest chapter was in Colorado, it also had outlying chapters in California, New York, Utah, and Arizona. Many of its members were extremely dedicated, having presented hundreds of lectures and exhibits about Indians and the Mesa Verde cliff dwellings.

The Peabody-McClurg fight became public on February 23, 1906, when the *Denver Post* wrote an editorial, "Make It a National Park." The *Post* began, "Mrs. Gilbert McClurg and the Cliff Dwellings Association are fighting Mrs. Peabody and her cliff dwelling bill."[12] The editorial further stated that Mrs. McClurg's opponents accused her of simply wanting to maintain power by keeping Mesa Verde under her thumb, that is, under the control of the Colorado Cliff Dwellings Association. Mrs. Decker, national president of the Federation of Women's Clubs, wrote that she "prayed" Virginia would refrain from making a public rebuttal to the *Post* editorial. Her prayers were in vain. A few weeks later Virginia's reply appeared in the *Rocky Mountain News*.

For starters, she called the *Post* "Scurrilous Penny-a-liners" who were busy searching for "some trifling incident to distort, some praiseworthy labor to minimize, and some difference of opinion to magnify." However, she denied that she and Lucy Peabody were having a fight. They were, she said, merely having a "difference of opinion." Then she stated her position: the most "pernicious feature" of the impending bill was that it would put the ruins "under exclusive control of the Department of the Interior who would be empowered to give permission to museums, universities and college to indulge in 'excavations and gatherings.'" The *Post* was trying to "bury" the Cliff Dwellings Association in the "grave of the national park."[13]

Lucy severed ties with the Colorado Cliff Dwellings Association and in so doing siphoned off many other disenchanted members, including Mrs. Decker. In a seven-page typed letter, Virginia tried to persuade Mrs. Decker to change her mind and to remain a member of the association. Virginia also revealed that she was hopping mad. "Who can show any newspaper article in which I have attacked Mrs. Peabody?" she wrote. "But from the *Pueblo Chieftain* to the *New York Tribune*, I can show those wherein she has misrepresented and vilified." She went on to say that she was no longer idealistic about women working together: "I do not have to look far to see the greed for office; the slander, the double dealing; the wise good women duped by the schemers; the lack of loyalty; the personal point obtruded to the sacrifice of the cause; the inability to see or understand, the political wire-pulling; the undermining of faith."[14]

As the debate got hotter, Virginia made a fundamental tactical error: she remained in Colorado while trying to gain support for her position. Meanwhile, Lucy Peabody went straight to where the action was, Washington, D.C., and assumed the role of official spokeswoman for the proposed Mesa Verde National Park. She enjoyed the quiet support of Dr. Edgar L. Hewett of the Bureau of American Ethnology, although he was careful to preserve his cordial relations with the McClurg faction, too.

Lucy Peabody won: the Hogg Bill was approved on June 7, 1906. Two weeks later its deficiencies were rectified by the passage of the Brooks-Leupp Amendment, which provided that all prehistoric ruins situated within five miles of the boundary of the park would be administered as part of the park. President Theodore Roosevelt signed this amended bill into law on June 29, 1906, finally creating a Mesa Verde National Park that was complete with ruins.

It is not clear if Virginia and Lucy ever reconciled, but Virginia Mc-Clurg's interest in Mesa Verde never waned. She once wrote, "My heart would have broken long since had I not been sustained by the consciousness of rectitude."[15] Under her regent generalship, in 1911 the Colorado Cliff Dwellings Association contributed one thousand dollars for the reconstruction of Balcony House. And in September 1917 Virginia wrote, costumed, and directed a pageant, "The Marriage of the Dawn and the Moon," performed in the Spruce Tree House. The event required twenty-four actors, singers, and dancers, all of whom were transported, presumably, from Colorado Springs.

Eventually the Colorado Cliff Dwellings Association disbanded and became affiliated with the Archeological Institute of America. However, two curious incidents occurred after Mesa Verde National Park was created. First, although Lucy Peabody became known as the "Mother of Mesa Verde National Park," she committed a serious blunder in her choice of Mesa Verde National Park's first superintendent. (Technically she didn't do the appointing, but her wishes were heeded.) Lucy backed Major Hans M. Randolph of the Denver National Guard, a man described as a "likeable and cooperative person . . . but an out-and-out politician."[16] He became the first superintendent of Mesa Verde, but a few years later the Department of the Interior filed formal charges against him that resulted in his suspension and the eventual termination of his services.

The second curious incident was the construction of the Manitou Cliff Dwellings near Colorado Springs. Although many records have been lost, there is reason to believe that after Mesa Verde National Park was finally established, Virginia McClurg tried to have her husband installed as its first superintendent. Since she was not successful, in a fit of pique she apparently decided to build her own Indian ruins in Manitou Springs, near Colorado Springs. A prospectus for the Manitou Springs ruins, printed in 1907, stated: "Cliff Canyon, near Manitou [Springs], is an exact counterpart of many of the canons in Southern Colorado where the cliff dwellings were made, and the work of carefully removing the whole of Cliff Canyon undertaken. More than a million pounds of rock have been brought to the new location and the houses erected in exact dimensions and appearance, stone by stone."[17]

W. S. Crosby directed the work, which was begun in 1906 and completed in 1907. The new ruins replicated parts of Spruce Tree House, Cliff Palace, and Balcony House. A brochure stated that world-traveled scientists and archeologists gave their unqualified endorsement of the ruins and "pronounced them . . . a splendid contribution to education by making easily accessible the so long buried wonders of this race." Under "Important Information," in language that sounds suspiciously like Virginia McClurg's, the brochure noted, "Only the ignorant or malicious minded will tell you that a visit to these Ruins is not worthwhile because the prehistoric Cliff Dwellers did not build them here personally!"[18]

During Virginia's lengthy involvement with prehistoric Indian ruins she remained a serious writer; her poems appeared in newspapers and in publications such as *The Century, Cosmopolitan, Success,* and the *Review of Reviews.* Often she wrote about Colorado subjects, such as wildflowers or Pikes Peak. A book of her poems, *Seven Sonnets of Sculpture,* published in Boston, received high praise and inspired one critic to comment, "Her work has a sculpturesque dignity and delicacy of which few—if any— women poets have seemed capable."[19] In 1928 Colorado College gave Virginia an honorary degree and in 1933 published, posthumously, a book of her poems, many of which had long been out of print.

Virginia Donaghe McClurg died on April 30, 1931. Lucy Peabody died in Denver on September 19, 1934. Today, both women are largely forgotten, as is their feud. Most visitors have no idea that Mesa Verde National Park has been called the "Women's Park" because its creation was due almost solely to women.

4

The Mountains: A Refuge

For the female mountain climbers, hikers, and skiers, Colorado's mountains offered a diversion. For Virginia Donaghe McClurg, Lucy Peabody, and members of the Colorado Cliff Dwellings Association, the mountains secreted the remnants of an intriguing ancient civilization. And for yet other women, such as Susan Anderson and Katherine Garetson, the mountains served as a refuge and the chance for a good life denied them in cities.

SUSAN ANDERSON

Susan Anderson was born in Monroeville, Indiana, on January 29, 1870, and lived there long enough to regard it as the place she always wanted to move back to. At some point in her early life, however, she moved with her family to Kansas, later graduating from Wichita High School. Her portrait at that time shows a very pretty young woman, who, one can imagine, had her pick of beaux. However, because her father had been thwarted in his desire to study medicine, he insisted that she go to medical school and become a physician. Although Susan had almost no interest in studying medicine, she was "a dutiful daughter" and enrolled in the University of Michigan Medical College, one of the few good medical schools that admitted women. (One neighbor in later years who met Susan's father found him to be an "ornery old cuss . . . who bossed her around.") In addition to taking the standard courses, Susan did some special work in pathology and studied a new course, bacteriology. She had no instruction in pediatrics or psychiatry, since none was offered, and her practical training did not include any contact with patients.[1]

In 1897, at the age of twenty-seven, Susan graduated from the University of Michigan Medical College with extremely high grades. She was one of thirteen females in a graduating class of sixty-four, exemplifying a national trend. As Barbara Solomon points out in her book *In the Company of Educated Women*, the number of women physicians in the United States rose from fewer than twenty-five hundred in 1880 to approximately nine thousand in 1910, 6 percent of the nation's total.

After receiving her medical degree, Susan Anderson went to join her brother and her father in Cripple Creek, west of Colorado Springs, where gold had recently been discovered. She began practicing medicine in the brawling boomtown and later commented that the miners accepted the situation of having a lady doctor "with surprising gentleness" and didn't bother her at all. "Some were a little bashful about having their barroom wounds sewed up by a lady," she said, "but they learned to accept it. The only one that didn't accept it was my father who insisted Cripple Creek was no place for a lady. He finally—after three years—prevailed upon me to leave."[2]

Susan went to Denver but disliked it because "people just didn't believe in women doctors." She then moved north to the town of Greeley but again found that her sex was a barrier to practicing medicine. To support herself she was forced to work as a nurse, for which she was completely untrained. As she became more and more discouraged, her health broke down. "I couldn't even diagnose what was wrong with me, myself," she said. Susan finally concluded that she had tuberculosis. As autumn faded into the short days of winter, her thoughts dwelled on a vacation she'd taken the previous summer to the Western Slope, where the air was sharp and the valleys were green and spacious and contained by high mountains. This shining image so contrasted with the dry plains of Greeley that she made up her mind to move to Fraser, to die or be cured.[3]

In December 1907 Susan took the Moffat train over Rollins Pass to the raw settlement of Fraser, born in 1905 when the railroad laid tracks through the townsite. Fraser consisted of twelve houses and nearly as many saloons. One of the coldest places in the nation, it was often isolated from Denver in winter when the brutal winds of Rollins Pass drifted snow across the tracks, closing the route for days, even weeks.

Susan rented a room from the Charlie Warners and got a job as a grocery store clerk. Before long, as word got around that she was a licensed physician, people began calling on her for emergencies. Her first patient was a horse, about whom she later said, "I'm afraid I never got his name." He was badly cut up from a barbed-wire fence, and after Susan sewed him up, he removed the stitches with his teeth. Still, she managed to pull him through.[4]

Apparently Susan passed muster, for her calls increased. Gradually her own illness evaporated in the frigid air, and she developed a full practice of what she called "just plain practical medicine for the benefit of the people." Many years later she recalled that it took people in the area a while to realize that she was competent. "I had two good reasons why I simply had to make good," she said. "First I had to prove a woman could be a good doctor. And secondly, I graduated from a great school. I couldn't bring shame upon the school."[5]

During those first years some of the lumberjacks played crude jokes on Susan. For example, a big Swede once walked into her examining room at a logging camp and unbuttoned his fly. He said, "I want you to look at this." Susan replied, in a professionally solicitous tone, "What's the trouble?" "Nothing," the Swede replied, "but isn't it a beauty!" Furious, Susan shot back, "The examination just cost you $10.00, payable now." (This was an exorbitant fee; she usually charged a buck.)[6]

Gradually, much of the initial skepticism in the Fraser Valley about a female physician changed to: "Call Doc Susie. She'll come if she has to walk." At first she needed a guide to take her to remote ranches, but within a few years she could find her own way. "Oh, I've skied into ditches—never was much of a skier," she once said. "And I've lost my way, now and then, in a blizzard, but nothing to get worried about. Once all the townspeople thought I was lost and had searching parties out for me—but it was silly, I wasn't lost."[7]

Doc Susie went to her patients any time of day or night, no matter if it was 30 degrees below zero or colder, by whatever means of transportation was available—her own feet, skis, snowshoes, horses, sleighs, the train, and, in later years, automobiles. Once she walked twelve miles to tend to a woman at the Box Factory Lumber Camp, above Tabernash. Another time she hailed the train on a bitter winter night and rode as far as Parshall, where a man met her with a team and sled. They rushed up the Williams Fork, barely in time for Doc Susie to deliver a baby boy in Milner.

Knowing how she loved to dance, logging camps often put on a dance in her honor when she came on a call. Since Susan was a good-looking woman, five foot three or four, with a slender waist, her romances caused a lot of speculation. One story, perhaps apocryphal, had her snuggling up to a married man while he drove her back home in his wagon from a lumber camp where she'd attended a patient. The man protested, but Doc Susie persisted. Finally, he gave her a powerful shove, and Susie landed in a snowbank, followed shortly by her medical bag. Another alleged romance ended when Susie and a man quarreled over the shape of a window for a door in Susie's house. She insisted it be a diamond; he insisted it be a square. One rumor had it that Doc Susie had been "sweet on a man" who was in some kind of business in Fraser. If true, nothing came of it. Her exceptional education must have put her out of step with most prospective suitors. At one time she told a neighbor that the men she didn't want, wanted her, and the ones she wanted, didn't want her. When she was in her eighties, Doc Susie chuckled when she told a reporter, "I could have [married] if I hadn't flown off the handle so much and said 'pooh' so many times."[8]

The Denver, Northwestern and Pacific Railroad, known locally as the Moffat Railroad, employed doctors in towns that the line ran through, which in 1911 included Fraser, Hot Sulphur Springs, Yampa, and Steamboat Springs. Susan became a railroad doctor and thus had a free pass on the line. Although a brochure described her as a physician and surgeon and although her office was equipped with a surgical table, she in fact probably performed very little surgery. At the University of Michigan Medical College, she'd become so upset while dissecting her first cadaver that she'd seriously considered dropping out of medical school. So, most likely, Doc Susie performed only emergency surgery.

She didn't use chloroform—or any drugs—to ease the pain. According to Ruth Phillips, whose family came to Fraser in 1908, Doc Susie thought that if word got around that she didn't have any drugs in her house, no one would try to break in to get them. Glenn Wilson, a former Fraser resident, well remembers that Doc did not use any anesthetic when she pulled out one of his molars. Nor did she use any when one of his friends cut his arm badly. "I think we did this out in the yard for the proper light," Glenn recalls. "But Doc Susie had these little curved needles for sutures and she was working there and she said, 'I've got to take these into the garage and get them sharpened.'"[9]

By all reports, Doc Susie's practice of medicine was "typical pioneer work," and she was good. Dick Mulligan, a long time resident of the Winter Park area, recalls that when she bandaged up his smashed big toe and then sent him to Denver General Hospital, a physician there gave high praise to her dressing. She also earned high marks during an emergency that took place in 1940, when a trainload of sailors passed through Fraser. A young sailor rammed his arm through a train window, cutting it so deeply that a tourniquet was required to stop the bleeding. A message was sent ahead to the station in Fraser that a doctor was needed, and Doc Susie was dispatched. She brought her supplies to the depot and boiled water. The train pulled in and stopped, and the pharmacist for the naval troops requested that Doc Susie climb aboard. "No," she replied, "I'm all set up. The boy's got to come out here."[10]

The sailor was carried out. As Doc began her work, the rest of the troop train exploded into Fraser, throwing snowballs and gorging on food and beer. Susie told the injured sailor that he could cuss if he liked because that was the only pain-killer he was going to get. Then she stitched him up and dressed his injury with her usual care, knowing it would be two days before the train reached California and the boy received more medical attention. Several weeks later a naval doctor wrote Doc Susie a letter of commendation saying that when the bandages were removed, everything was perfect. The sailor's mother sent Doc a new Hudson's Bay blanket.

Pneumonia was a common killer in the Fraser Valley, which is eighty-five hundred feet above sea level. Until 1928, when the Moffat Tunnel opened, Fraser was often isolated for days at a time, so that it fell to the local doctors to treat pneumonia cases. Doc Susie's remedy was simple and, apparently, often effective; it involved a Number 2 galvanized washtub, water as hot as the patient could stand, and lots of blankets. Ruth Phillips recalls that Doc Susie twice cured her brother-in-law with this method. "She'd always give them a hot bath, no matter who they were—the biggest, roughest men . . . and she'd cover them up and they'd stay covered—even if she had to sit on them, they'd stay covered."[11]

Doc used patent medicines, some of which are displayed in the Grand County Historical Association Museum in Hot Sulphur Springs, Colorado. For sore throats, she swabbed with Dobells, wickedly powerful stuff that people swore actually burned off a layer of skin.[12] Doc Susie rarely wrote prescriptions for medicine, preferring to dispense the numerous free samples she received in the mail. This did not endear her to the local pharmacist.

Doc Susie had a soft side to her, and often had a gentle way with patients. "When I was about four years old," Ruth Phillips recalls, "I broke my arm. . . . I can't remember the pain or anything, but I can remember when she came in, she was so kind and her voice was so sweet. She made you feel safe. She got her some cardboard and she made her a splint. She padded it all with cotton and she wrapped it up and tied it together with—I don't know—string or what not. I can still remember her voice."[13]

In the mid-1920s Doc Susie became coroner of Grand County in the middle of her predecessor's term. Shortly thereafter, a particularly vicious murder by hanging occurred near Grand Lake, but the body of the victim, Fred Selak, wasn't discovered for a month. Two local men were arrested for the crime and put on trial. As coroner, Doc Susie presented medical evidence that contributed to sending the men to the gallows. She felt so guilty that she refused to run for coroner after her term expired.

But Doc had a hard side to her, too, and didn't hesitate to stick up for her convictions. Once she gave a tongue-lashing to a man who was considering joining a club that served liquor. She passionately disapproved of alcohol, for she was convinced that it ruined many a home. In 1924 she was deputized. On one occasion she assisted the sheriff in uncovering six pints of "hootch" in the occupied bed of a woman in Fraser. The woman's husband was tried, fined three hundred dollars, and sentenced to thirty days in jail.

Although Doc Susie found her niche in the Fraser Valley and seemed to enjoy her life there, she apparently never completely adapted, especially during the bitter winters. Throughout her life she remained nostalgic for roses, filling her house with etchings of roses on windows, embroidered roses on her pillowcases, photographs of roses on calendars, and pictures of roses from seed catalogs, which she pasted on the walls. Once, when someone asked her if there was anything she would most like to have or do, Susie "sighed and wistfully said, 'I'd still like to go back to Indiana and have a garden of roses.'"[14] At least twice, Doc Susie actually did move back to Indiana. One of her trips was paid for by the residents of Fraser, who took up a collection. Doc loaded all her belongings into a boxcar and left town. But a month later she was back. Things had changed back in Indiana, Doc said, and she had decided that Fraser was her real home.

Certainly, she behaved like a die-hard local when the Moffat Tunnel was officially dedicated on February 26, 1928. The completion of the Moffat Tunnel, slightly longer than six miles, was a major event for residents of the Fraser Valley, giving them for the first time a fast, reliable way to Denver in winter. The tunnel took four years to build. Most families in the valley knew someone who either was cutting timbers for the tunnel or was working on its construction. The labor was hard and dangerous, taking the lives of nineteen men. Since Doc Susie was a physician and coroner, she was intimately involved with some of those accidents. So she, as well as many other locals, eagerly anticipated the ceremonies that were to inaugurate the tunnel's use and that were scheduled to take place at East Portal, on the Denver side. Though this inconvenienced Doc Susie and her friends, they decided to simply walk east through the tunnel in time for the dedication and to then catch a ride back on the first train west through the tunnel.

However, the officials of the Denver and Salt Lake Railroad announced that they would not permit anyone to walk through the tunnel. This meant that everyone from the Fraser Valley wanting to attend the dedication would have to take the night train over Rollins Pass, which would put them at East Portal nine hours before the ceremony. Fraser Valley residents were incensed. Whose tunnel was it, anyway? They grumbled that the *Denver Post* was stirring up such a self-serving hoopla that it was diverting credit for the tunnel away from the people who had really sweated and worried it into completion.

Doc Susie masterminded a protest, revealed when the first train through the Moffat Tunnel emerged at the West Portal. She and a dozen others held up a large sign that read, "We Built the Tunnel—Not the Post." An offended dignitary quickly ordered the section men to destroy the sign, but not before a photographer could grab a shot, which the *Rocky Mountain News* gleefully printed the next day.

In one respect, the Moffat Tunnel eased life in Fraser Valley because it brought big-city amenities, such as good doctors and hospitals, much closer. On the downside, however, the termination of scores of tunnel paychecks wounded the local economy. The Great Depression nearly finished the job, and hard times stalked the area. Everyone, including Doc Susie, tightened belts. However, since her wants and needs had always been simple, she survived reasonably well. Doc Susie owned her log cabin and had no utility bills because she didn't have any electricity or running water.

(Water came from a well in her backyard.) Her property taxes were laughably low, and the townspeople cut and split a good supply of firewood for her every fall.

Doc Susie ate very little and sewed her own clothes or made do with what people gave her. She adopted the clothing fashion of the early 1900s and retained it for the rest of her life, which confused new doctors at Colorado General who didn't know her reputation for making accurate diagnoses. In winter she wore a dress down to her ankles, long underwear, and the traditional boots that the local men and some of the women wore— German felt socks and rubber overshoes. In summer she wore cotton dresses, several petticoats, black button shoes, and a little "kind of brown pillbox" hat that was for trips to Denver.[15]

As Doc Susie grew older, her habit of saving things became more pronounced. Always one to pick up things she found in the street, such as a nail or a piece of string or a copper wire, she now began saving other objects, such as grapefruit seeds, which she collected in a little dish. (As one local said, "What in the world would you save grapefruit seeds for in Fraser?") By the time she was sixty or so, Doc's acquisition of papers had gotten so out of hand that her office was "a tiny space surrounded by tons of old magazines, newspapers and cardboard boxes, stacked from floor to ceiling and reached by a narrow path which wended its way through a hallway done in the same paper and cardboard decor." The clutter was not reassuring to prospective patients who'd never met her before, such as skiers injured at Winter Park. One man commented that if you were a patient seriously ill, you'd be dead by the time Doc Susie cleared off her examining table. This, however, wasn't true, for Doc by this time examined patients on her bed.[16]

Some said that Doc Susie wasn't clean, but one longtime friend refutes that, saying: "I mean—if anybody can be clean with a lot of clutter, she was clean. Because my mother-in-law worked with her at baby cases and she said, 'You never saw anybody so clean.' She said that before she would even go over she'd bathe and scrub and wash her hair and clean her fingernails until she was just shining. Put on all clean clothes."[17]

Although many Fraser Valley residents admired Doc Susie and understood her, others saw her as an eccentric old lady, not to be quite trusted as a physician. In Doc's later years, her income was erratic and often inadequate. She charged "whatever the patient could afford—money, eggs, a chicken, a piece of beef, garden vegetables, a load of firewood or nothing." Glenn Wilson thinks that frequently Doc collected the "nothing." He remembers that once when he and Doc were chatting in town, a young man strolled by and Doc muttered under her breath, "There goes one that isn't paid for."[18]

"I don't doctor for money, I doctor for results," Doc once told a black family that was passing through the valley and was worried about paying her for treating their child.[19] Still, somewhat surprisingly, Doc Susie did manage to save money. Friends frequently saw her roll bills up in a four-inch roll of adhesive tape and put it in her medicine chest. She also maintained a bank account.

In 1947, when Doc Susie was seventy-seven years old, she went back to Michigan for her fiftieth reunion of the University of Michigan Medical College. To pay her way, the townspeople of Fraser took up a collection, which included a percentage from poker games at the local pool hall.[20] Doc Susie decked herself out in a dress and coat of a fashionable length that came just below her knees; she smiled broadly for her portrait, snapped just before she stepped on the train. The university feted her, wrote articles about her, and presented her with a tiny pin decorated with a gold *M* and a blue *Emeritus*. Susie was also presented with a photograph showing the five members of her class of 1897 who were still practicing medicine. Several years later her neighbor, Hazel Briggs, used that photograph to prove that Doc Susie was at least sixty-five years old and was therefore eligible for an old-age pension.

By the time she was in her seventies, if not before, Doc Susie no longer kept regular office hours. One neighbor recalled that if you wanted her, you began knocking on doors. Since Doc Susie was always welcome to stop at most houses in town for a bite to eat, anyone who needed her could eventually track her down, given enough time. During all the years that Doctor Susan Anderson lived in Fraser, she practiced medicine. In her later years, when she had become frail and arthritic, she maintained her practice only because there was no one else to take over. By the time she was eighty years old, she'd given up night calls, except for emergencies, and didn't like maternity cases because she figured she wasn't up to them. However, she was still able to go into Denver several times a year, mostly to shop and to eat at different cafes and to visit friends.

When she was eighty-six, Doc Susie had a stroke and was moved into the Good Samaritan Nursing Home in Denver. Although she recovered enough that she could talk, according to her friends she was never the same. Once, when Hazel Briggs and Minnie Cole went to visit her, they found Doc all dressed up, sitting in a chair "waiting for somebody to come to take her to Indiana."[21]

She died at the age of ninety, on April 14, 1960. Doc Susie was buried in Cripple Creek, as she had often said she wanted to be, next to her beloved brother, who had died in the flu epidemic of 1900. Once again the residents of Fraser rallied on Doc's behalf, paying for her tombstone. Today, those who knew her remember Doc Susie as "a character, a fine doctor—and certainly a saint if there ever was one."[22] In Fraser, there is a street named "Doc Susie."

One usually thinks of homesteaders as men, accompanied by a brood of children and brave helpmeets wearing sunbonnets. Of course there's a lot of truth to that stereotype, but it needs to be balanced. As Nell Brown Propst points out in her book *Those Strenuous Dames of the Colorado Prairie*, many single women homesteaded on the plains of Colorado. Probably fewer homesteaded in the Colorado mountains, although figures are hard to come by. It seems likely that two of the earliest were Kitty and Annie Harbison, who each filed on a 160-acre claim near Grand Lake, on the Western Slope, in 1896. Since their father was ill and their younger brother was not inclined to hard labor, they did most of the work. The Harbison sisters always wore long skirts, which, though they dragged in the manure, showed that the owners were ladies. After Kitty and Annie proved up on their claims, they tended their dairy farm, raised the daughters of a neighbor whose wife had left him, and ran a summer resort famous for its Sunday chicken dinners. Today their homestead is just inside the boundaries of Rocky Mountain National Park.

Kitty and Annie perhaps coped better, at least initially, than did women like the inexperienced Margaret Duncan Brown. In 1915 she and her husband, who had worked in a bank in Cripple Creek, moved to a ranch near Craig, Colorado. Three years later her husband suddenly died from influenza, leaving Margaret, a gentle southern woman, completely on her own and in debt. She discovered unsuspected grit. To everyone's surprise, especially hers, she became a successful sheep rancher, homesteaded several new tracts of land, and lived quite happily by herself for forty-seven years.

In between chores, she kept a diary, which is the basis for a charming book, *Shepherdess of Elk River*.

As we have seen, Esther Burnell Mills filed on land near Estes Park, although she married Enos Mills before she proved up on it. Katherine Garetson, a homesteader who preceded Esther by several years, liked Esther and offered her advice and encouragement. However, Katherine saw a timid, hesitant Esther, rather than the fearless one Enos Mills described in his book *The Adventures of a Nature Guide*, which is the basis for the Esther presented here in Chapter 2. (Enos not only was in love with his subject but also was an advocate for women homesteaders and nature guides.) One suspects that Katherine Garetson's portrait is the more accurate, because Esther was originally a city girl from Cleveland. Certainly we know that Katherine Garetson was utterly untrained to cope with the rigors of homesteading in the Colorado mountains, because she tells us so.

Only a few years after Doc Susie moved to Fraser, where she regained her health and professional integrity, Katherine Garetson moved to Tahosa Valley, near Longs Peak. Like Doc Susie, Katherine was escaping from something, although in her case it was financial dependence on relatives. Katherine Garetson's tale of homesteading "on the Big Owl" describes her transformation from an ignorant greenhorn into a veteran mountain-dweller. The specifics are, of course, about Katherine, but in another, larger sense, she is describing a metamorphosis that took place all over the West. She was but one of the thousands of city people who, with more pluck than sense, gambled on their ability to satisfy the requirements of homesteading so they could acquire government land without a big outlay of cash.

Katherine Garetson, and other women like her, pulled it off. Her story underscores the half-truth of "Go West, young man." The Colorado mountains, at least, could be the land of opportunity for a young woman, too.

KATHERINE GARETSON

In 1914, when Katherine Garetson was thirty-seven years old, she took a step that, as she put it, "is the most serious thing you can do, aside from marrying."[23] She filed a three-year residence claim on 160 acres two miles south of Longs Peak Inn in Tahosa Valley. Nothing in her background suggested that she would succeed. Having grown up in St. Louis, Missouri, she was, by her own description, "soft, sensitive, shy—an easy mark."

However, her life, which had previously been "made safe by a prosperous father," was interrupted by a "financial upheaval," and she was forced to move in with her sister, Helen Dings, who was married and had two sons.

Katherine spoke of herself as "average." She wrote: "Like all good American girls, I could sew and cook and read and write and think. . . . My home was in St. Louis and I had observed other lives carefully enough to be overwhelmed with the knowledge: 'The city is so hard a place for people who are poor and sensitive that many choose to die by their own hands.'"

One of Katherine's young nephews, McClelland (Mac) Dings, was very sick with what was feared to be the beginning of tuberculosis. The family physician advised taking the boy to Colorado, and so in 1909 the Dings family and Katherine headed west to Colorado. Mac was so weak that he mostly got around on a little burro rented from Sam Service in Estes Park. (Eventually he recovered and was a Longs Peak guide for several seasons.) The family sampled a few local resorts until they discovered Longs Peak Inn, which was to their liking. They stayed there for the rest of that summer and returned for several more until 1913, when they built their own cabin on two acres purchased from Enos Mills.

In the summer of 1914 Katherine walked out on the cabin porch to view a violent thunderstorm, which she found exhilarating. Suddenly, she saw two drenched figures hurrying to the porch for protection and invited them in to dry out by the fire. One, an old man who'd been working on the road, began talking about homesteading. As Katherine later wrote:

The words fell upon peculiarly fertile ground because I was seeking to escape from the return to St. Louis. Before he went away he tugged at some old papers in his pocket and finally produced two pamphlets for me. They had been published at Washington, issued by the General Land Office of the Department of the Interior. One was "Vacant Public Lands in the United States," but the other pleased me most; it was entitled, "Suggestions to Homesteaders and Persons Desiring to Make Homestead Entries."

. . . At last I deliberately took the leap as one who shuts his eyes and jumps. It took less than twenty minutes after I reached the land office in Denver to make out papers, swear an oath, pay sixteen dollars in fees and hear the registrar say, "The land is yours. All you have to do is to live up to the requirements of the law."

Katherine went back to St. Louis and persuaded her best friend, Annie Adele Shreve, to stay the winter with her. Annie was "steadfast, and keen for an adventure; she was gentle, not talkative, earnest and good-looking.

Pikes Peak, the only mountain over fourteen thousand feet that nearly abuts the
Great Plains, has lured would-be climbers
for over 180 years. The first recorded ascent
was made by members of the Long Expedition in 1820. Thirty-eight years later Julia
Archibald Holmes became the first woman
to climb the peak. This L. C. McClure
photo, circa 1910, shows America's most
famous mountain behind the second
Antlers Hotel in Colorado Springs on Pikes
Peak Avenue. Photo courtesy of the Colorado Historical Society, Denver.

Julia Archibald Holmes, an early-day feminist, was the first woman known to have climbed a mountain in Colorado. Wearing bloomers, she walked across the prairie with a group from Kansas and earned the disapproval of the only other woman in the party, who insisted that dresses were the only appropriate attire for women. Undaunted, Julia wore her costume for an ascent of Pikes Peak in 1858. Photo courtesy of the Department of Western History, Denver Public Library.

Anna Dickinson dared to wear pants for her ascent of Longs Peak in 1873. She was a successful public speaker whose fiery tongue lambasted slavery and extolled woman suffrage. Although many suitors wooed her, Anna turned them all down. Photo, circa 1870, courtesy of the Department of Western History, Denver Public Library.

Isabella Bird was an opinionated world traveler who once remarked, "The only waterfall I care for is Niagara." There are hints that the "desperado" of Estes Park, Rocky Mountain Jim, was wildly attracted to her, a fascination that was kindled when he guided her up Longs Peak in 1873. Isabella is shown here, circa 1895, wearing Manchu dress. Photo courtesy of the Department of Western History, Denver Public Library.

This view, looking west from the top of Twin Sisters, shows Tahosa Valley and the mountains that rise from it: (from left to right) Mount Meeker (13,911 feet), Longs Peak (14,255 feet), and Mount Lady Washington (13,281 feet). Anna Dickinson, Isabella Bird, Carrie Welton, and Victoria Broughm all climbed Longs Peak by going behind Longs as seen here, through the Keyhole (hidden by Mount Lady Washington), traversing along the west side, and taking the steep slabs on the south side (known as the Homestretch) to the top. After Agnes Vaille's death on Longs in 1925, cables were installed on the northeast side, making the ascent much shorter. This view of Longs Peak is the one that Walter Kiener, who was a fire guard on Twin Sisters, was subjected to almost daily for five summers, a constant reminder of the death of his climbing companion Agnes Vaille. Photo by Janet Robertson.

A group of Boulder schoolteachers take a walk near Boulder, circa 1890. Note the dress of the teacher in the foreground: hiking skirts, hitched up and pinned to make walking easier. Photo from the Rowland Collection, courtesy of Phyllis Smith.

This group of Colorado Mountain Club members on the Narrows of Longs Peak in 1914 typifies a pattern that persisted until the late 1970s: women went on their outdoor adventures with men, almost always following them. Photo from the James Grafton Rogers Collection, courtesy of the Colorado Historical Society, neg. no. F-15, 464.

Skiers pose at Breckenridge for their photo,
circa 1880. Note that each woman used but
one long pole, a technique typical at that
time. Photo courtesy of the Colorado Historical Society, neg. no. F-8277, 31, 163.

Esther Burnell came to Longs Peak Inn in
1916, seeking an antidote to her stressful
life in Cleveland. She fell in love with the
mountains and the inn's proprietor, the famous naturalist Enos Mills, whom she married in 1918. This photo, taken about
1920, shows Enos and Esther. Esther's sister, Elizabeth, became the first female guide
for Longs Peak. Photo courtesy of the Colorado Historical Society, neg. no. F-32,
200.

The young Pifer sisters, Anne (shown in
this photo) and Isabel, served as Longs
Peak guides in the early 1920s, beginning
and ending their long hike from the YMCA
grounds, near Estes, in darkness. Their re-
ward was a free dinner—sometimes—and a
long soak in one of the twelve tubs of hot
water on the premises. Their mother never
tried to discourage "those crazy Pifer girls,"
despite a near-catastrophe with a bear and
two cubs. Photo, circa 1922, courtesy of
the Dorsey Museum, YMCA of the Rockies,
Estes Park.

Although Eleanor Davis Ehrman and Albert Ellingwood used European climbing techniques as early as 1914, climbers in the vicinity of Boulder were climbing with ropes (which Eleanor and Albert occasionally used) as early as 1904. However, Eleanor and Albert made technical climbs all over Colorado and Wyoming, racking up first ascents, whereas the Boulder climbers didn't wander far from home. Apparently, the female members of the Boulder-based Rocky Mountain Climbers Club routinely climbed the rugged Third Flatiron in skirts. Photo, circa 1915, by Ernest Greenman, courtesy of Baker Armstrong.

One of the most active female members of the Rocky Mountain Climbers Club was Ermin Sweeney Greenman, known as "Ma" Greenman." Her husband, Ernie, a Boulder druggist, was known as "Pa." The pair, married in about 1902, shepherded many climbers up the Third Flatiron and avidly hiked other local peaks. Once when "Ma" was away visiting her home in Kansas, Ernie said to their five-year-old daughter, "Come on, honey, get on your tennis shoes," whereupon he took her up the Third Flatiron. Photo, circa 1915, by Ernest Greenman, courtesy of Baker Armstrong. Information courtesy of Dorothy Greenman.

Taken March 13, 1921, this photo shows
Colorado's early female mountain climber
Eleanor Davis Ehrman sitting on the Giant
Tooth Rocks of Sentinel Peak beside her
mountain-climbing friend Eleanor Bartlett.
Eleanor Davis was the first woman to climb
the Grand Teton in Wyoming, thereby
earning a membership in the largely male
American Alpine Club. This photo by
Harry Standley, a Colorado Springs pho-
tographer, is one of few extant showing
her.

Eleanor Davis Ehrman, here shown a few
months before her hundredth birthday,
walked with a cane because of an old injury
suffered in a fall on an icy step. Recalling
her climbing career nearly seventy years earlier, she remarked that heights had never
bothered her and that from childhood on
she'd had a kinesthetic sense. "You either
have it, or you don't," she said. Photo by
Janet Robertson.

The jagged Crestone Peak (right) and Crestone Needle were the last of Colorado's fourteeners to be climbed. Eleanor Davis Ehrman and Albert Ellingwood made the first ascents in 1916. Photo by Janet Robertson.

Marjorie Perry (second from left), shown here in about 1915, was an accomplished horsewoman and an avid skier who was largely responsible for bringing the Norwegian skiing champion Carl Howelsen (second from right) to Steamboat Springs. Photo courtesy of Mr. and Mrs. Robert Perry.

The Moffat Railroad crossed Rollins Pass, which, at 11,666 feet above sea level, was especially fierce in winter. Often the engine's rotary snowplow, touted as the most powerful one in the world, couldn't keep ahead of drifting snow. Frequently the train was delayed for hours—even days. In February 1928, when the train was stalled, Marjorie Perry and Elinor Eppich Kingery put on their skis and set off down the tracks; the conductor warned them they'd be killed. Photo by L. C. McClure, courtesy of the Colorado Historical Society, neg. no. F-32, 195, 196.

As part of the campaign to create Rocky Mountain National Park, Harriet Vaille (Bouck) and a friend arranged for three Arapaho Indian elders, an interpreter, a guide, and her cousin Oliver Toll to take a pack trip through the Estes Park area in 1914. (Since it was inappropriate for a young woman to accompany the men, Harriet had to stay behind.) The trip yielded Indian names for many of the geographical features of the area that did become the national park in 1915. In this photo Harriet, Enos Mills (in the foreground), and several Arapahos stand in front of what is probably Longs Peak Inn, a day or two before the pack trip. Photo by J. R. Griffiths, courtesy of the Colorado Historical Society, neg. no. F-44428.

Harriet Vaille Bouck's younger sister Agnes should be known for more than her dramatic death on Longs Peak in 1925. Although she was an avid mountain climber and devoted member of the newly formed Colorado Mountain Club, she was also a savvy businesswoman, far ahead of her time. Photo, circa 1920, by William Ervin, courtesy of Polly Bouck.

Agnes Vaille and Walter Kiener stayed the night at Timberline Cabin, near Jim's Grove, before setting out on their ill-fated winter climb of the East Face. In this 1932 photo, Hull Cook stands beside the dilapidated structure, which the Park Service officially closed in 1926. Photo by Everett Long.

Longs Peak, the northernmost of Colorado's fifty-four peaks over fourteen thousand feet, was first climbed by white men in 1868. (Indians trapped eagles on its top much earlier.) Addie Alexander of St. Louis was the first woman known to have climbed it, in 1871, followed by Anna Dickinson and Isabella Bird in 1873. Photo by Janet Robertson.

This diagram of the East Face of Longs Peak shows: the Kiener-Vaille route (---------), the site of Agnes Vaille's death (×), the Diamond (A), and Broadway (———).

Agnes Vaille's father had a rock shelter built (at the left in this photo) just below the Keyhole in memory of his daughter and her hapless rescuer Herbert Sortland. Photo by Janet Robertson.

In 1927 the newly constructed "Boulderfield Hotel" opened for business. Guests
could make reservations by phone from
Estes Park. Once at the hotel, they could
purchase sleeping space and meals and hire
guides to take them up Longs Peak. After
nine years the rock buildings had shifted so
much that they were declared unsafe and
were blown up. Photo, circa 1932, by Everett Long.

Here Dorothy Collier (second from right), who, with her husband, Bob, ran the high-altitude "Boulderfield Hotel" for nine summers, clowns on one of the donkeys that transported guests. At the "Boulderfield Hotel," nearly thirteen thousand feet above sea level, climbers could sleep on mattresses, dine on home-cooked food, and hire young guides to ensure that they reached the top of 14,255-foot Longs Peak. Photo circa 1930, courtesy of Dorothy Collier Bullivant.

"Tiny" Collier, daughter of Dorothy and
Bob, was the darling of the "Boulderfield
Hotel." From the age of six she had the run
of the mountain and could scamper up
Longs Peak faster than most adult climbers,
although she needed an occasional boost.
She loved living at the hotel and recalls that
"only nice people" stayed there. Photo,
circa 1930, courtesy of Dorothy Collier
Bullivant.

The well-educated writer Virginia Donaghe McClurg, shown here, championed the preservation of the outstanding prehistoric Indian ruins in southwestern Colorado. In 1900 she organized the Colorado Cliff Dwellings Association, which worked to call attention to the plight of the ruins. However, power struggles and politics tarnished Virginia's ultimate role in the creation of Mesa Verde National Park in 1906. It was Lucy Peabody—not Virginia McClurg—who became known as the park's "mother." Photo, circa 1889, courtesy of the Colorado Springs Pioneers' Museum.

One of Mesa Verde's outstanding ruins, the Cliff Palace, has been popular with tourists since the first of them struggled up to the site in the 1880s. Photo, circa 1910, courtesy of the Department of Western History, Denver Public Library.

Doc Susie wore a skirt of fashionable length, rather than the long ones she usually favored, when she posed for her picture, just before boarding the train to go to the fiftieth reunion of her medical school class. Regarded as an eccentric by some, she remained a dedicated physician in her adopted home of Fraser, Colorado, until she was over eighty years old. For Dr. Susan Anderson, this mountain community offered professional opportunities denied her in the cities and towns of the plains. Photo, circa 1947, courtesy of Glenn Wilson.

Doc Susie, shown here in a graduation portrait, chose not to marry. Although she claimed that she attended medical school only because her father insisted she do so, she was a dedicated professional until a stroke forced her to retire at the age of eighty-seven. "I don't doctor for money," she once said. "I doctor for results." Photo, circa 1897, courtesy of the Grand County Historical Association Museum Archives, Hot Sulphur Springs.

Annie (far left) and Kitty (far right) Harbison were among the earliest women to homestead in the mountains of Colorado. Each filed on a 160-acre claim near Grand Lake in 1896. The sisters ran a dairy farm and a summer resort known for its Sunday chicken dinners; some neighbors observed that the sisters worked harder than their brother. They always wore long skirts, even while milking the cows, to show they were ladies. Photo, circa 1910, courtesy of the Grand County Historical Association Museum Archives.

In 1914 Katherine Garetson, from St. Louis, took a step that, as she said, "is the most serious thing you can do, aside from marrying." She filed on 160 acres in Tahosa Valley, near Longs Peak, and later described her homesteading experiences in a charmingly candid account, "Katherine of Big Owl." This photo, circa 1915, shows Katherine, with two unidentified men, in the Big Owl Place, which she ran during the summers. Courtesy of the Estes Park Historical Museum.

Katherine Garetson's close friend Annie Shreve (left) lived with Katherine (right) during her first year of homesteading. Photo, circa 1916, courtesy of the Estes Park Historical Museum.

In 1887 Alice Eastwood escorted the famous English scientist Alfred Russel Wallace up Grays Peak (shown here with
Torreys Peak) so he could observe the exquisite flowers growing above timberline.
These fourteen-thousand-foot mountains
are so gentle that one could ride a mule to
their summits, and they are easily accessible
from Denver. Photo, circa 1915, by James
Grafton Rogers, courtesy of the Colorado
Historical Society, neg. no. F-32, 198.

In the late 1800s the botanist Alice Eastwood designed a garment that served as a
skirt or culottes, depending on the occasion
and how it was buttoned. This unconventional approach was typical of Alice, who
lived by Emerson's dictum "Scorn conventions and you always can." Although her
early years were spent in Colorado, where
she was educated and first became interested in botany, she is most closely associated with the California Academy of
Sciences, where she was curator of botany
until her voluntary retirement at the age of
ninety. Photo, circa early 1900s, courtesy of
Special Collections, California Academy of
Sciences, San Francisco.

Hazel Schmoll's father, who ran a livery
and guide service in the gold-mining town
of Ward, Colorado, taught his only child
how to "see" nature. In 1932 Hazel became
the first woman to earn a doctorate in ecology at the University of Chicago. At the
age of forty-eight, she returned to the
mountains near Ward, country that she said
was "like family" to her. There she taught
grade school and operated a summer resort.
This photo shows her on the porch of
Range View Ranch, probably about 1950,
when Hazel was sixty years old. Photo
courtesy of Western Historical Collections,
University of Colorado Libraries, Boulder.

In the 1920s the young botanist Ruth Ashton (*left*) made the first comprehensive collection of plants in Rocky Mountain National Park (which led to a master's degree and a book) and attended the famous Yosemite School of Natural History. Ruth was never appointed park naturalist, probably because of the sexist attitudes of the time. So she concentrated on teaching and writing books. This photo was taken when Ruth was in her twenties or early thirties. Courtesy of Sue Gentle.

Above: Ruth Ashton Nelson at the age of ninety, at her beloved Skyland Ranch near Estes Park. Photo taken in 1986 by Janet Robertson.

In 1971 some of the most remarkable botanical research in the world was carried out
in one of these rock cabins, since razed, on
Trail Ridge Road in Rocky Mountain National Park. Katherine Bell and her assistant, Emily Dixon, wintered in one of the
cabins while studying kobresia, a common
tundra plant. Photo, taken in 1972, courtesy of Jean Weaver.

Katherine Bell, twenty-six years old, spent the winter of 1971 in the rock cabin without running water or electricity and warmed only by a defective oil heater. An extraordinarily motivated scientist, Katherine carried out her studies at great physical and psychological cost. This photo shows Katherine in the spring of 1972, when she continued her research. Courtesy of Jean Weaver.

Emily Dixon Fose, Katherine Bell's assistant, stands on the site of the rock cabin in which the two women barely survived the winter of 1971. Behind Emily is the Knife Edge, a portion of Trail Ridge Road where the winds typically exceed one hundred miles an hour. Once Emily saved Katherine's life by feeding her M&Ms so she could climb out of a hole. Photograph taken in 1987 by Janet Robertson.

Elizabeth Cowles (Partridge), transplanted to Colorado Springs as a bride, became the first Coloradan to regard the world's mountains as her playground. She taught climbing, photographed, wrote and lectured about mountains, and threw memorable parties for climbers. In 1950 she was a member of the first party of Westerners to reconnoiter the Nepalese approach to Mount Everest—the approach by which it was subsequently climbed. This photo, taken in the 1930s, shows Elizabeth on the Jungfrau. Photo courtesy of Archives, American Heritage Center, University of Wyoming, Laramie.

Although a Ladies Hiking Club sprang up in Fraser, Colorado, in 1915, there is no record of women ski touring without men until the early 1970s. Here the Wednesday Ladies of Boulder, going strong since 1972, ski to Black Lake in Rocky Mountain National Park. Photo taken in 1978 by Janet Robertson.

In 1980 Louise Shepherd, an Australian, and Jean Ruwitch, an American, became the first women to climb, free, the formidable Diamond of Longs Peak. This photo, taken by a tourist who had climbed Longs the easy way, shows Louise (left) and Jean after their epic climb. Unlike many good female climbers of the 1970s and 1980s, Jean and Louise did not make their ascent to prove that female climbers were the equal of males. Rather, it was simply a pleasurable day's outing. Photo courtesy of Jean (Ruwitch) Goresline.

Coral Bowman was one of the finest female climbers on two continents. Here she is shown on the poster for her climbing school, Great Herizons, perhaps the first American school for technical climbing owned and run by a woman, for women. Coral sought to teach climbing in an unintimidating environment. Photo, circa 1981, courtesy of Coral Bowman Wilber.

DANCE
IN A
VERTICAL
WORLD

great Herizons

Rockclimbing School
for Women and Men

P.O. BOX 1811
BOULDER, CO 80303
(303) 499-1381

Gudrun (Gudy) Gaskill, skier and mountaineer, will be most remembered for seeing
the 470-mile Colorado Trail through to
completion. Conceived in 1972, the trail
lagged in construction until Gudy took on
the role of its "Supermom." It was officially
dedicated in 1988 and is one of the most
beautiful long walks in America. These
1987 photos by Janet Robertson show
Gudy in her trail-crew garb.

Beatrice (Bettie) Willard instructs a class in
alpine ecology on Trail Ridge Road in
Rocky Mountain National Park. She conceived the idea of the park's conducting in-
depth seminars and taught the first class, offered in 1962. Bettie is one of the world's
experts on alpine tundra. Photo taken in
1983, courtesy of Archives, Rocky Mountain National Park Headquarters.

Estella Leopold, a paleontologist with the U.S. Geological Survey in Denver and daughter of the renowned conservationist Aldo Leopold, studied the famous fossil beds in Florissant, Colorado. For three years she and her friend Bettie Willard, a plant ecologist for the Thorne Ecological Foundation in Boulder, worked with local conservation groups to save the beds from development. Finally, in 1969, their dream was realized; six thousand acres were set aside as a national monument. Photo taken in 1966, courtesy of Sam Alfend.

Forrest Ketchin, an avid outdoorswoman, spent a summer and fall scrutinizing the overused Indian Peaks Wilderness from the viewpoint of a cultural anthropologist. By interviewing campers and observing the effects of camping on the area, she produced a map that helped persuade the U.S. Forest Service to control use of the area by banning fires and requiring camping permits. Photo taken in 1982 by Janet Robertson.

Elizabeth Nitze Paepcke fell in love with
Colorado after a 1917 visit to Estes Park.
She and her family stayed at Longs Peak
Inn and befriended the naturalist Enos
Mills, whom Elizabeth calls an important
influence in her life. The town of Aspen,
her frequent home since the mid-1940s, has
benefited from her generous gift of a nature
preserve in the heart of town, as well as
from her founding of the Aspen Center for
Environmental Studies. Photo taken in
1977 by Chris Cassatt.

One of America's earliest female taxidermists as well as a first-rate naturalist, Martha Maxwell was decades ahead of her time.
Although she had some successes—for example, representing Colorado at the American Centennial Exhibition in Philadelphia
in 1876—her life was filled with the frus-
trations of being a reluctant mother, an unhappy wife, and a dedicated, innovative
scientist. Photo circa 1876, courtesy of the
Colorado Historical Society, neg. no. F-41,
727.

The Denver artist Helen Henderson Chain is here shown painting a landscape, her favorite subject. She climbed many of the mountains she painted. Although the great Thomas Moran praised her rendition of Sierra Blanca, it is her famous student Charles Partridge Adams whose paintings are known today. Photo, circa 1880s, courtesy of the Department of Western History, Denver Public Library.

Mount of the Holy Cross, publicized in the 1800s by the painter Thomas Moran and the photographer William Henry Jackson, lured religious pilgrims to view its gigantic natural cross of snow. The artist Helen Chain was probably the first woman to ascend the mountain. Photo, circa 1915, by James Grafton Rogers, one of the founders of the Colorado Mountain Club, courtesy of Western Historical Collections, University of Colorado Libraries.

Anne Ellis, who grew up in the mining
town of Bonanza in the 1880s, described
her memories in one of the most remarkable autobiographies of a woman in the
West, *The Life of an Ordinary Woman*
(1929). She countered the many tragedies
of her life with spirit and humor. Though
she never finished grade school, the University of Colorado awarded her a Master of
Letters degree in 1938. Photo, circa 1900,
courtesy of Anne Matlack.

Muriel Sibell Wolle, shown here with her
dog, Chipper, spent many summers sketch-
ing the abandoned mining buildings that
she saw fast disappearing from the Colorado mountains. Her classic book *Stampede
to Timberline* (1949) established Muriel's
reputation, and she wrote several more
books about ghost towns of the West.
Photo taken circa 1943 by Victoria Barker.

In 1939 two writers from Colorado Springs, Belle Turnbull and Helen Rich, moved to the mountain town of Breckenridge in Summit County. After purchasing a primitive house on French Street, they devoted their free time to writing about the real West as they saw it reflected in the local people. Belle produced a novel in verse, a prose novel, and two volumes of poetry, of which *The Ten Mile Range* (1957) is the better known. This photograph shows Belle in her high school prom gown, 1904. Photo courtesy of the Department of Western History, Denver Public Library.

After her move to Summit County, Helen Rich worked as a caseworker in the county welfare department during the day and wrote at night. Two of her novels, *The Spring Begins* (1947) and *The Willowbender* (1950), were published by New York houses. A third novel about the legendary dancehall girl Silverheels was rejected. Photo, circa 1950, courtesy of the Department of Western History, Denver Public Library.

As small children, Alice and Helen Dickerson moved up a canyon near Fort Collins with their parents, the last homesteaders on the Buckhorn. The sisters have lived there ever since, practicing a hospitable, self-sufficient life-style that harkens back many decades. Alice holds one of her collage paintings and Helen displays two of her pine-needle baskets. Photo taken in 1987 by Janet Robertson.

Olga Schaaf Little, whose German parents moved to Durango, Colorado, in about 1900, was the only woman in the state—if not the country—to run a packtrain of mules like the one shown here. For thirty years, winter and summer, Olga delivered supplies to the mines in the rugged La Plata Mountains and carried ore (and sometimes a corpse that needed burying) back down to Durango. Photo courtesy of the Department of Western History, Denver Public Library.

Chauffeuring passengers up the narrow Big Thompson Canyon was a man's job, but Vena Apgar (Snyder) showed that a mother of three could also perform it with great skill. After the birth of their first son, Vena's husband bought her a Stanley Steamer like the one seen in this photograph from the early 1900s. He taught her how to drive it up the narrow mountain road between Loveland and Estes Park and how to cope with the boiler. Photo courtesy of the Department of Western History, Denver Public Library.

Helen Dowe was the country's first woman to serve on a U.S. Forest Service fire lookout. In 1919 and 1920 she lived on the Devil's Head station in Pike National Forest from May to October. Photo, circa 1920, courtesy of the USDA Forest Service Regional Headquarters, Denver.

Muriel MacGregor, a lawyer and the only
child of a wealthy rancher near Estes Park,
refused to sell the valuable property she had
inherited. Living in near poverty, she kept
the MacGregor Ranch intact, willing it to
the public. This photo was taken in 1925 at
her graduation from Colorado College.
Courtesy of the MacGregor Ranch, Estes
Park.

We called her 'A. A.'" Katherine also acquired a dog, a Great Dane named Gypsy, whom she kept for only one year; he ate huge amounts of food and intimidated visitors.

Her plan was to live on the land, to cultivate it, and to run a tearoom in the summer in order to acquire cash. She and Annie lived in the Dings cabin while their own was being built. They visited with their neighbors at Longs Peak Inn: Enos Mills; his Swedish employee, Alfred; the manager of Longs Peak Inn, Charlie; and John Dickinson Sherman, an editorial writer for the *Chicago Tribune* who was on a year's leave of absence and who later homesteaded in the area. "Alfred had much concern over my preparations for the winter," Katherine noticed, "and Mr. Mills, while pretending that it was a matter-of-fact thing for a woman to brave a Rocky Mountain winter, must have been aghast at times over the foolhardiness of my exploit. Nothing would have induced me to go into that undertaking had I known what things could happen; what the life was like."

Alfred told me that I would freeze to death on a single bed. He wagged his head with a "No, no, that won't do!" when I said I had bought cots for A. A. and me. I must have a double bed and tons of comforters below and above my body, and furthermore, learn the trick of rolling up tight in the covers so that no speck of my bodily warmth could escape. He told me I must secure a tank that would hold at least fifty gallons of coal oil. Wood-stacks and stacks of poles for stove wood, must be placed around the house like a barricade, and a lot of it sawed up before the first deep snow came. He showed me how to swing an axe; how to lift and wriggle a pole on to a sawbuck; and how to saw with the big coarsetoothed saw.

Finally the cabin was finished; it consisted of a large front room with many windows on three sides and a lean-to with two tiny bedrooms and a storeroom in the middle. Katherine and A. A. ordered a six-month supply of food from Estes Park. As it turned out, they badly overestimated the amount they needed.

On the thirteenth of November a wagon drawn by four horses pulled up the mountain, bringing a tremendous load of provisions. I had never seen so many tin cans, sacks and boxes of food outside a grocery store. I felt as if I had invested in a department store. This stuff was piled in one corner of the main room of the cabin amidst shavings and boards, crated beds, stacks of water pails and coal scuttles, tubs and dishpans and brooms.

Our first night was the most tragic of my life. Coyotes, wild with excitement over the light in the wilderness, howled and shrieked to blood-curdling tunes. We bravely went to work to have supper. Although the cook stove had been set up, no table was built, so we laid boards over carpenter's horses and found some boxes to sit on. We decided to cook just one thing for the evening meal and that happened to be spaghetti stewed in diced bacon and tomatoes. We unpacked the new skillet and after washing it carefully, turned into it the can of tomatoes, the bacon and then the boiled spaghetti. The skillet wasn't iron—or at least the inside of it was enameled with some strange preparation.

When we sat down to our first meal we tried to be jolly; probably we were silly; we were both afraid of the night and the long winter ahead of us; and we were desolately lonely and homesick. We each took a mouthful of the spaghetti and stopped. It was vile. The strange enamel had soaked off—perhaps the acid of the tomatoes had helped it—and the flavor of our one and only dish was nauseating. It didn't really matter because neither of us could have eaten that night. We couldn't even swallow water. The new coal oil lamps burned queerly. Without ceremony we unpacked the bedding and crawled in—to cry, to turn, to toss about, and to wonder why we ever did it.

By the time Katherine and Annie had arranged their furniture, kitchen paraphernalia, and food, the "all-winter snows began," and they were committed to life at eight thousand feet in the Front Range. They called their house Big Owl Lodge, derived from a poem written by their neighbor Charles Edwin Hewes at the Hewes-Kirkwood Inn. Later Katherine changed the name to the Big Owl Tea Place. Once a week A. A. walked to the Wind River Ranch, a mile north of Longs Peak Inn and two miles from the Big Owl Lodge, where she bought a gallon of milk from the Hardings. "When the ground became rough from old snow melted and refrozen into ragged ice, and snow drifts alternated with long bare stretches of frozen trail, we found it took her all day long to make the round trip for the milk, and so at last we gave up trying to have fresh milk and took to 'tin cow'— the custom of the country."

Aside from a housewarming, and holidays, the big excitement was picking up the weekly mail.

The manner in which we worked steadily towards Saturday, and let our excitement increase till that night, reminded me of the way city working men and women look forward to "Saturday Night." Saturday was our mail day; letters had to be ready to send by four o'clock and by six or seven the carrier was met with his incoming pouch. Nothing mattered on Saturday: life was a scramble. And on Sunday morning we were more apt to be cross than happy. We had to get ourselves in hand for another week of mountaineering, and learn to regard the back-home, city interests in their true light: of no consequence, so far as we were concerned.

I am sure the majority of brides act as I did about my new house. I tried to be a perfect housewife. I observed the old-time weekly regulations; on Monday I washed; on Tuesday, ironed; cleaned lamps and scrubbed on Wednesday; mended and fussed about on Thursday; Friday wrote letters; and Saturday cleaned house hard. This naturally made Saturday the worst day of the week, even had there been no matter of mail! I was always tired and out of breath when we went out at noon for the weekly journey. We had to go to Alfred's cabin, the Old Original at Longs Peak Inn, over two miles north. The Inn was the Longs Peak Post office. Alfred would make a gala day of our coming and serve a meal (often a delicious dinner) at about three o'clock. Then we sewed. He played his phonograph. It seems to me that went on for many a restless, fidgety hour, till one of us, during repeated trips to the point of vantage outside the cabin, sighted the two mountain ponies and the mail wagon. Up to that point we were all friendly, talkative, affable. As soon as the pouch was brought in we were all silent. Sorting out the handful of letters was so solemn a matter, we did it with lumps in our throats! It seems to me somebody was invariably disappointed. Never did all the right, hoped-for letters come. We would load up our shoulder packs, light the lantern and start home, often in a high wind. As soon as we had lighted the lamp and built the fire in the heating stove, we'd sit down and try to digest the week's mail. The room always looked the same way on mail night: mittens, caps, overcoats, overshoes, haversacks, and wrappings from parcels and newspapers, in confusion on table and benches. We often had a loaf of bread sent up on the mail wagon from the village [Estes Park] store. At about nine o'clock one or the other of us would build up a hot fire and broil bacon, making sandwiches with the fresh bread. How many a night I stood over the heater eating hot bacon sandwiches, while A. A. and I told each other how "mean" certain innocent individuals were for not having written. Perhaps the Saturday excitement of Mail did us good; on the other hand, it may have interfered with a settled content[ment] which this life in the mountains could have brought us, had we been able to throw off all interest in the life from which we were hopelessly cut off.

As the weeks wore on, the stoves began belching out more smoke than heat. Katherine and A. A. endured the bitter cold and half-cooked meals until a man "from over the Range" stopped by and listened to Katherine's complaints. "He calmly said: 'All you need to do is to clean out the stoves and take down the pipes and blow out the chimneys. It's customary to clean out the pitch once a month.'"

Eagerly, the women anticipated their first Christmas dinner at the Big Owl, which was to be for nine people, including the two children of the Hardings at Wind River Ranch. "A fine drifting snow worked steadily for two days and nights before Christmas [but] when the day came with blazing sunshine we forgot about the snowy days and prepared the feast, supposing the road would be reasonably clear." The Hardings started out but found the road badly drifted and turned back. Charlie came to break the news to the women. Katherine noted: "We howled. Yes, we howled." The five adults (Katherine, A. A., Charlie, John Sherman, and Alfred) ate dessert and then sat around the table in the dusk while John Sherman told a Christmas story. "We were all of us homesick—desperately so. Charlie cried, 'Oh look!' The east, seen from the row of front windows was growing light; we all knelt on the bench under the windows and in profound silence watched a great silver moon ride into the sky accompanied by clouds. We felt as if we were listening to music. It was a sweet and solemn ceremony."

The women's nearest neighbors were at Longs Peak Inn. In January, John Sherman and Charlie left, and since Enos Mills was on a lecture tour, only Alfred remained. Charlie Hewes was two miles away, but as Katherine explained, "Due to his habits of a recluse, we failed to think of Mr. Hewes as a neighbor; in fact we never thought of him at all." Katherine and Annie became "wearied with continued monotony." One day they decided to walk south to the "hamlet" of Allenspark. They had heard that the postmaster, a former bartender, was "becoming a noisy and ardent socialist; it was worth our while to make his acquaintance." So, setting off early, they arrived at noon. They could find only one inhabitant, a man who was leaning on his shovel in front of his shack.

We told him that we had walked about eight miles to make the acquaintance of the postmaster. I am afraid one question we asked was; "Is he young?" Another, "Is he married?" He gave us a sly look and shook his head; and then he said the man we sought had taken his wife and child down the canon on a visit that fine day. Watching us narrowly to see how we stood this blow, he went further. He asked: "Be you lookin' for a man?" We turned and fled.

The winter wore on, and then one morning in April, as Katherine wrote:

I went before seven for a walk on the Hill. It had rained all the day before and I knew sunlight on wet things was worth going out to see. The pasque flower, our hoary crocus, was blooming in clumps. The beauties held moisture on stem and blossom and how they glistened with the sun shining on them! Scattered among them were buttercups and sweet ellysium. I stood close to a white rabbit and watched him wiggle his nose. He nestled in a bed of kinnikinnik against a red rock wall, and of course he assumed that he was not seen for he is sure of this protective coloring — white in winter and brown in summer. . . . Never had I stumbled on such variety and beauty and wildness—no, not in all the years I had been visiting this land—as I discovered my hill to be. It was too good to be true. It made my heart beat fast to think the winter was behind us.

In spite of Katherine's rejoicing, her troubles were far from over, for she and A. A. were completely broke. They lacked the money even for stamps, which had to be sent to them "from home." To add to their woes, a neighbor, Ted, stopped by and pointed out that if Katherine intended to comply with the conditions of the Homestead Act, she would have to clear the land and put in crops. Katherine replied that she had assumed she would be exempt from this stipulation because of the barrenness of the soil and the short growing season at eight thousand feet.

Ted, unmoved by her explanation, said firmly that if a government agent wandered by and saw that she hadn't begun the clearing, it was likely that the big cattleman of the district would "git" her claim. So Katherine began clearing the land.

I gave up two hours a day to splitting and sawing the logs that were down. We had a little tin express wagon which I would trundle into the back door loaded with firewood. It was my way of tackling the most difficult phase of homesteading by women—clearing the land. At night I did ache so I could hardly get to sleep; there were gashes and blood blisters on my hands. I didn't do it right, but I made headway. Thus I cleared half an acre, waiting till spring came with its thaw to get out the tall stumps. When the ground became soft I used to run downhill and fall against one of them till stump and I went rolling to the stream.

Katherine hired two men to build an addition to her cabin for a gift shop and washrooms, and she ordered new chairs, tables, teapots, coffeepots, trays, and a coal oil stove for what was to be a tearoom, all of which cost money that she did not have. And then another blow fell. It became obvious that the improved road from Lyons to Allenspark to Longs Peak Inn was going to cut an entirely new swath through the woods, leaving the Big Owl Tea Place on the abandoned part of the road.

Surprisingly, however, business was good. Partly this was because customers wanted to see the "Women Homesteaders." And partly it was because the Big Owl Tea Place was a charming oasis in the forest. Gradually, by trial and many errors, A. A. and Katherine learned to deal with customers, even when they came in droves, and to offer fewer items on their menu. Tourists eagerly bought up the Russian dolls, runners, towels, aprons, and pillow tops that the women had sewed in the winter.

Still, by the end of the summer, Katherine was so deeply in debt that the women agreed that A. A. should secure a position as a teacher in Wyoming. After she left with a tearful farewell, Katherine became very depressed and "degenerated and lived like a stray dog." One day a new friend, Bill, told her that she'd better go back to St. Louis for a few months. She did.

Her lethargy continued. And then, she later recorded, "after Christmas it dawned on me that inertia would last forever if I was not strong enough to snap out of it." Katherine called on a business friend of her father's, a "casual acquaintance of the whole family" who didn't know her, and asked him to loan her one thousand dollars. The man wrote out a check, refusing to let her sign a note. He sent her away with, "My child, I don't want to make any money out of you." She returned to the Big Owl in February.

Katherine battled mice, pack rats, and, worst of all, loneliness. She began talking to herself, even having arguments between "Self Number One" and "Self Number Two." Yet through it all she began to detect a growing self-esteem. "Isn't it odd," Katherine wrote, "that a human being, living like a hermit, should begin to have a sacred care for the spoken word? It came to me. And isn't it odd that such a recluse should grow tolerant, fair and kindly towards others? It came to me."

The days took care of themselves. The weather gods were with me. Never was such an open, stormless spring experienced in these mountains. . . . In my uninterrupted days I was forever going over into that 'Somewhere-else of the Imagination.' I lived for hours in Kipling's India, in Stevenson's South Seas and in Baghdad of the Arabian Nights.

. . . Day after day I went up to the rocks on the hill and sewed until sundown, dreaming in the sun, happy and hopeful. There were very few people in the hills then. I went occasionally to the Inn for mail but as I now had my own lock box I seldom saw a soul there, not even Alfred. . . . This solitude threw me on my own resources. I didn't care. It gave my imagination full swing so that I dwelt in a bright world created to my taste.

. . . It was during these sunny days on the Hill that I made the elaborately cross-stitched curtains out of an unbleached muslin bed spread; the famous curtains which have hung in the tea room ever since and been admired by everyone who knows Russian peasant art. . . . I had a hard time keeping the threads for my embroidery. The [pack] rat stole so many skeins that I had to finish the curtains with a much lighter shade of blue than the one with which I had started. He used to carry off my thimble, too, but this I was always able to recover before it went down under the house.

Katherine hired men and teams to clear and fence her land and to put in three acres of oats and one of potatoes. She was quite confident that her cultivated land would add up to eight acres; the Land Office inspector who measured the fenced fields announced that it was four.

When summer came, Katherine worked up enough nerve to reopen the tearoom. A. A. would not be there to help, having decided to spend the summer in St. Louis. However, Katherine's sister, Helen, and Helen's son decided that instead of opening up their cabin, they would live with Katherine to keep her company and to help. Since the road that ran by the Big Owl was no longer being repaired (and, as Katherine said, "Mountain roads are bad at best—even the petted, popular ones"), a new method of delivery had to be worked out. Katherine arranged for the mail driver, Emil, to deposit supplies on the Dings cabin porch. Then, at night, Katherine, Helen, and her son hauled them two miles down to the tearoom.

The summer was neither a rousing success nor a disaster, although Helen returned to her own house rather abruptly after she discovered that a pack rat had taken her best silk stockings as nesting material for its new babies. Since the bad road forced customers to walk downhill a half-mile to the tearoom, "not much money was taken in. . . . On the other hand, little was spent." The rye crop didn't come up and the potatoes were small.

Yet with a new pride Katherine wrote, "Although I risked no money that second business season, and though I made no effort to attract the public, I was visited by eight hundred tourists and paid all the running expenses for the four months." The confidence that Katherine was gaining was evident from the observations she made when she met another young woman who decided to homestead.

About the time Big Owl closed for the season I entertained two unusual and very interesting young women. They were gentle, unassuming girls, wearing city clothes which in that day meant long skirts, high black shoes—to say nothing of long hair. We were beginning to expect sport clothes, so these girls seemed a little old-fashioned, a bit quaint and modest. They were enjoying the first experience they had ever had of outdoor life and the West; staying for a few weeks at Longs Peak Inn, they were being introduced to Nature. They were the most eager pupils Enos Mills ever had. One of the sisters was dark-haired, the other red-haired, and their names were Bessie and Esther Burnell. Although they came for a short vacation they fell in love with our country as I, myself, had done, and Esther, at least, was destined to "take root." She was not well. Someone had suggested to her that she spend the winter with me. I liked her but plainly said that I preferred to be alone. If I could not have my little A. A. I would have no one. That was that.

Esther set about finding a homestead of her own. Glorious hikes we had, looking over unentered tracts of land. Together we drew plans for her cabin—forty different ways of building. The minutest details of food and utensils and clothing were worked out. I entered into her plans with genuine delight. I overflowed with the expression of bottled-up experiences and emotions. One deep impression was made upon me by watching this other girl from a city go through what I had known. One by one she battled with fears that had made the venture a struggle the first year. I watched her efforts to overcome her fear of being far from human beings in the night; her handling of the money-end of it all; her fear of what construction the gossips would put on her isolation. Indeed, there was so much that was hard at the start, that my heart was wrung for my own old self. Finally she filed on land four miles the other side of Estes Park and I saw very little of her after she went to the Village to supervise the building of her cabin.

After Katherine paid out precious cash to have her addition converted into a winter living room, she went back to St. Louis for Thanksgiving. On December 1, she returned to Estes. Emil, the mail driver, picked up her and her "grub" at a hotel.

That morning was utterly bleak. Heavy, dark sky, a keen north wind with snow flurries. Emil was so bundled up all I could see of him was a red knob of nose and two twinkling water blue eyes. Esther Burnell was staying at the hotel waiting for her cabin to be roofed, so she stood at the window watching us start up the mountain. She looked frightened, piteous; and she told me afterwards that I might have been starting for the North Pole from the way it looked to her. . . . She knew I was headed for a place where no one would welcome me—only a bare, unheated, lonely little frame cabin at the rim of a forest. I didn't dare pity myself. That was one thing I had learned not to do under any circumstances—indulge in self-pity. As we started she ran out, calling frantically, "Have you matches?" Our latest sensation had been a newspaper account of two women who froze to death on a claim in Montana, the grocer having overlooked putting matches in their box of grub.

Katherine's third winter at the Big Owl was the "dreariest ever known in the mountains. The sunshine . . . never came. The days were dark, threatening, for weeks at a time." She covered her seed potatoes with all the bedding she didn't use herself and built a fire in the Wilson heater to prevent them from freezing. Still, Katherine was by now a "seasoned mountaineer," and when she did not see a human being for three weeks she didn't feel the lack. After a storm dropped a foot of snow, Bill stopped by, presenting her with some rabbits. Katherine wrote:

I greeted him. I stopped in the middle of the greeting, frozen as stiff as he looked. That voice of mine came hesitatingly and frightened me. I suffered a nervous chill. Here was something familiar—the sound of my own voice, and yet it had been so long since I had heard it that I didn't think of it as my own. Most uncanny was the experience and never to be repeated by me.

I talked poor Bill nearly to death until five in the evening when he went away home. That very night I began a practice which I have stuck to religiously when living alone, that of reading aloud and talking to myself. In another week I was treating the stove, my shoes, water pails and brook like members of the family—as if they had personality as well as ears. That laughable trait of "talking to one's self" is as necessary to one who dwells in solitude as is the daily food and nightly sleep.

By the time Christmas came, the "back of the house . . . was snowed up clear to the roof." Katherine could not sleep a whole night through. "By one o'clock I began to grow restless, then chilly, then too cold to lie in bed. Night after night before three in the morning came, I was up and building a hot fire in the heater, heating hot water for a cup of malted milk and toasting my bed clothes." The first year she had learned that hot-water bags often froze solid and split. "But flat-irons and stove lids could be reheated in the night. While this was taking place I often sewed a little, hugging the stove as tight as I dared."

On December 1 Katherine and Esther had arranged to meet each other on Christmas Day. Since their claims were sixteen miles apart, they had agreed on a spot midway, by a little stream eight miles north of the Big Owl, beyond Lily Lake. There had been no communication between the two women since. On the appointed day Katherine thought she would go mad if she stayed "in that gloomy cabin and looked out all day upon dull grey air and dead white land."

Hardly realizing what I was doing, I pulled down the shoulder knapsack, tossed into it a can of tomato soup, coffee, bread, bacon, can opener and coffee pot; put on my wraps and my snowshoes and away I flew towards Estes Park, hoping Esther would remember our tryst. The daybreak was lovely and made me hopeful. Still, it wasn't likely that her acquaintances in the Village would overlook inviting her to Christmas dinner and that would be too good for a lonely homesteader to miss. All the way I was anxiously watching the weather and also longing ardently for that companion. I made up my mind not to wait for her at all but in the appointed place build my fire, cook my Christmas dinner of soup and coffee and hot bacon sandwiches, and enjoy the fire in the snow, then trot home as fast as I could go. Thinking all this with a lump in my throat, I turned the edge of the forest through which, like a white serpent in a dark green country, twisted the road. We bumped right into each other!

Together we exclaimed, "I didn't think you would come!" and both of us were near tears, so much had we hoped to find each other.

Down by the stream we scooped away the snow where we built a great fire, without any difficulty, finding plenty of dry twigs and dead limbs of the trees. The ice over the middle of the stream was not hard to break for water so the coffee pot was soon boiling. Of course the ground around the fire where snow melted fast was wet, nay muddy. Esther found newspapers in her knapsack which made fairly good rugs. We talked excitedly for an hour, telling each other what the home folk had sent us for Christmas and all that had happened since we parted in November. She had moved into her cabin, although it was still at sixes and sevens because she was learning to hammer and saw, making her own bed and chairs.

The weather was sorry enough; scattering flurries of snow did not dim the fire which blazed away magnificently. Besides the great red flames and her head of red curls, the world was white. She looked wonderfully pretty, animation transforming her into a beauty. Her eyes are the exact tint of her hair. We acted like mad-caps, declaring that this celebration was a tribute to the God of Winter.

An hour was all either of us dared to tarry. While it was still daylight, we said goodbye and I trudged back up the mountain to my isolated home. . . . Now and then I passed deserted cabins, once homesteaders' shacks, or else summer homes. Nothing cheers the solitary wanderer in our hills like a whirl of smoke from a dwelling. All habitations, that Christmas Day were without smoke, dead, and I would not look at them. It was pitch dark long before I reached Big Owl but, accustomed gradually to the darkness, I did not lose my way.

In January the hens that Katherine had purchased began laying. On each egg she marked the name of the hen who had laid it and the date because "I had entered them in a contest for best layer." She gave some of the eggs to Julian of Lily Lake; his wife, Mary, had fun deciding "whether they'd boil Biddy's big brown egg or Yellow-Belly's small one."

Until March, Katherine experienced "real happiness." She "responded to every mood of Nature, sensitive to impressions that would have been impossible under normal living conditions." And then what had seemed an ample supply of wood gave out. She traded her seed potatoes and hens for more wood cut by men at a nearby sawmill. April and May "were like another winter tied onto the tail of the one that began on the tenth of September—already unbearably long."

Smallpox broke out at the sawmill, making it off limits for visiting. And because it took so much energy to surmount a fifteen-foot snowdrift that had formed on the road, Katherine rarely went to Longs Peak Inn for the mail. In the middle of that bitter spring she ate the last fats in her larder. Her meals no longer contained any bacon, ham, lard, butter, olive oil, or canned milk. They consisted only of "sugar, dried fruits, corn meal (worms had to be carefully sifted out before using) and a lot of desiccated vegetables which Doud had enthusiastically recommended, altho he had not tried them himself but had fallen for the advertisement of them."

One evening Katherine was "just snowshoeing around, up the road for amusement" when she "topped a high snowdrift in the middle of the road" and met Miss Spencer, who owned land south of Longs Peak Inn. Utterly astonished, Miss Spencer took a moment to recover and then announced, " 'There's big news. America has entered the World War. I'm going to get into Red Cross work!' "

The thawing snowdrifts cut deep gullies into the road above the Big Owl and Katherine "spent five hours a day with shovel and wheel barrow, filling in the ruts with wet sand. It was killing work," she wrote. "I longed so for the wagon with food to get to Big Owl that I kept writing the store keeper that my road was almost passable." Katherine discovered that a road gang was working three miles south of her and begged the men to bring her some bacon, canned milk, butter, and white bread from Allenspark. They brought it, and by eleven o'clock she was in her kitchen "hysterically making hot bacon sandwiches. Mind you I had been without any kind of fat or meat for weeks. I ate awhile and cleared it all away and washed the dishes; then, not feeling satisfied, did it over again. I kept this up till seven at night, one complete performance after another."

In the beginning of the summer Katherine hired a man named Walstrom to build her a bedroom cabin and to plant oats, timothy seed, and potatoes. In the fall he and his bride helped dig up the potatoes and took their half share, as had been agreed upon. The tearoom was more profitable than it had been the previous summer, perhaps because Katherine was better known and the road was in better condition.

She looked forward to November 20, when her three years of home-steading would be over, and wrote: "All my plans led up to that date. After final proof—what? I never thought beyond that date; it was the goal." After the tearoom closed for the season, she worked at the entrance to Rocky Mountain National Park, established during Katherine's second year of homesteading and situated near the Big Owl. Katherine was delighted to be outside all day and pitched an A-tent for shelter near Fawn Creek. At night she slept in her cabin.

On December 6 she stayed with an acquaintance in Estes Park while on her way to Denver, where she was to wrap up details to prove up on her homestead.

Now, I was destitute of city clothes so had ordered from my old-time tailor in St. Louis a new traveling suit. My friend went to the express office for it and had it ready —pressed and everything—for me to put on when I arrived in town. Dear me! How red-skinned, wind-blown, and rough I was! I saw it in the long looking glass in my room. At Big Owl I used such a tiny mirror I didn't know anything at all about my looks. What a raw country woman I had become! I can't say I enjoyed that evening—especially when some very different town young people came in to play cards.

The next day Katherine and some neighbors went into Denver. After she met the lawyer and testified in private at the land office, she took the train back to St. Louis. But her return was no "triumphal entry" because "the War and the War only, mattered." She took a menial job, "dreary work and wretched pay. . . . I was shabby; and food was scarce and queer at home; and troubles and war gloom piled up around us. My days and nights were spent looking towards my return to Big Owl."

In March the land office sent Katherine a big envelope, which she assumed contained her patent. Instead, it was a document saying that the Forest Service contested her right to the patent on the grounds that she had not complied with the Homestead Act in the matter of cultivation. Later, Katherine found that the Forest Service had treated all six other home-steaders in her National Forest Reserve in the identical way.

Her friends and family advised her to forget it all and to settle down in St. Louis and "be a sensible citizen." But that was no longer possible. As Katherine wrote: "If I had any hopes of being a sensible city woman again, I might have heeded their advice. Three years of life on that claim in Colorado had given me an overwhelming love for the western world. I hated that life in St. Louis, so cramped, so far removed from the natural life, so stupid and dull. I wanted to die rather than submit to such a drab way of living."

Katherine visited with a friend, a Judge Quincy, who gave her money and advice and letters to Denver friends so she could procure the services of the "best land lawyer" in Denver. She returned to the Big Owl and, in effect, started all over. A neighbor came one day asking if Katherine would board some carpenters and stonemasons while they built three cottages; she agreed. A. A. came back and helped. And Katherine set about cultivating the land again, planting potatoes and oats. She restrung fence and re-measured. Much to her immense surprise and pleasure, the local cattleman, Fred Robinson, said he would do everything in his power to help her because she had been such a good neighbor. He reminded her that he had grazed the forty acres on the eastern segment of her homestead from the very beginning and that this would weigh in her favor, compensating for the fact that she didn't have enough arable land to cultivate twenty acres.

The tearoom made money even though its prices were high and it "did not have much good food" because of the war. The oats Katherine had planted now flourished. "A ripple of excitement ran through [the] community in August when . . . Esther Burnell proved up on her homestead and married Enos Mills—all on a summer's day." (Katherine is mistaken in this; Esther never did prove up on her homestead.)

Burns Will, one of the first national forest rangers in the area and a friend of the supervisor and ranger who had instigated the protest against Katherine, took up her cause and that of the other local homesteaders. Enos Mills also used his influence in Katherine's behalf, as did Mr. Bond, the local state representative. That winter Katherine went back to St. Louis, where she earned money as a stenographer. Then she and A. A. worked as solicitors, earning ten cents for each interview with a woman in her home. They averaged four dollars a day and by early April had saved enough money to go back to the Big Owl. The day after her return, Katherine, despondent over the injustice against her, set off on a walk to Longs Peak Inn for the mail, "loitering, watching birds, pretending nothing hurt."

As I came home through the Inn yard, I tore open a long envelope without noticing who the sender was.

This was from Washington. I stood stock still, not realizing at first what I was reading. A thrill ran through my body at sight of Woodrow Wilson's signature. I glanced up and saw Enos Mills standing in the path in front of me. I handed him the document. His eyes danced with delight.

"Congratulations, Neighbor!" he cried; then added gently, "Indeed, you have earned your patent!"

Katherine Garetson operated the Big Owl Tea Place from 1915 to 1934. At some point she made it a Russian tearoom, complete with a samovar. Her nephew Mac Dings recalled that it was considered a very expensive place and that some people, such as horseback riders from the Stanley Hotel in Estes, occasionally became indignant over the high prices. However, another Estes Park resident remembers the Big Owl Tea Place as being "the prettiest thing you ever saw."[24]

Apparently Katherine continued her pattern of migrating to Missouri for part of the winter. In the 1930s, after Burns Will became state representative, she went to Denver to work for the state government. After Colorado went wet, Katherine became head of the Colorado Liquor Licensing Board, a job she held until her retirement. During her last years she lived with a nephew, Frederick Dings, in Seattle, Washington. Katherine died in 1963. In 1985 the Big Owl Tea Place building, which had become a private residence, suffered a major fire and was razed.

In 1871 a young Englishwoman, Rose Kingsley, visited Colorado and observed, "In the frank unconventional state of society which exists in the West, friendships are made much more easily than even in the Eastern States, or still more, in our English society."[25] Fifty years later Rose would probably have observed that the "frank unconventional state of society" could now be found in the mountains of the West, rather than in its established towns and cities. As examples she could have cited Susan Anderson and Katherine Garetson, who gained control over their lives only after they took to the hills.

5

The
Gutsy
Lady
Botanists

In the 1800s Emanual D. Rudolph, compiling information from available lists, found that 1,185 women had some kind of "active" botanical connection; mostly they made plant collections and belonged to botany clubs. Of this number, only a few dozen, at most, made what could be called, possibly, a significant contribution. Still, botany was obviously considered a suitable subject for young women to study; in 1887, an article appeared in *Science* titled "Is Botany a Suitable Study for Young Men?" Nevertheless, botanist Alice Eastwood probably made it look too easy when in the late 1800s she deftly made her professional way in a field dominated by men. It seems entirely likely that her unique personality opened doors that would have remained closed had she been less confident and vital. Certainly, two Colorado women who followed her, Hazel Schmoll and Ruth Ashton Nelson, had a rougher time of it; Hazel finally gave up, whereas Ruth was forced to change her goals. It wasn't until the 1970s that a woman, Katherine Bell Hunter, undertook botanical research so innovative and dangerous that it was considered a remarkable endeavor for any botanist, male or female.

ALICE EASTWOOD

Alice Eastwood was born January 19, 1859, in Toronto, Canada, the first of three children. When she was six years old, her mother died. A few years later Alice's father put her and her sister, Catherine, in a Catholic convent school, horrifying his Unitarian relatives. For the next six years he then wandered from job to job, visiting his daughters only once. Although the girls didn't learn much in the school, Alice described it as "lovely"—filled with trees planted by the resident French priest, and with lilacs, where she and Catherine played house.[1] They had no toys but learned to sew, knit, crochet, and tat. "Indeed I mended my clothes and stockings from the beginning," Alice wrote. "We had no luxuries and no feasts. I remember being given a spoonful of honey as a birthday treat." Occasionally Alice visited an uncle who was a physician and experimental horticulturist; he taught her the Latin names for a wild red raspberry, *Rubus odoratus*, and a partridgeberry, *Mitchella repens*.

Eventually Alice's father landed in Denver and sent for her. However, once there, she discovered that he and her brother, Sidney, were staying at the cheap Carr Hotel, quarters deemed unsuitable for a young girl. So Alice became what today we would call a nanny for the two young children of the Jacob Scherrers, a wealthy cattle-ranching family. She was treated more like a daughter than a servant and was encouraged to read books from their well-stocked library. When the Scherrers moved to the cool mountains for the summer, Alice had her first encounter with some of the brilliant wild-flowers that lived there. They impressed her.

After her father built a combination store and living quarters on Larimer Street in Denver, Alice moved in. While attending the Arapaho Street School, she hauled water, cooked, washed, cleaned house, worked at out-side jobs, and excelled in school. One of her teachers saw that Alice had become "crazy over botany" and gave her copies of *Gray's Manual*, the classic book on botany by Asa Gray, and *The Flora of Colorado*, by Parry and Coulter. Alice used them as references and as a means of learning the plant families and genera on her own, since there was no one else to teach her. While still in high school she started a plant collection. In 1879 she graduated as valedictorian of her high school.

Thanks to Jacob Scherrer, Alice landed a summer job teaching primary children in Kiowa, about thirty miles southeast of Denver. The pupils brought her wildflowers, eggs, bird nests, rocks, and whatever else caught their eye. Alice capitalized on their natural curiosity, and she got along well with them. "The children were so good," she later wrote, "that they needed no punishment. Some of them needed brains." In the fall, she taught eighth grade at East High School in Denver, an experience she later called the "most difficult" of her life. Alice was about five feet tall and barely older than some of her pupils and had had no experience disciplining boys bigger than she. Her job, substituting for all the teachers of the school, frequently forced her to study harder than her pupils so that she could keep ahead of them in a subject that was new to her. Alice instructed in physiology, American and English literature, Greek and Roman history, Latin, zoology, calisthenics, geometry, chemistry, bookkeeping, astronomy, algebra, and even drawing, which she'd never studied before. When teaching English, she often corrected two hundred essays a week.

Although her salary was only $475 a year, she managed to save enough money to spend summers in the mountains. By sewing her own dresses and living frugally, Alice even saved enough to indulge in her only extravagance, purchasing botany books. At the end of her first year of teaching, she bought the *Manual of Botany of the Rocky Mountain Region*, by John Merle Coulter, and hopped a train west to Georgetown. After several days she was able to accomplish her goal of climbing Grays Peak, a fourteener named after America's botanical guru, Asa Gray, who had climbed it in 1872. On its slopes Alice made her first acquaintance with the exquisite jewel-like flowers that grow above tree line.

Her trip to the high country was habit-forming. Thereafter, every summer she made arrangements to get into the Colorado mountains on plant-collecting expeditions. Gradually, her fame as a collector spread. A member of the Denver School Board gave her a letter of introduction to the railroad magnate David Moffat. She visited him and came away with free railroad passes on the Moffat Railroad, which enabled her to collect plants in such distant parts of the state as Steamboat Springs, Silverton, Ouray, and Grand Junction. She later acknowledged her benefactor's "courtesy and kindness" by naming a penstemon for him, having collected it along railroad tracks near Grand Junction.

On a train trip to the Western Slope, a salesman persuaded Alice and a clergyman from St. Louis to visit the beautiful Uncompahgre Canyon, between Silverton and Ouray. The pair made arrangements to ride horses there, which presented a problem for Alice. Although she wore a skirt that was unconventionally short—it came to the tops of her button-top shoes—she slept in a thoroughly conventional nightgown, which was long-sleeved, full-gathered, and bulky. If she wrapped it in her raincoat and a storm came up, it would get wet. Finally, remembering the advice of a friend, she rolled it up and wore it as a bustle. The arrangement was awkward and uncomfortable, though, especially since she was riding sidesaddle, so on the return trip she simply wore the nightgown under her dress. To add to her troubles, a local reporter read the Beaumont Hotel register and wrote in the *Ouray Journal*, "Miss Alice Eastwood of Denver and the Reverend Porteous of St. Louis are making a tour of the mountains on horseback." The Denver newspaper carried the item also, and Alice worried that it would be picked up by a St. Louis newspaper. It wasn't.

In July 1887 Alice escorted an Englishman, Alfred Russel Wallace, up Grays Peak to collect alpine flowers. The arrangements had been made by James Baker, the principal of East High School (and later president of the University of Colorado), who had told Dr. Wallace that Alice was the "only person in Denver" who could competently guide him up Grays Peak. Wallace, one of the most famous scientists of his time, was in the United States on a lecture tour. He had conceived a theory of evolution at nearly the same time as Charles Darwin, but, being much younger, had generously deferred to him.

On a brilliant, clear morning in mid-July Alice and Dr. Wallace took the train to Graymount, west of Denver, and spent the night in a rude two-story log "hotel." They then hiked up to the Silver Plume Mine, ate a hearty noon meal, walked some more, and spent the night at a working mine in Grizzly Gulch. The mine manager, a Mr. West, joined them the following night in a hut owned by the mine, thirteen thousand feet above sea level. By hanging a blanket across the single room, dividing the men's sleeping quarters from Alice's, the trio observed proprieties. In the morning Alice fried pancakes and brewed coffee. After breakfast Mr. West went back to his mine, Alfred Wallace began strolling up Grays, and Alice tidied up the cabin and washed the towels and dishes. Then, stepping out into a morning that was marvelously bright and bracing, she hurried to catch up with her charge. They made their way up the peak amid spectacular bursts of pink moss campion, white arenaria, and sky-blue alpine forget-me-nots and through a color riot of columbines, paintbrush, clovers, and penstemons. Wallace told Alice that the alpine gardens reminded him of his honeymoon in the Alps.

After standing on the rocky summit of Grays Peak, they started down. However, the carpet of flowers so bewitched them that they neglected to pay close attention and lost their way. Alice's long skirts and bulky plant press hampered her when she stepped over fallen logs, but finally, just before dark, the pair stumbled in to the mine. By morning they had revived enough to enthusiastically collect new wildflowers in Grizzly Gulch which later found their way into the Eastwood herbarium.

For ten years Alice taught at East High School. Her starting salary gradually doubled to one hundred dollars a month, enabling her to purchase a corner lot in Denver in partnership with her father. It proved to be a shrewd investment: they eventually sold the lot for twenty thousand dollars "during the height of the boom." Alice took her half of the money and invested in Denver property, on which her father built, and in two houses in Durango, which she rented out. At the age of thirty, suddenly finding herself financially independent, she decided to devote the rest of her life to botany.

In June 1889 Alice met Theodore A. Cockerell, who was studying natural history in the town of Westcliffe. (Later he would become a well-known entomologist and naturalist and would assist Alfred Russel Wallace in preparing the second edition of Wallace's book *Island Life*.) Theodore and Alice botanized in the Wet Mountain Valley, and Alice was later elected secretary of the Colorado Biological Association, which Theodore had founded. After Theodore returned to England, Alice wrote him a letter, which he found "rather effusive . . . as is her wont." She said that she had learned a great deal from him, "in some respects more than from anyone else," and that she hoped to repay the obligation to her fellowmen.[2]

James Baker persuaded Alice to teach for one more term at East High School; then, in early December, she headed out to California, where she collected plants and made good professional contacts. In the spring she migrated back to Colorado and visited her friends the Wetherills at their ranch on the Mancos River near Mesa Verde. Alice had first met the Wetherills when she'd stopped at their ranch as a tourist and had paid for a guided tour of the Indian ruins. They'd become such good friends that the Wetherills regarded Alice as a relative, and she often camped out with Al and Dick on the rim of Cliff Canyon, collecting plants while the brothers dug in the prehistoric ruins they had discovered. Alice Eastwood was, in fact, the first woman to collect plants for scientific purposes in what is now known as Mesa Verde National Park. However, none of her specimens found their way into the Mesa Verde National Park Herbarium, which did not exist at the time she was collecting. (Incidentally, although both Alice Eastwood and Virginia Donaghe McClurg were frequent guests at the Wetherill ranch in the 1880s and 1890s, there is no evidence that they knew each other. We do know, however, that Al Wetherill admired them both.)

The following fall the Brandagees, botanists whom Alice had met on her recent trip to California, invited her to help organize a herbarium for the California Academy of Sciences in San Francisco. She accepted. By combining her fifty-dollar-a-month salary with her income from the Durango property, she was able to live modestly and to still have enough money left over to purchase botany books. During her stay she wrote an essay on the mariposa lilies of Colorado for the October issue of the academy's publication, *Zoe*.

So distinct, so individual are those blossoms, that they seem to have souls. They speak a wonderfully enticing language to draw the wandering insects to their honeyed depths. . . . The bands of color on both divisions of the perianth are bewildering, impossible to describe; but more than aught else, they cause each flower to say proudly, with uplifted head, "I am myself; there is no other like me."

. . . To see the different kinds of insects hovering over these plants, alighting on the flowers and crawling slowly through the viscid hairs of the honey glands is to understand how this race of lovely hybrids came to be. Not in vain do these flowers set off their beauty and store their sweets.[3]

In May 1892 Alice took a train east for a prearranged trip with Al Wetherill. He met her on the Denver and Rio Grande line at Thompson's Springs, Utah, with two riding horses and one packhorse. Their plan was to follow a cattle highway to the Wetherill ranch so that Alice could collect plants. Since it was late in the day, they stayed the first night at a "sort of hotel" in Thompson's Springs. As Alice later recalled, "The woman in charge was suspicious and asked, 'Are you married?' Al was standing by. I said, 'No.' 'Are you going to be?' Again I answered: 'No.' It was certainly embarrassing for Al who had no intention of asking me."

Near Moab they stayed for several days with a lonely Mormon widower while Alice collected plants and the horses rested. Alice made strawberry shortcake, a dish new to the widower and his young son. Once the widower realized that Alice was not Al Wetherill's prospective bride, he proposed to her. She declined.

Alice and Al then left for Monticello but lost the trail and had to spend a cold night out. The next day, after a cloudburst, they took refuge in a cave; Al unsaddled Alice's horse so she could wrap herself in the sweaty saddle blanket while he started a fire. The smoke drove out swallows that were nesting in the cave and Alice was instantly remorseful that innocent birds had paid for her own comfort.

At Monticello they picked up two more horses that belonged to the Wetherills but that had either drifted back or been stolen from the ranch. Then Alice and Al headed out. After taking a shortcut that didn't work, they got caught in a rain. Since night was fast approaching, Al used a rope to lower Alice and the gear over the side of a steep box canyon called Montezuma. He then tied the five horses together and left, hoping to find an easy way into the canyon.

Alice "rigged up the pack cover as a wind break and then lit a fire." She stayed up until nine, hoping Al would appear. After eating a little food, she lay down to sleep. "I wasn't at all worried about myself," she wrote, "because I knew if I followed the creek up that I would reach Monticello eventually and I am a good walker." The next morning she spread out her plant specimens on rocks to dry in the sun and climbed down to the river to find Al, scattering pieces of paper on the ground so he'd have a trail to follow up to her ledge. When a strong wind came up, she quickly scrambled back to rescue her plants. Finally, in the early afternoon, Al arrived, exhausted. He ate the few scraps of food that were left, and Alice cooked oatmeal in creek water "thick with adobe mud." Then Al slept the rest of the afternoon.

At six in the morning Al and Alice set out, riding until nine that night. Montezuma Canyon proved to be a labyrinth of passages, which they struggled through with the horses, up and down steep walls. By now they were famished. But even on empty stomachs they delighted in encountering many plants new to them. They slept out a second night. At noon the next day they reached the San Juan River and knew they weren't far from Mancos. Al unsaddled the horses so they could rest, and Alice put her plants out to dry. Suddenly a "whirlwind lit into them," scattering the plants. Alice threw herself down to protect them. Al brought the saddle blankets and covered the plants as Alice gingerly lifted herself up. The plant specimens and the paper scraps with pertinent information written on them were hopelessly mixed up. Alice painstakingly untangled them, matching them up properly. Years later she confessed that the incident had disheartened her, that it was the first time during the entire trip that her spirits had been low. (Al Wetherill wrote that Alice, whom he called "The Lady," would have wept if he hadn't been there, although she was not the "weeping kind.")[4]

By following the San Juan River, Alice and Al found their way to the Hills Ranch on McElmo Creek and finally to the Wetherills' Alamo Ranch at Mancos. They'd covered over two hundred miles. Alice wrote, "I have always felt that I can never repay Al for taking me on that trip." She decided that getting off and on a tall saddle was hard on the horse and hard on her. To her everlasting regret, she had failed to collect one particular plant because she was too weary to dismount and mount again. She never rode sidesaddle again.

Alice returned to Colorado with the intention of remaining there. In Denver she resumed work on a botanical book, prepared a collection of plants for display in the Denver Public Library, joined a discussion group, attended operas, read avidly, and enjoyed her friends and family. "How I loved the [Colorado] mountains and the flowers," she later wrote. However, the Brandagees recognized Alice's abilities and wanted her to return to California. They offered her a joint curatorship of botany at the California Academy of Sciences, to be shared with Katharine Brandagee. Alice put off giving them a definite answer. In addition to being reluctant to leave her home, she was also quite taken with a young eastern journalist who'd come west because of ill health. His death finally decided her, and in December 1892 Alice moved to California.

In 1893 she published *A Flora of Denver*, underwriting the cost herself because she was unable to find any other financial backing. The book wasn't promoted and lost money. Her father was irritated by the impracticality of the venture and destroyed all remaining copies. (Alice later put out a second edition, describing additional species.) In 1893 the Brandagees left San Francisco, taking their private herbarium and botanical library with them. Alice was appointed curator of botany at the academy and editor of *Zoe*. Now thirty-four, she had finally found what was to be her lifelong botanical niche.

On her many collecting trips for the academy Alice rode astride and wore a costume of her own invention.

At that time, 1893, the only woman who was permitted to wear trousers was Dr. Mary Walker in Washington and she had been a nurse in the Civil War. I had to compromise so I designed and made my own. It was a blue denim and the skirt was fastened to the waist. The skirt was open in front and behind and fastened for walking by buttons and button-holes concealed by a flap. When I rode, the buttons on the front were fastened to the holes of the corresponding one in the back so it made a perfect riding skirt and not so clumsy as the later divided skirt. The front of the waist was buttoned and the watch pocket concealed by a jacket effect something like a [bolero] which made it a little less plain.

Except for the short skirt, I was to the rural public "au fait." Indeed my costume was much admired and greatly approved by the men. Never heard what the women thought. They probably envied my independence. I've been told more than once, "You can do it but I can't." Emerson says, "Scorn conventions and you always can."

In 1895 Alice made what was apparently her last collecting trip with Al Wetherill, riding from Mancos past Bluff and Mexican Hat to Willow Creek, all in Utah, and back to Mancos. They spent an uncomfortable, hot night sleeping on the floor of a ranch. "How I wished I could have been outside on the gravel instead," Alice lamented. "However, we were then too near civilization to disregard convention. My reputation meant nothing to these people but Al's did."

As usual, they found new plants, which Alice named. She distributed the duplicates to the Gray Herbarium in Cambridge, Massachusetts, considerably enhancing her professional reputation. In 1900 she contributed to Joseph Young Bergen's *Elements of Botany: Key and Flora*. At some unknown time she donated the Colorado species of her herbarium (which was the first one in the state) to East High School. The collection made its way eventually to the Colorado State Museum and ultimately to the University of Colorado at Boulder.

Alice was devoted to her work at the academy, even using part of her salary to hire assistants. California became her permanent home, with a six-year hiatus caused by the San Francisco earthquake of April 18, 1906. Many years later Alice said that the earthquake was "an experience I am not sorry to have had if it could have been without the terrible loss." She described that memorable day in a letter published in *Science* magazine.

The earthquake did not frighten me as it was felt less where I lived than in other parts of the city. . . . After getting breakfast, I went down to the academy. I could not get in. The store next door was open and they were taking things out, and I knew there was a door of communication with the front building. It was still as death. I had to climb over the demolished marble staircase at the entrance of the museum, but found the stairs going up the front building all right. When I reached the top a yawning chasm stretched between the two buildings as the bridge had been thrown down. I tried several doors but every one seemed to have deserted the place. . . . We went to the back and saw that the fire was on Mission Street. . . . We again entered by the store next door and when we came to the front hall found Mr. Loomis, Mr. von Geldren, General Foote, Mrs. Newell and John Carlton. . . . Porter pulled me up the ruins of the marble staircase and we entered the museum, the door of which was now open. The marble staircase leading up to the top was in ruins and we went up chiefly by holding on to the iron railing and putting our feet between the rungs. Porter helped me to tie up the plant types and we lowered them to the floor of the museum by ropes and strings, tied together. Not a book was I able to save nor a single thing of my own, except my favorite lens, without which I should feel helpless.

. . . I do not feel the loss to be mine, but it is a great loss to the scientific world and an irreparable loss to California. My own destroyed work I do not lament, for it was a joy to me while I did it, and I can still have the same joy in starting it again. . . . The kindness of my friends has been great. I did not know that I had so many or that their affection for me was so warm and sincere.[5]

While the academy was being rebuilt, Alice spent most of her time working and studying at the great herbaria of the world: the Smithsonian, the New York Botanical Garden, the Arnold Arboretum, the Kew Gardens, the British Museum, Cambridge University, and the Jardin Des Plantes. In 1912 she returned to California to resume her position as curator of botany at the academy, now situated in the Golden Gate Park.

For fifty-seven years Alice Eastwood was associated with the California Academy of Sciences. During her long career she published over three hundred articles about botany, two hundred of them after she was fifty years old. By the time she was eighty years old, the academy's herbarium contained over three hundred thousand specimens, accumulated largely through her zeal. On her ninetieth birthday, at her request, Alice retired as curator of botany. The next year she was designated the honorary chairperson of the International Botanical Congress in Sweden, which she traveled to by herself. In a supremely happy moment, she was permitted to sit in the chair of Linnaeus, the father of the binomial system of biological nomenclature. She died in October 1953, during her ninety-fifth year. The Alice

Eastwood Hall of Botany, part of the California Academy of Sciences, was dedicated in 1957, one of many honors given to the woman who had collected plant specimens throughout California, especially the Bay Area, as well as in Oregon, Alaska, Nevada, New Mexico, and Baja California.

Yet Alice never forgot the Colorado wildflowers that had sparked her life's work. In her memoirs she wrote, "What grand times I had in the southwestern part of Colorado wandering around alone over those beautiful mountains where the alpine regions far surpass in abundance, variety and beauty of the flowers anything I have seen in any region." The task of classifying the plants in Alice's Colorado herbarium fell to Hazel Schmoll.

HAZEL SCHMOLL

Hazel Schmoll was born near McAllister, Kansas, on August 23, 1890. A year later she moved with her parents, William (Will) and Amelia Hauberg Schmoll, to Caribou, Colorado, a silver-mining settlement, and a year after that they moved to Ward, 9,250 feet above sea level, about twenty-five miles west of Boulder. At the time, Ward's gold mines were so active that the town supported five hotels, two drugstores, two meat markets, two livery stables, two newspapers, three restaurants, a bakery, a laundry, two confectionery stores, and five saloons. It was the commercial hub for nearly five thousand people and a wonderful place for a kid to grow up. Hazel later wrote, "As a small child, I never ceased to be thrilled at hearing the mine whistles in Ward [there were fifty-two working mines] blow morning, noon and night, and seeing the men filing down the mountain swinging their dinner pails as they came from work in the gold mines."[6]

Hazel's father worked in the mines for one month. Then he bought a livery and began renting out horses and guiding people into the mountains. In 1900 a fire destroyed the Schmolls' house and Will's livery as well as most of Ward. By this time the gold mines had begun shutting down permanently, and so the town was never completely rebuilt. Many residents pulled up stakes, but Will Schmoll had faith in the scenic attractions of the area and built another livery. He was an outdoor man, the first person to guide tourists on trips to see the glaciers west of Ward in the Arapahos, now known as the Indian Peaks Wilderness. Often he helped rescue stranded mountaineers. His good reputation spread, so that frequently clients had to wait for "quite some time" to hire him as a guide. He took parties as far north as Rocky Mountain National Park and as far south as Mount Evans. Reportedly, he once took the Theodore Roosevelts over the Divide, but since such stories are as prolific as fireweed, it's hard to know if this one is true.

Hazel began riding when she was quite small. At first she sat on a sidesaddle, since her family was well aware that the first woman in Ward who had dared to ride astride, in about 1894, was "severely criticized." Often Hazel followed her father on horseback, and she later wrote: "It was my father who taught me to know and love the wild flowers. His keen sense of observation was something he retained to the last and always filled me with awe. These contacts with nature have given me a background which I would never exchange for their equivalent in book knowledge." When Hazel was old enough to wander by herself, her mother would make a lunch for her. Then she'd mount her albino horse, Snowball, and, with her black cocker spaniel walking by her side or riding in front on her saddle, she'd head for the mountains. Sometimes she went with friends.

Ward "used to have very good times." There were dances and traveling shows, chicken suppers sponsored by the Ladies Aid Society, a town band, and drilling contests for the Fourth of July. In late summer it was easy to fill pails with the wild berries that grew rampant in the logged-over areas. Hazel and other kids would go to the mining dumps, pick out a few rock specimens, and sell them to the tourists in town. In winter during recess they careered down the middle of town on sleds, starting at the railroad and ending, three-quarters of a mile later, at Lefthand Creek.

Hazel was an only child, raised by German parents—and aunts and uncles—who had definite ideas about bringing up children. Her mother saw to it that she received lessons in painting and elocution. Her aunt, Rosena Hauberg, an artist whom Hazel described as "adventurous," gave her lessons on a piano hauled up from Denver. Hazel sang and played the piano in Sunday School. She graduated from the eighth grade in Ward. "That school is something for which I am grateful," she later wrote. "We didn't have classes in art and music . . . and we may have missed some of the social amenities, but we had a college graduate for a teacher and we knew our basics."[7]

The Schmolls were hardworking and taught Hazel to be the same. At age four she began delivering one-quart and two-quart buckets of milk to the townspeople, morning and evening, a job that ended when she moved to Boulder, where she lived while attending the Boulder Preparatory School at 17th and Pearl Streets. In 1909 Hazel entered the University of Colorado. Her mother began taking in sewing to pay for her education. Hazel found the university "hard work," especially writing themes for English, but she rejoiced in the "greater freedom and wider contacts with people." She decided that she wanted to teach botany only if it meant she would be outside, and she considered majoring in German. Finally, though, she settled on biology with an education degree. One of her professors was Theodore Cockerell. She spent the summer of 1912 at the university's mountain laboratory at Tolland run by Dr. Francis Ramaley. Shortly before Hazel graduated from the University of Colorado, her aunt and uncle took a trip east and discovered that there was going to be an opening for a biology teacher at Vassar College in New York. They told Hazel about it. She applied and was accepted. It caused "quite a stir," perhaps partly because, as Hazel says, "I was terribly shy."[8] She found Vassar stimulating but apparently not intimidating, for she later wrote that she had "a much better background in spelling and geography and arithmetic" than many of her contemporaries.

At Vassar, Hazel was the envy of the other girls and women because she came from a state in which women could vote. When she began teaching there, New York women were still fighting the suffrage battle, and Hazel eagerly took up their cause. While knocking on doors, she wore pants. During her last year of teaching at Vassar, 1917, New York granted women the vote.

Hazel then enrolled at the University of Chicago to earn a master's degree in a new course, ecology. It was exactly her kind of botany, although she found that collecting plants in a long skirt was a nuisance. So with the approval of her professor, Henry Chandler Cowles, Hazel waited until she was safely out of Chicago and then discreetly changed into pants. In the spring of 1919 she received her master's degree and was elected to the Sigma Xi honorary. Hazel also became a member of a purely social group called the A.O.E. (Ancient Order of Ecologists). In one letter she declined an invitation to attend an A.O.E. meeting in Chicago—she was living in Denver at the time—signing her name as "Viola bicolor."

Hazel returned to Colorado and within a year was hired as state botanist. One of her tasks was to properly mount and identify the plant collections of Alice Eastwood and Ellsworth Bethel. Hazel found that her male colleagues were nice to her, but she couldn't accept their attitudes toward other people. Many years later she cryptically told an interviewer, "You think women could be catty, but you ought to work where you've got some men that are."[9]

Although Hazel's attitudes about plant ecology sound quite contemporary, today it is jarring to read her ideas, typical of the time, about "varmints." For example, at a Nature Protection and Conservation Conference at the University of Colorado she stated that although coyotes were pretty, it was not desirable to leave them on the range because they would "destroy birds' nests, eat the eggs, and kill other young animals." And, she further stated, woodchucks, or whistling marmots, were "particularly obnoxious to the rancher because they eat vegetables."[10]

As state botanist, Hazel worked on committees with the National Forest Service, the National Park Service, and local garden clubs. She became a lobbyist for the Colorado Mountain Club and was instrumental in the passage of the state's "Columbine Bill," which imposed a fifty-dollar fine for pulling columbines up by the roots or for picking more than twenty-five blossoms in a single day. Hazel also collected plants at Chimney Rock near Pagosa Springs and in the early summer of 1925 made the first systematic plant collection of Mesa Verde National Park, to be used as a basis for the park herbarium. Her assistant, Deric, was ten or so years old and was the son of the park superintendent, Jesse Nusbaum. In May, Hazel and Deric collected a white milk vetch that grew in the piñon-juniper forest at 7,150 feet. Later named for Hazel, "*Astragalus schmolliae*," it was described as a "narrow endemic on Chapin Mesa."[11]

After the position of state botanist was eliminated in 1925, Hazel decided to study for her PH.D. in ecological botany at the University of Chicago, first taking a six-month European trip financed by her aunt and uncle. Once in school she earned money by scrubbing floors, selling newspapers, and managing her father's business affairs. After she received her doctorate in 1932, Hazel stayed in Chicago, although she did not find a good job and had to eke out a living. She rewrote a high school biology textbook, worked in the Field Museum, and substituted for a professor at an Illinois junior college. Finally, she'd had enough, and in 1938 she moved back to Ward.

It is interesting to speculate why, at the age of forty-eight and armed with her hard-earned doctorate, Hazel never again worked as a professional botanist. After all, Alice Eastwood had carved out a remarkably successful career in botany even though she had only a high school diploma. But Alice, unlike Hazel, was confident to the point of being commanding (or even imperious, according to some who knew her in her later years). In addition, Hazel was trapped in the Great Depression and was the only child of ailing, elderly parents. Then too, perhaps she was just plain homesick for Ward, about which she once wrote, "This country has been my life—it's as close to me as my family."[12]

Hazel decided to do something "whereby I could share what I knew about plants in the out-of-doors with others." She had a lodge built on a 205-acre spread, owned by her family, that faced a panorama of the "high snow-patched peaks of the Front Range." It is a stunningly beautiful site. For over thirty years she ran her guest ranch for adults, advertising in the *Christian Science Monitor* and by word of mouth. (Hazel had become a Christian Scientist in 1922.) She took in only those guests who neither drank nor smoked, and through the years she made loyal friends with hundreds of people. Hazel took obvious delight in guiding her guests on horseback into the Indian Peaks to view "superb peaks, waterfalls, glaciers and glacial lakes," just as her father had. She answered questions but never forced botany on anyone. Although Range View Ranch sometimes lost money, Hazel said she "loved making converts to nature. I never liked to learn just for myself. I'm not that much of an intellectual."[13]

In the winter, when the ranch was closed, Hazel checked on her scattered tracts of mountain property, often driving in her red jeep. She wore her favorite clothes, either old slacks or blue jeans. Once, when relatives sent her money to purchase new clothes, she enthusiastically told friends that she'd purchased a new suit. Incredulous, they said, "Hazel, how wonderful!" before she explained that it was a snowmobile suit to keep out the cold.

Hazel was "property rich, money poor," having inherited quite a few tracts of land from her parents and aunts and uncles. In general, she was loath to sell her land, although she did once try, unsuccessfully, to sell 158.6 acres at Duck Lake. For three years, during World War II, she taught school in Ward for one hundred dollars a month. Following her parents' principle that "true happiness comes from unselfish service to others," she served on the school board and on Ward's town council and was a volunteer in the fire department.[14] She was also precinct committeewoman of the Republican party until she resigned at the age of eighty-five "because of increasing demands" on her time.

By 1967 the population of Ward had shrunk to about twenty. An out-of-state developer eyed Hazel's considerable land holdings and tried to pressure her into selling. She refused. On January 15, 1968, arsonists set fire to and burned all of Hazel's garages and stalls in Ward. On May 27 someone apparently put a bomb in each of the five office rooms on the second floor of her stone building and completely demolished it. Hazel speculated that the developer was involved in some way, although nothing was ever proven. In her Christmas newsletter she wrote: "Pathetic are those people whose home training has not taught them not to steal and destroy property belonging to other people and who have not been taught to be grateful for our rich heritage. Compensation for the loss of so much is found in the group of fine young people who have moved to Ward this winter and appreciate what Ward has to offer them."[15]

The "group of fine young people" were hippies. At first Hazel was skeptical of them. Gradually, however, she came to realize that they were not exploiters and that they wanted to live compatibly with the old buildings and with the land, just as she did. Many of her young neighbors came to regard Hazel as a treasure. For years she had been keeping a diary, and using this plus her fine intellect and memory, Hazel became the town authority on water rights, property rights, and history, as well as on the dates that the first mountain bluebirds arrived, how much snow had fallen in a specific year, whether the wildflowers were early or late, the date that the fall colors peaked, and so on. Her house became Ward's unofficial municipal library. Men and women flocked to her glassed-in porch, full of plants and sunlight, to talk to her while sipping tea. For her part, Hazel became a regular at the weekly town socials at the Mill Site Inn. One new friend called her "the warmest, sweetest, most hospitable, most generous person I have ever known."[16]

In 1978, when Hazel was eighty-eight years old, the town of Ward gave her a certificate of appreciation for "public service, unprecedented faithfulness in attendance, exemplary toleration and understanding of new persons and ideas and devotion to the historical integrity of the Town of Ward as a public official and leader of Civic Affairs."[17]

Today Hazel lives in a nursing home in Wheat Ridge, a suburb of Denver. One day the contents of her diaries will be known. It seems certain that they will constitute an unprecedented documentation of the natural history, sociology, and history of Ward, Colorado, the final gift of Hazel Schmoll, one of Colorado's first ecologists.

RUTH ASHTON NELSON

Ruth Ashton Nelson, though a contemporary of Hazel's, had a very different sort of career in botany. However, her professional path was not easy, either.

Ruth described her childhood as "eventful."[18] She was born in 1896 in Boston, the first of three children. Her parents, Grace and Willard, ran a settlement house they had established, but after Grace's health broke down, the family moved to a farm on Martha's Vineyard. Because the colonial farmhouse in which they lived had but a single fireplace, the Ashtons spent winters elsewhere. Often they stayed in Rockford, Illinois, where Ruth's paternal grandfather lived; he hoped, in vain, that Willard would someday take over the family department store. One winter Ruth's parents met a promoter of rental vacation homes and were persuaded to spend a summer in Estes Park, Colorado, in 1905.

From the children's point of view, the summer was glorious. Their parents rented two burros from Sam Service for Ruth and her sister, and the family explored Bear Lake, which was desolate from a recent forest fire, and Bierstadt Lake, where they beheld the famous view of Longs Peak that the artist Albert Bierstadt had painted. For their mother's birthday, Ruth and her sister picked a bouquet of forty different kinds of wildflowers, one for each year, to put on her cake. However, the end of that summer also marked the end of the Ashtons' marriage. Willard purchased ranch property in Horseshoe Park, in what is now Rocky Mountain National Park. In 1907 or 1908 he and his brother built a hotel, Horseshoe Inn, from plans drawn up by Frank Lloyd Wright. Willard sold the property sometime around 1915, and the buildings were later razed.

After the divorce Grace and her three children shuttled between Illinois, Iowa, Martha's Vineyard, and Colorado, never staying in one place for more than a few months. Until Ruth entered the eighth grade, she didn't have a single uninterrupted school year. Grace firmly believed that children could learn more from the outdoors than from a formal education, and so despite a few set-tos with the Vineyard Haven public schools, she managed to keep her children at home, tutoring them herself. Grace loved flowers and would send Ruth out to collect leaves, which Ruth then compared with the illustrations in Asa Gray's classic manual on botany.

In 1912 Ruth's mother took the children back to Colorado, this time to the Glen Isle Hotel near Bailey, where she arranged to take a pack trip. The party—consisting of Grace, her three children, a guide, two burros, and two horses—rode through South Park, "blue with great sheets of gentians," presumably over Hoosier Pass to Dillon, and then down the Blue River to Kremmling. Finally, eleven days after setting out, they arrived at the town of Hot Sulphur Springs. For two months they camped out at the edge of town, eating at a hotel that is still standing today. While Grace "took the waters" for her health, the children attended the local two-room schoolhouse. As the nights became cooler, the family put slickers over their bedrolls. By the time Willard arrived to take the children to his home in Fort Collins, frost covered the slickers at night.

Another summer, Grace and the children stayed in the Estes Park area at Stead's Ranch and at Mrs. McPherson's Moraine Lodge, which has since been converted into a museum in what is now part of Rocky Mountain National Park. Apparently Grace asked Enos Mills for advice, for he wrote a letter assuring her that with a competent guide she would be safe on the Grand Lake trail "or any mountain trail."[19] When in her teens, Ruth began attending a small boarding school for girls on Cape Cod, and after graduation she enrolled at Mt. Holyoke College. Because of illness she received her degree in English two years late, in 1924. While making up credits at the University of Wisconsin, Ruth met the Dawsons, who ran a small camp, Ekalelea, near Longs Peak Inn at the base of Twin Sisters. Mrs. Dawson hired Ruth to teach nature study and horseback riding.

That summer Ruth made her first and only climb of Longs Peak, riding a horse to the Boulderfield and then clambering to the top. Mostly she hiked and rode with the campers, pointing out the flowers, birds, and animals "as well as she could." After camp was over, Ruth rented a cottage on the Big Thompson River from the Clatworthys. She spent what turned out to be a bitterly cold winter in Estes Park, having decided to homestead in the area and to start her own camp for girls. However, after exploring the country on foot, she became convinced that the only parcels of land left for homesteading were on barren rocky ridges, so she bought 240 acres that had already been proved up on. It was high, airy country, southeast of Estes

Park, complete with a primitive three-room cabin that faced Longs Peak and its snowy neighbors. Ponderosa pines edged broad meadows that promised a wildflower garden come spring. Ruth named her place Skyland Ranch.

The next summer she took a job as information clerk in Rocky Mountain National Park. In the fall she began work on a master's degree in botany at Colorado A&M (now Colorado State University). For the next few summers, while working for the Park Service, she made the first comprehensive collection of the plants in Rocky Mountain National Park. As information clerk, Ruth recorded the daily statistics supplied by rangers on the number of automobiles, carriages, saddle horses, and pedestrians that had passed through each of the park's three entrances. Mainly, though, she stood behind a counter and answered all kinds of questions: "How far is it to there?" "Where can you get to ——?" and "What's the name of this flower?" Informally, and without any official recognition, Ruth also gave naturalist talks "when there wasn't anybody else to do it."

Ruth decided that naturalists had a lot more fun (and made a lot more money) than information clerks. So she enrolled in the famous Yosemite School of Natural History, conducted in California. She thought this training, plus her unique knowledge of Rocky Mountain National Park's botany, would lead to an official appointment as a park naturalist. It never did, a fact that Ruth attributed to a strong prejudice against women. She was about twenty-five years too early. It wasn't until 1955 that the park hired its first female naturalist, Ruth Ewald Gay (see page 151).

Ruth Ashton worked as an information clerk in the summers of 1925, 1926, and 1927. On her days off she roamed the high mountains and valleys of the park searching for new plants. Her vasculum (collecting can) was a nuisance on a horse, so she usually hiked, often by herself. Since there were so few people knowledgeable enough to help her identify species, she sought the help of Aven Nelson, curator and founder of the Rocky Mountain Herbarium in Laramie, Wyoming.

Aven, whose wife had recently died, arranged for Ruth to receive five hundred dollars as his assistant at the herbarium during the winter of 1930–31. At the time, he was seventy-one and Ruth was thirty-four. A romance developed. Aven's children and grandchildren were shocked when he and Ruth were married in Santa Fe, New Mexico, on November 29, 1931, although they gradually became reconciled to the marriage and in time fully accepted their father's young bride.

In 1933 Ruth's book *Plants of Rocky Mountain National Park*, which also served as her master's thesis, was published by the government printing office, with a price tag of twenty-five cents. Today it remains a popular, concise aid for amateur botanists. The Nelsons' marriage lasted twenty-one years, until Aven's death in 1952 when he was ninety-three and Ruth was fifty-six. Being married to such a famous botanist opened new doors for Ruth. For example, in 1934, when Aven was president of the American Botanical Society, Ruth accompanied him to Europe—her first time there—for the International Botanical Congress in Prague. And the Nelsons took joyous collecting trips together, including one to Mount McKinley (Denali) National Park in 1939.

However, many of Ruth's friends felt that she was also stifled by her marriage to Aven. Only after she was widowed, for example, did she resume long visits to her beloved Skyland Ranch, which Aven had found boring because it lacked a large variety of plants. And after Aven's death Ruth began teaching seminars for the Rocky Mountain Nature Association as well as adult education classes in Colorado Springs. She also wrote the *Handbook of Rocky Mountain Plants* and *Plants of Zion National Park: Wildflowers, Trees, Shrubs and Ferns*, revised *Plants of Rocky Mountain National Park*, and assisted Rhoda Roberts in writing *Mountain Wild Flowers of Colorado*.

Friends have described Ruth as a "shy, retiring and very private person," not easy to know, who came alive in the midst of flowers, wild or domestic. "The smile, the utter delight in beholding a flower, the joy of recognition, make her eyes sparkle and bring a chuckle of pleasure."[20] Professionally, Ruth exuded a solid confidence. Perhaps no one saw this side of her more clearly than Tom Blaue, who illustrated her book about the plants of Zion. The two embarked on what turned out to be a four-year project when Ruth was in her mid-seventies and Tom was in his early twenties.

Tom found Ruth to be "teacherly" rather than "motherly"; she was demanding of him and, most of all, of herself.[21] "I think I've never met a more deliberate lady," Tom said of her. "She went to bed every night thinking about what she was going to do the next day. There wasn't too much casual about her in the sense that she never, to use the modern terminology, 'went with the flow of things.' She had plans and agendas and schedules and she adhered to them quite closely." It amused Tom, and other friends, that Ruth was slightly ashamed of her passion for chocolate.

Tom found that Ruth rarely, if ever, missed anything. She assumed a certain posture when she was looking for flowers, "which was all the time. She'd throw her hands back and kind of clasp them behind her hips. She had about a three-quarter list and it was a pretty good angle for scouting ten feet in front of her. That's the way she walked everywhere. She was in that pose about 100 percent of her waking hours and it served her quite well."

Ruth tended to be careless when a plant caught her interest. She would climb over rocks and logs and poke her hand into bushes, not thinking about whether or not one of Utah's many poisonous critters lay hidden there. It worried Tom. He knew that her religion, Christian Science, would have condoned, though not encouraged, her seeking medical help, and he once asked Ruth what she would do if a rattlesnake bit her. She said she didn't know. Fortunately, her reaction was never tested.

Once, on a scorching hot day, Ruth scolded Tom, who was becoming more and more uncomfortable and distracted as the temperature rose. Ruth had caught him looking at a bird in the sky. "She kind of snapped at me—it was the only time that she did—and said something like, 'Tom, you'd get more done if you'd keep your eyes on the ground.'" Since the criticism was so utterly out of character, Tom figured the Utah sun had overheated Ruth, too.

While collecting in Refrigerator Canyon on September 20, 1974, Ruth discovered a new species of composite, a sagebrush, later named for her: *Spheremaria ruthiae.*

Plants of Zion National Park was Ruth's last book, although when she was well into her eighties she revised her previous two. Her personal favorite was the *Handbook of Rocky Mountain Plants*, illustrated by a good friend, Dorothy Leake. However, she considered the Zion book to be her most beautiful, and at the time of its publication she insisted, despite Tom's protests, that he receive prominent billing as the artist.

While in her seventies, Ruth took car camping trips with friends and collected plants. She was even able to backpack into the Grand Canyon and in Rocky Mountain National Park, thanks to Dee Godesiabois, who carried a disproportionate share of the equipment and food. Although Ruth lived in a retirement home in Colorado Springs in her later years, she managed to spend at least part of each summer at Skyland Ranch, even in her ninetieth year. She'd enlarged the original cabin and spruced it up, but she had retained the privy and limited running water. The wildflowers in the meadow, many transplanted by Ruth, delighted her, as they always had. By this time Ruth's memory betrayed her, yet an essential quality of her character shone through. Her friend, the well-known alpine ecologist Bettie Willard, described Ruth's character in the foreword to *Plants of Zion National Park*: "This woman has a deep affection for, devotion to, and comprehension of the land and its diverse plant cover. . . . She expresses profound quiet reverence for the natural world through everything she says and does."[22] Ruth Ashton Nelson died on July 4, 1987.

KATHERINE BELL HUNTER AND EMILY DIXON FOSE

Katherine Bell Hunter and Alice Eastwood shared several characteristics. Both women were uncommonly good musicians and seamstresses who were described as brilliant. And both were so passionately dedicated to botany that they endured extreme physical hardship—even danger—to pursue their goals.

However, by the time Katherine arrived on the scene, nearly a century after Alice, the methods and tools of botanical research had changed considerably. Then too, Katherine and her assistant, Emily Dixon (Fose), embarked on a project that was unusual even for their era. The following account mostly concerns that project. It is replete with detail, thanks to Emily, who was most generous with her time and words.

From Emily's point of view, the project began rather casually. In May 1970, after graduating from a small school in Chattanooga, Tennessee, with a degree in biology, she'd landed a summer job working as an aide in Rocky Mountain National Park. At the season's end she had decided not to return to the South, where she'd grown up, but instead to stay in Colorado, where she could experience a climate with seasons and "see what winter was like."[23] Emily had saved enough money to live modestly in Estes Park.

On Friday, January 22, 1971, she returned to her rented room and found a note taped on the door.

I'm looking for a girl to act as a field assistant for my graduate research for the rest of the winter. Bob Haines, at the Park Headquarters thought you might be interested. I'll be living at Rock Cabins beyond Upper Hidden Valley and studying winter environments and physiologic ecology of an alpine plant. What I need is someone who could stay up here, help with rather simple field work and in keeping us going in cold without water or electricity. I can pay about $350/month (supplied by Dept. of Botany, University of Alberta). If you are interested, could I talk to you? I have another couple of girls who might do this; but since I need someone as soon as possible and they may not be able to quit other jobs readily, I would like to know if you're possibly interested and available.[24]

The writer of the note, Katherine Bell, came by the next day. She was twenty-six years old, about five feet six, with dark hair and rosy cheeks, a woman of "great enthusiasm and tremendous intellectual curiosity."[25] After talking for several hours and discovering that they were both devout Christians, Emily and Katherine decided they would be compatible enough to work together.

Then they moved quickly. The cabin they were to live in, located just above timberline, was already stocked with food, mostly canned goods, which Katherine had taken up by car in the fall before the snows had closed Trail Ridge Road. So on Monday they drove down the canyon to Fort Collins to get outfitted at Jax Surplus Store. On Tuesday they went up to the Rock Cabins, where Katherine would conduct research crucial to her doctoral thesis.

The Rock Cabins were located about a mile and a half from the top of the upper lift of the Hidden Valley Ski Area, which is accessible from the 10,400-foot level of Trail Ridge Road. Rocky Mountain National Park officials had considered the cabins' proximity to the ski area as a significant factor in their decision to permit Katherine to headquarter there. Before Katherine and Emily's stay, no one had lived in the Rock Cabins during the winter for more than several weeks.

Since neither Katherine nor Emily had ever been on skis before, Dave Stevens, a research biologist for the park, spent the morning helping them learn to ride the T-bar. The women were using cast-off cross-country skis; they didn't know how to wax them properly for easy gliding on the flat and downhill surfaces and for effortless climbing on the gentle inclines. (By the time they made their second trip up, Katherine and Emily were able to wax their skis correctly, which was an enormous improvement.) Their backpacks, stuffed with bedding, clothes, cameras and film, and some scientific instruments, were extremely heavy. After riding to the top of the ski lift, they took their skis off and laboriously walked on alternate patches of snow and bare ground, taking an indirect tack to avoid the willows. Finally, they reached their home. It was a lonely outpost on the tundra, 11,400 feet above sea level.

The Rock Cabins, which had been constructed in the 1930s to house the men who had built Trail Ridge Road, were made of local stones. In 1971 the southern building was used as a garage and the northern cabin as a bunkhouse. The middle cabin, where Katherine and Emily would live, was the only "winterized" cabin. Although the Rock Cabins are no longer standing, the site is easy to find; it lies on the Ute Trail, indicated by a sign, 1.8 miles west of Rainbow Curve on the north side of Trail Ridge Road.

The women's new home consisted of one room, sixteen feet by twenty, and an alcove in the southwest corner. A Norge furnace squatted in the center, surrounded by a couple of armchairs, two or three straight-backed chairs, two beds, two tables (one of which was hinged and dropped from a cabinet), a counter and sink, a cookstove with oven, and a bookshelf made of bricks and boards. An interior door joined the alcove and the main room, and there were two exterior doors. However, the exterior door on the north wall was on the lee side of the cabin and was thus blocked by high snowdrifts.

Since Katherine was nervous that the Norge fuel-oil furnace might explode and burn the cabin down, Emily tried to clear the way to the north door. She shoveled a path outside but gave up when it was drifted over by the next day. "So," Emily recalls, "we just accepted the fact that there was only one entrance to the cabin. And we used the big drift by the door as our water source."

Their cabin had windows on two sides, but only the one on the south let in light. Katherine and Emily took the shutters off one of the two east windows and covered the windows with heavy plastic. Frost frequently collected on the plastic, obscuring the view, but the windows did at least let in light. Often when Emily and Katherine were returning home after being in the field, the plastic reflected the light in such a way that the cabin seemed to wink at them.

Although the site was several hundred feet above the dominant tree line, slightly above the cabins was an island of krummholz ("crooked wood") trees on the lower slopes of Sundance Mountain. This stunted forest was an indicator of what the women would discover: the Rock Cabins lay in a place that was relatively sheltered from horrendous winds but was still windy enough that the dry snows of winter did not accumulate. And, most advantageously, the cabin site was surrounded by gentle tundra, so Katherine could conduct all her research within a half-mile of her quarters. It also offered views of deep, forested canyons and high, cliffed mountains. On a clear day Emily and Katherine could see one of the most spectacular silhouettes in all of the park: the massive block of McHenrys Peak, whose north face plunges into the great cleft known as McHenrys Notch. But clear days were rare. As Katherine wrote, "Glimpses of snow-plumed peaks only occasionally broke the monotony of ground blizzard and roaring wind."[26] The view, of course, was incidental, for Katherine was there to carry out a research project whose difficulties she could only guess at. She was prepared to give it her all.

Katherine, born on May 9, 1945, was the oldest of three children. Both her parents held doctorates in mathematics, and from the time she was a young child they had made it clear that they expected Katherine to excel intellectually. She graduated from Agnes Scott College in Atlanta, Georgia, with a B.A. in philosophy. For her master's degree in botany, which she earned at Wake Forest University in North Carolina, she spent a year studying an alpine rush, *Luzula spicata*, at the Institute of Arctic and Alpine Research (INSTAAR) near Ward, Colorado. While there, she became interested in why a sedge, *Kobresia bellardii* (not named for Katherine), remained green in winter—a possible indication that it carried on photosynthesis—and why it grew in snow-free habitats. Katherine decided to try to answer these questions in a thesis for her Ph.D. at the University of Alberta in Canada, supported by a grant from the National Science Foundation.

The Rock Cabin site on Trail Ridge Road had not been her first choice; she had preferred a site on Niwot Ridge where she could have used INSTAAR's well-tested winter-support systems. However, after Katherine had found out that the fees charged by INSTAAR would be prohibitively high, she approached the officials of Rocky Mountain National Park, where she had spent several family vacations.

They gave her the go-ahead, insisting only that an assistant live with her and that she maintain daily radio contact with park headquarters. Dave Stevens recalls that he never had any doubts about Katherine's staying at the Rock Cabin. "She was a pretty strong little lady," he later said. "I thought, though, that if things were too bad that she would come down on her own. I wasn't going to tell her to not do it—I'm pretty liberal about those things. I always figured that if we had to, we could go get her. We figured that with Emily up there one of them could get down to report if something happened."[27]

Katherine's plan was to study kobresia's habits during each of the four seasons. She had actually begun her studies in the summer of 1970, assisted by her sister, Martha. But a series of snags had delayed the start of her winter research. First, she and her fiancé, who was to have been her winter assistant, had broken off their engagement. After much effort, Katherine had found a replacement; however, the replacement had come down with mononucleosis and had had to drop out at the last minute. By winter Katherine was desperate. She must have been overwhelmingly relieved to find Emily on such short notice.

For the first five or six weeks of their stay at the Rock Cabin, things went well. To test the "autecology of kobresia," Katherine's formal task, she planned to study it under several conditions. One was in its natural, nearly snow-free habitat. The three others were "unnatural habitats," one created by transplanting kobresia to a site that accumulated snow, a second by transplanting kobresia to a windy fell-field (rock-strewn area), and the third, by placing snow fences in such a way that snow accumulated, for the first time, on existing kobresia. Katherine had prepared all but one of her study sites earlier, when Trail Ridge Road had still been open; the exception was the site containing snow fences, which could be erected only under winter conditions. Katherine also put up anemometers, a hygrothermograph in a weather shelter, and a solorimeter. Finally, she installed maximum-minimum recording thermometers in the kobresia sites.

Emily's role was to "help with the chores of life and to be there in case two people were needed in a situation . . . and to do some of the grunt work in the field." Most of the time, the two women went from site to site, taking temperature and wind readings "day after day after day." Every few days they measured how tall the green shoots of kobresia were. As Emily explains, "She'd dictate and I'd copy down. She'd take the readings and I'd record them." Always, the wind blew, stopping only when an upslope storm moved in from the east. When that occurred, Katherine and Emily needed their snowshoes for walking on the new, soft snow. But within hours after the wind resumed, the snow was blown hard and unyielding again, so they could walk on it easily.

After their first trip out to Estes Park, the women modified their backpacks. They dropped the sack to the lowest place it could be attached to the pack frame, which was at about shoulder level, to minimize the surface that the wind could slam against; this made a "tremendous difference" in the effort it took to walk. "We got to where we could walk in steady winds of seventy to eighty miles an hour," Emily remembers. "And we could walk in gusting winds of sixty to seventy. Gusting is much more difficult than steady. A calm day made it a little bit hard . . . because we were so used to leaning." After a few days Emily and Katherine noticed that they were both breathing differently. "It wasn't something we developed—we noticed it," Emily recalls. "We had regular chest expansion, but we also elevated our shoulders. Your diaphragm works on the bottom end vertically, and your shoulders work on the top end vertically so it increases the capacity of the chest."

The women became quite good at estimating wind speeds. (Several years after their winter in the Rock Cabin, however, they found out that the anemometers they had used hadn't been built to accurately measure high wind speeds in cold temperatures; their readings had read possibly as much as 35 percent too low.) Emily and Katherine soon could estimate the wind's velocity within ten miles an hour without going outside. By going outside, they could estimate it within five miles an hour.

The wind became a fact of life. It blew almost constantly and sucked out the few BTU's the furnace managed to exhale. "Old Norge," as Katherine and Emily fondly called it, was not performing well. Its fuel tank sat outside the cabin, above ground, which probably chilled the fuel oil enough to make it sluggish. And to compound the problem, the pipe that ran from the furnace to the tank had a crimp in it. Inside, the pipe often iced up. The Norge consisted of an inner shell, where the fire was, and an insulating, outer shell. The outer shell should have been too hot to touch, but Emily and Katherine discovered that they could comfortably hold their hands against it to warm them. And when their feet were "really cold," they could remove their outer boots, keeping on socks and other clothes, open the furnace doors, and rest their feet against the outside of the inner shell.

Gradually, Katherine and Emily developed housekeeping routines. Since Emily had grown up as "Daddy's little helper" and was the more mechanical of the two, she became the handyman who fetched the snow and did the shoveling. She also pumped up the Coleman lantern, the only source of light in the evening. At first the women did not realize that it was necessary to put a finger over the hole of the pump while pumping, although they eventually figured it out. Emily laughingly recalls that they had to learn a lot of things by trial and error.

Katherine did the cooking; Emily cleaned up. "Cooking" meant going into the alcove and retrieving cans of food that could safely be eaten frozen solid. ("Of course, it turned out that the cans she kept under her bed in the main room were also frozen solid, too," Emily recalls.) Then Katherine would take the top off with a can opener, turn the can over in the pan, remove the bottom, and put the pan on the stove. After a while, when the contents had thawed enough, she would remove the can and finish heating the food. Katherine later wrote that "only the sense of taste remained a source of pleasant novel experience and the difficulty of cooking in temperatures below freezing made us frequently avoid the effort necessary to concoct tasty dishes."[28]

Cleaning up was a chore that Emily remembers well.

Washing dishes got to be a real art. You got a bucketful of snow from the pan that had been sitting on the furnace for two days and you put that on the stove to melt it down. Then you got a second bucketful and poured that into the pan so you could keep that hot. You got a third bucketful of snow to put on the stove to begin melting. You used the first water to wash the dishes and then you put them in the sink for the soapy water to clean them. You had to have the rinse water already heated because if you washed the dishes and then melted the rinse water, the soap suds would have frozen to the dishes and you couldn't get them off. There was no question of drying. You just waited and after a while you chipped the ice off.

Shortly after moving up to the Rock Cabin, Katherine and Emily had decided that they'd wash down to the waist anytime the temperature warmed up to 45 degrees, which it occasionally did after supper when the butane cookstove had been on for a while. As it turned out, though, they often skipped their baths, sometimes for weeks at a time.

Before going to bed, Katherine frequently rewrote the day's field notes and sometimes "did a lot of stuff with test tubes and sugar water," as Emily put it. In fact, Katherine was using sugar water to measure water potentials in leaves and roots. Sometimes Katherine played her recorder and Emily played her harmonica. They rarely turned on their battery-operated radio. Emily had more time than Katherine for recreational reading and once remarked that she didn't think she would ever, "under any conceivable circumstances even worse than Trail Ridge, get to where it was too arduous to read." She read fiction almost exclusively—*Doctor Zhivago*, the complete works of Gilbert and Sullivan, some Conrad Richter. Katherine gave her the complete *Hobbit* series as a birthday present, but since Emily "wasn't much on fantasy," she found it hard to get into.

On a typical night Katherine would turn in around ten o'clock. Emily usually stayed up a little later, "to have some space." She described her nightly ritual in a letter to her parents. "Going to bed is easy," she wrote. "Just take off stocking cap, coat, sweat shirt, wind pants and boots and climb in. That leaves me lightly dressed; T shirt, thermal shirt, sweater, thermal pants, corduroys, knee socks, wool socks and thermal socks." When it turned colder, Emily modified the ritual, removing only her boots when going to bed.

Katherine used a sleeping bag so old that the down had shifted into clumps that left cold spots. Nevertheless, she offered her Hudson's Bay blanket to Emily, whose old Dacron bag had been sewn "before Dacron was good." So Emily, who slept on top of an inch-thick foam pad, was warm. Katherine, however, was often cold and usually slept badly. Oddly, the women never brought additional bedding up to the cabin. As Emily explains:

It never occurred to either one of us. I think the cold froze our brain cells. It just never dawned on us to do anything like that. The one thing that dawned on us—the one thing that we did to make the cabin warmer was that we used a roll of masking tape and we chinked the cabin on the inside. After the first or second day we got out the tape and filled in all the holes. It was so drafty in there that you could hardly light a candle.

The morning temperatures depended to a large extent on the wind velocities. During one bitter three-week period the cabin never once got up to freezing, and on several days Emily recorded in her diary that it was 12 and 15 degrees when they arose. (The coldest outside temperature recorded during their stay was −21 degrees Fahrenheit.) These were the extremes, but the cabin was never truly comfortable or even close to it. Carrying out fieldwork in clothes heavy enough to protect them from the cold was tough. As Katherine wrote:

Apart from maintaining general body warmth, the most critical problems lay in the use of hands. Down mittens are warm, but their bulk makes only clumsy manipulation possible. Wool inner mittens with windproof covers were not quite as warm, but with practice we did such delicate tasks as taking field notes, attaching lead wire to a potentiometer, and opening plastic sacks without removing the mittens. It was usually futile to plan work requiring use of silk gloves or insulated ski gloves before late March. Removing outer mittens was not wise either, since hands numbed within a minute or two and snow blew into the empty mitten openings. It was helpful to carry a pair of thin gloves in a snowfree pocket, but we rarely used them except in relatively good weather.

Frost-covered glasses also caused major problems, and these remained unsolved. Emily was dependent on glasses, and she was unable to keep them cleared. I had difficulty using sunglasses. Their protection from both light and painful blowing snow was offset in mid-winter by their tendency to ice up. A solid steam-deterrent product helped somewhat, but was not completely satisfactory.

A few other items of equipment were most helpful. Soft-lead pencils wrote best at low temperatures. When paper tended to ice up, soft-surfaced note cards could be scratched and read later. A heavy dandelion digger was (to a limited extent) effective in removing roots from frozen soil. Electrical tape (especially Scotch Brand 300) held better than other sorts, but even that had to be replaced frequently. An Ensolite foam pad provided protection while we were kneeling or lying, but it tended to blow away.[29]

Katherine and Emily never set an alarm clock; they just got up when they felt like it. After dragging out of bed, they finished dressing, an easy routine because each had but one set of clothes. Katherine would boil water for breakfast—three packets each of quick oatmeal and cups of hot Tang, a rather meager meal, considering the circumstances. Emily would clean up. Then they'd gather up whatever they needed and go out for morning fieldwork. When it was really cold, they didn't brush their teeth because, as Emily explains, "Brushing teeth involved going outside and getting your hand wet at the same time so we didn't do that unless there was no chance of frostbite in the two seconds that we'd be out."

Katherine and Emily would come back to the Rock Cabin for a lunch that almost always included hot Jell-O. Then they would go back out. On rare occasions, if Katherine had work to do they would stay inside during daylight hours. Sometimes—far too rarely, they later came to find out— they played games. Emily especially remembers one that Katherine invented, in which they pretended that a signboard by the road, carved on both sides with the words *Rock Cabins*, was their mailbox.

We would come down off the work place across the road [Tombstone Ridge], come to the "mailbox" and take turns getting the mail and making up what was in the mail that day. Then we would make up the mailman's route. Sometimes he would come up Trail Ridge and go back through the Big Thompson Tunnel. Sometimes he would go back by way of what is now the Indian Peaks Wilderness. Or he would go over the Moffat Tunnel road—whatever it would take to get back to the Eastern Slope.

Originally, Katherine had planned to work five days and to go down to civilization on weekends. However, after the first trip down she realized that she would lose a full day in leaving and returning. Feeling extreme pressure—largely self-imposed—to do her research, she modified her plan so that Emily and she worked ten days and went down for two or three.

On a summer day on the tundra it is almost impossible to comprehend the weather conditions that Katherine and Emily endured on the first part of their trip "down to the valley" for their break. The temperatures were not dramatically low, usually between zero and freezing, but, coupled with the near-constant high wind, they produced a wind-chill factor that was extremely dangerous. Occasionally, blowing snow obscured all but a few yards of the route. Emily and Katherine would set out wearing their expedition-type down parkas with tunnel and fur ruff, clutching their skis so the wind couldn't snatch them out of their hands. Since neither was a proficient skier, they had decided it would be quicker and safer to walk the gentle grade of Trail Ridge Road to Hidden Valley, a distance of three miles, rather than to descend the slopes of the ski area, a distance of one mile. (Twice, during unusually severe conditions, park officials did manage to convince Katherine that the two women should walk to the ski area and be carried down to the bottom on ski patrol toboggans.) When the snow was blowing, they postponed the trip down and in fact didn't even venture outside.

Until their first trip down on the road, Katherine and Emily had no notion of the difficulties they would encounter at a place which they named Windy Gap, but which the locals called Knife Edge. Windy Gap is seven-tenths of a mile west of Rainbow Curve; it is the six-hundred-foot portion of Trail Ridge Road that straddles the ridge, allowing one to see, simultaneously, Hidden Valley to the southeast and Hanging Valley to the northwest.[30] The first time down, Katherine tried to cross Windy Gap standing up. In a few seconds she realized that the wind was too strong, so she lay down on her stomach and began slithering across. The wind picked her up, blew her a few feet, and dropped her. "At that point," Emily recalls, "we said, uh-oh, better do Plan B."

"Plan B" was to lose forty or fifty feet of elevation and to walk gingerly across a snow surface that was sometimes slabbed so hard it supported their weight and was sometimes, only a few steps later, so soft that they punched through. Emily and Katherine learned to walk very carefully so they wouldn't injure themselves on rocks and tree stumps hidden in the snow. Crossing Windy Gap usually took about an hour.

Katherine and Emily estimated that the wind speed at Windy Gap was one hundred miles an hour. Emily very distinctly remembers mentioning this figure to other people and sensing that they didn't believe it, although "they never came out and said so." Several years later a researcher, Dave Glidden, confirmed the women's estimate, speculating that the extreme winds in this spot are caused by the Bernoulli effect, which he defines as "pressure differences introduced by the sharp separation—Knife Edge ['Windy Gap']—between Hanging Valley and Hidden Valley." In 1981 Dave Glidden recorded a 201-mile-an-hour wind on top of Longs Peak and said his winter research in Rocky Mountain National Park indicated that "alpine and subalpine winds are severe and exceptionally turbulent, with maximum recorded gusts ranking among the highest which have been published for known weather stations, including Antarctica."[31]

After Windy Gap, it was a straightforward walk around Rainbow Curve into the forested part of the road to the bottom of the upper ski lift. There, Katherine and Emily caught a ride to lower Hidden Valley, where Katherine's car was parked, and headed for the home of Joyce and George Bennett, just outside Estes Park.

The Bennetts were very warm, Christian people whom Emily had met at church the previous fall. Not having children of their own, the Bennetts "adopted" many young people, including Emily. After they met Katherine, they adopted her too. She was "so dear" to them that they couldn't bear to call her anything but "Kathy." Joyce found Katherine to be "a very feminine person and a very tender person, not just emotionally, but physically as well. . . . She was too fragile a person to endure the things she put herself through."[32]

The Bennetts' home became Katherine's and Emily's home. There they showered, did their laundry, and generally relaxed, although Katherine always checked in at park headquarters and occasionally had to drive down to Denver or Fort Collins to solve a problem with an instrument. And after a few weeks of living at the Rock Cabin she began checking in regularly with two Estes Park physicians, Dr. Sam Luce and his wife, Dr. Julia Martin. Katherine was worried because she was steadily losing weight. It was a new worry for the woman whom one friend described as "chunky" and "quite muscular."[33] She had carefully planned the meals on Trail Ridge so that she and Emily were consuming twice as many calories as they normally did. Yet they both lost weight, Katherine more than Emily.

Katherine increased her intake. Both she and Emily modified their diet so it included a higher proportion of fats and carbohydrates; Katherine estimated that their daily food consisted of 35 percent fat, a little more than 40 percent carbohydrates, and a little more than 20 percent protein. They drank approximately four liters of fluid daily. After quite large meals the women became chilled more quickly than usual, so they heeded Dr. Martin's advice to eat numerous small meals. Katherine and Emily began carrying "nibbling food," such as peanuts, raisins, and small candies, in their parka pockets. It helped. "Katherine kept M&Ms with her at all times," Emily recalls. "She even kept them by the bed. She would wake up shivering at night because her bedding wasn't warm enough, and she would eat some M&Ms and that would give her enough energy to get her back to sleep again. But she'd wake up sometimes two and three times a night for M&Ms. She never left the cabin without some in her pack—I guess we both probably did that."

On one occasion Emily saved Katherine's life. Katherine had stayed out to dig a deep gap between an eight-foot drift and a rock. Emily had gone back to the Rock Cabin, mindful of an earlier procedure they'd agreed on: anytime one of them wasn't back at the cabin by a certain time, the other would immediately leave on a search, not waiting to see if the person was just a little late. They understood that a few minutes could mean the difference between life and death. So when Katherine didn't show up at the agreed-on time, Emily set out and discovered her in the "hole," too weak to climb out. Emily fed her M&Ms. "There wasn't anything else I could have done," she recalls, "short of shovelling for three hours or so." In a little while Katherine gained enough strength to dig herself out.

Joyce Bennett recalls: "Those girls would eat like they had not had anything to eat since they'd left, and particularly liquids. They'd just drink and drink and drink because they were so dehydrated. And they'd sleep a lot." Emily remembers heaping their plates with potatoes at the Bennetts', "just anything to get more calories." She and Katherine craved fresh fruits and vegetables, since they could carry only small amounts up to the Rock Cabin. Katherine lost between ten and fifteen pounds and Emily about ten. Dr. Luce is quite sure that although Katherine was "deprived calorically, she was never deprived nutritionally." Altogether, he and Dr. Martin saw Katherine a half-dozen times or so, sometimes just for a quick chat. Finally, after she'd been living on Trail Ridge for several months, her weight stabilized, and she stopped her visits to the two doctors.[34]

February 25, Emily's birthday, began with a literal bang. At about two in the morning Emily abruptly woke up when the inner door in the alcove blew open. Katherine was already awake, having slept very little because she was cold. The women staggered around and discovered that the wind had lifted the latch of the outer door and this in turn had blown open the inner door. They shut the doors, went back to bed, and lay awake. For half an hour the wind shook their cabin nonstop.

The next day Katherine baked a cake to celebrate Emily's turning twenty-two. That in itself made the supper special, since they almost never ate desserts (Emily had trouble digesting sugar). Their meals usually included just meat, starches, vegetables (mostly canned green beans), and hot drinks. Katherine presented Emily with the complete set of the *Hobbit* books, and the women went to bed. The night was uneventful; the wind dropped back down to its normal fifty miles per hour or so.

At about this time, when the women had been living in the Rock Cabin for a month, Katherine became badly frostbitten "in an embarrassing place" while sitting in the outhouse. Jack, as Katherine and Emily called the outhouse ("we thought we were on too-familiar terms with him to call him John"), faced northeast. Jack's back wasn't filled in solidly with dirt; when the prevailing westerlies came down into the pit, they went straight up. As Emily explains, "A sixty-mile-an-hour tail wind zapped Katherine." Although it later made a humorous tale, Katherine's frostbite was fairly severe and painful. She and Emily vowed that it wouldn't happen again. They found a makeshift chamber pot, which they dubbed Jack, Junior. At first, they planned to keep it in the alcove, but one sitting persuaded them to use it in the main room, which was slightly warmer, and to store it in the alcove.

Sometime after the women's first month in the Rock Cabin, a crest cloud, which sits on top of a mountain, settled over the general area of the Rock Cabins for a week. "It dominated everything," Emily remembers. Even Katherine, who insisted on doing fieldwork no matter what the weather conditions, decided not to go outside because frenzied ground blizzards erased all reference points. The women stayed inside for several days. Katherine baked some whole wheat bread, and the fragrance and added warmth from having the oven on cheered them both. She and Emily did indoor work.

The wind devoured what little heat Old Norge managed to produce. The thermometer fell and couldn't seem to climb back up again. It was at this time that the Rock Cabin's interior temperature didn't warm up to freezing for three weeks. "It's no big deal to go out in the cold if you're warmly dressed," Emily later commented. "It *is* a big deal to not have any place to get warm and to [have to] stay cold." Emily and Katherine came to dread the crest cloud because it almost always brought wind.

Sometime around the fifth or sixth week after Katherine and Emily had moved up to the Rock Cabin, the cold, the winds, the repetitiveness of the chores, the constant togetherness, the hunger, the monotony of the food, the lack of privacy, the absence of fun, and the hard work of simply surviving all came together. And it was too much.

The easy camaraderie between Katherine and Emily became strained. They spoke less and less to one another. After supper, instead of discussing the peculiarities of men or the nature of eternity, as they had done so easily in their first weeks, they retreated silently into their own worlds. At night, when tensions had run high during the day, Katherine and Emily tacitly acknowledged that Norge would be considered a dividing line of their territories. Katherine would sit on her side of Norge and do her research or reading and Emily would sit on the other side. She would hunker down so that Katherine couldn't see her, and turn the pages of her book very, very quietly. For Emily it was "a carryover from sixth grade when I would be hoping my mother wouldn't tell me it was time to go to bed. It was a sort of 'If she doesn't see me and doesn't hear me, maybe she'll forget about me and she can't tell me to get to work.'" The women adopted another strategy to escape from each other: in the evening Katherine would go to bed earlier than Emily, and Emily would linger in bed in the morning, long after she was awake and Katherine was up. Emily, who had never needed any urging to assist Katherine in her work, now became reluctant; Katherine prodded and became bossy.

Katherine felt compelled to obtain her winter data because not doing so would cost her a whole year. She possessed an intrinsic motivation to accomplish what she'd set out to do. For many years she had loved botany and intellectual challenges and, according to Joyce Gellhorn (Greene), "getting to inquire more in terms of depth into the real mechanisms behind why plants do certain things." But those who knew Katherine best felt that her extraordinary motivation came from far more than a love of botany. Joyce, a Boulder botanist, high school teacher, and writer, thinks it stemmed partly from a congenital foot problem that had been partially corrected when Katherine was in high school but was painful all her life. "Katherine wanted to get this research done and it was more than intellectual curiosity," Joyce says. "It was proving that she was physically capable. She was a person who just always pushed herself. She had a compulsion to do what she found difficult."[35]

Many years later Katherine's husband said: "She was very bright. There were no standards for her, never a 'that's good enough for someone of your talents.' She was a genius, and people expect geniuses to be able to accomplish more than themselves, to an unknown degree. And somehow, because of the gifts, there's little honor or praise in those accomplishments. It's considered a gift, not an accomplishment."[36] Emily put it somewhat differently, saying that Katherine "had the biggest inferiority complex I have ever seen. She was convinced that she could do no right. No matter what she did, it was not good enough. She was convinced that she was utterly worthless and the only way she could have any worth was by outdoing anybody's expectations. You know human nature; if you expect me to do 6 and I do 8, you will assume it is normal for me to do 8 and ask me for 9." Throughout her ordeal on Trail Ridge Katherine never hinted to her major professor that she was working and living under almost impossible conditions. So he innocently made what he considered to be reasonable demands of Katherine, without any knowledge that they created great hardship for her.

Ironically, as the stresses between Emily and Katherine began building, the relief provided by their trips to Estes Park diminished. Since they both usually stayed at the Bennetts', their crying need to be separated was not met. And although life at the Bennetts' was restful—they didn't have television—two days was simply not long enough for Emily and Katherine to re-enter civilization. Emily explains:

We noticed fairly soon after we started the research on Trail Ridge that when we would go down to Estes, there was just too much bombarding our senses. We were so tuned into the very simple act of staying alive that we couldn't handle how to drive a car *and* watching traffic. [Katherine had to pull off to the side of the road and stop whenever there was any other traffic.] The longer into the project it got, the worse it got. We couldn't look at the scenery *and* look at traffic. We couldn't stand walking through a crowded sidewalk. Too much was going on. It was too busy.

It wasn't nearly so bad at first, but after a month or so it was pretty desperate. I remember that once, later on, we could hardly stand it when we had to drive on the Foothills Highway to Boulder. We were so isolated from sensory stimulation up there on Trail Ridge. We lost our capacity to cope with what was ordinarily no big deal.

The Bennetts began noticing that Katherine and Emily tried to avoid each other and that, when they couldn't do that, they often snapped at each another. While Emily showered, Katherine would sit down at the piano and play classical music, which she did superbly. (She was also an accomplished cellist.) Then while Katherine showered, Emily would disappear. One night, when Katherine was so exhausted that she fell asleep in front of the fireplace, she suddenly woke up screaming; she had dreamed that the Rock Cabin had caught fire.

Emily recognized that she and Katherine were reaching a crisis. Her feelings are evident in her diary, which was the sole "human document" of their experience, since Katherine kept only scientific notes. She remembers:

My working hypothesis at the time was that first we burned up body fat and after that was gone we had to burn muscle in order to create warmth. And that created a terrible mental strain. We both went bananas. I was just reading my diary last night, particularly the places where I was just going totally wacko. My recollection is that I was feeling paranoic and schizophrenic—that half of me was saying, "She's out to get me," and the other half was saying, "You idiot! She's working harder than she's making you work. And she's not out to get you." And then the first half of me was saying, "Oh, yeah?"

And that's when I said, "That's it. I can't do this any more." That's when I took a long break. I went down to Estes for ten days, as I remember it.

Katherine arranged for Bernice Weldon, the friend of an acquaintance, to come up and stay with her at the Rock Cabin to fulfill the park's requirement that she not be by herself. Bernice recalls that the wind was so strong she had to crawl from rock to rock. One time she stayed in the cabin for the day while Katherine went out. Bernice looked at the room critically, was appalled, and decided to mop the floor. However, when the wet mop froze to the floor she gave up and decided to apply her energies instead to the dining table. Its surface was a mosaic of food samples that had spilled when Katherine and Emily had poured food while shivering uncontrollably. It needed a good scrubbing. But after the wet dishcloth froze on the table, Bernice again gave up. She stayed at the Rock Cabin for less than a week, but the experience confirmed her admiration for Katherine and Emily. "People living in the valley have no concept of high country winter conditions," she later wrote.[37]

Bernice's departure left Emily in a dilemma, for she knew that if she didn't return, Katherine would never get a replacement and would not be able to complete her winter study of kobresia. And Emily didn't want that to happen. She also realized that although Katherine could have fired her, she hadn't because she didn't want to ruin Emily's employment record. "We couldn't stand each other in the short term," Emily says, "but we loved each other, we really did. We were very close."

Emily decided to go back to the Rock Cabin. She arrived, mentally refreshed, and was shocked at the change in Katherine. "She was worse off than she had been before," she remembers. Their roles were reversed. Now it was Emily who would say to Katherine: "Okay, it's time to get to work." Or: "Okay, now you've been out too long. Your toes are starting to get cold. It's time to go to the cabin. I'll finish up here." Emily explains that Katherine was "just like a little kid. That's all that was left of her. She was a shell of herself physically and mentally. It was terrible."

Shortly after Emily's return, spring arrived, a week before the official date. Even though the wind and temperature didn't change, the snow's texture was transformed into granular "corn" literally overnight. Signs of animal activity appeared everywhere. Throughout the winter Katherine and Emily had been surprised by the variety of wildlife and evidences of wildlife that they had observed—eagles, ravens, elk, pikas, fox, coyotes, rabbits, ptarmigan, finches, and mice. And although they'd never actually seen the occupant, they'd monitored a weasel's hole with a heat-sensing instrument. But as the days lengthened they began seeing several species of new birds each day. On March 12 Katherine spotted some elk with their calves.

On April 6 Katherine and Emily took a hike, the only one for pure pleasure that they took together during their three months on Trail Ridge. They walked up to the Rock Cut and watched eagles soaring over Forest Canyon Overlook. Nearby, pikas were calling. Katherine said it was their mating call, which hardly anyone ever heard. On the way back they saw a bighorn sheep, a ram with a fine set of horns. During their last week the winter winds became almost docile.

On April 18 Emily and Katherine left the Rock Cabin for good. Before Katherine returned to Edmonton, she arranged for Jean Weaver, a long-time Estes Park resident and avid outdoorswoman, to stay with her at the Rock Cabin the following April; Jean consented on the condition that the Norge stove be repaired. Katherine then returned to Canada to analyze her data. She never took a real break. Emily visited her family in the South, where she "warmed up a little," and took a three-week vacation to the West Coast with a friend. After she came back to Rocky Mountain National Park, she worked as an aide for the summer.

For Katherine and Emily the winter of 1971 did not end in April. It changed them physically. Although neither sustained the classic symptoms of frostbite—white skin and blisters—each suffered a more subtle frostbite, or cold damage. Katherine suffered frostbite of her thighs, as well as her toes, hands, and face, from lying on the ground while taking measurements.[38] Emily had cold damage to her fingers, toes, ears, cheeks, and nose. Emily—and presumably Katherine—was for years supersensitive to cold, quickly losing sensation in her toes and fingers even in fifty-degree water. Katherine suggested that Emily take vitamins B and C. Emily today is no longer as sensitive to cold as she used to be, "for whatever reasons." She can tolerate a slightly wider range of temperatures without discomfort.

The ordeal on Trail Ridge altered Katherine especially. During the next year she received professional counseling. She learned what Emily and she might have done to make their living and working on Trail Ridge acceptable and even in some ways pleasant. Expedition-weight down sleeping bags would have guaranteed warm nights in bed. Katherine and Emily should have planned a four-day work week, taking a break every weekend. Instead of shooting for two four- or five-hour work sessions every day, they should have settled for one four- or five-hour period, devoting the rest of the time to play and to survival chores. Most of all, they should have incorporated play and fun into their routine every day by listening to talk shows and music on their radio, playing cards and board games, playing their musical instruments regularly, and making up more games like "mail-man."

The following April, when Katherine and Jean Weaver lived at the Rock Cabin for a month, things went well. Jean was seventeen years older than Katherine and had lived in Estes Park for twenty-one years. She had taught downhill skiing at Hidden Valley and regularly ski toured and hiked. However, even though she knew her way around Colorado winters, the almost perpetual wind on Trail Ridge affected her. She found that the wind was fatiguing and "did things" to her mentally. "On days that it blew hard," she recalls, "after a while I would start making mistakes, like writing down a '5' instead of a '7.' And I would be really tired at night."[39] Jean and Katherine worked on weekdays but went down to Estes every Saturday morning, returning to the cabin on Sunday afternoon. The snows were so deep that they always bypassed Windy Gap and instead skiied from the Rock Cabin to the Hidden Valley ski lift. Even Katherine, having been coached by Jean, enjoyed the run down.

Although that April wasn't as cold as the winter months, it was hardly springlike. The women strung a clothesline between the cabin and the outhouse so they wouldn't get lost in a whiteout. And the wind blew on all but three days. One day it slammed Katherine down so hard that she broke her coccyx. An hour later it blew Jean down, but she wasn't hurt. Despite her injury, Katherine continued working. Jean recalls that Katherine's hands were very sensitive and often bled, perhaps from cold damage she'd received the previous year. Yet she was basically very cheerful and always solicitous of Jean. In fact, as April unfolded, Katherine became more and more relaxed, tremendously relieved that she was coming up with the data she needed to complete her dissertation. One day she was "almost ecstatic" because she and Jean were able to visit each of her instrument sites four times—the all-time record. Of course there were problems. But Jean was impressed with how philosophical Katherine became when things went wrong. Katherine was sure that she could cope, and she usually did. Although Katherine was good at fixing broken instruments, her troubles with marmots were another story. Marmots are the West's woodchucks, roly-poly and cute to many people. Katherine hated them. They didn't merely nibble on her instruments; they ate them.

Katherine and Jean slipped easily into using their imagination and having fun. Almost daily they checked for mail in the "Emergency Telephone" sign-mailbox and chewed out the mailman when he left mostly junk mail. When they walked Trail Ridge Road, which was still closed to traffic, they kept a sharp eye out for cars coming too fast, and sometimes Jean had to suddenly pull Katherine out of the way of a careless Winnebago that had driven too close. At the end of the workday, usually five o'clock, Katherine and Jean came home and hugged the stove, saying, "Good Norge." Norge had been repaired and spent the days pulsing warmth into the Rock Cabin, so that it was actually cozy at suppertime.

Once, inexplicably, Katherine and Jean saw a jackrabbit at timberline, far above his usual habitat, and took a picture to prove it. Another morning they woke up to a land infiltrated by two-inch feathers of rime ice clinging to all the surfaces of their world—cabin, outhouse, instruments, rocks, trees, tundra. Glitters danced off the crystals as the sun climbed the sky. Katherine said it was the experience of a lifetime and they should forget about working until they'd photographed and admired as much as they wanted to. They did, for several hours, until the rime ice vanished in the sun and wind.

Toward the end of April, Katherine and Jean took a walk up Trail Ridge Road to the Tundra Curves. Katherine wanted to ascertain how the building of the road forty years earlier was affecting a field of kobresia. The road had created a new snowdrift, which now blanketed the kobresia every winter. When the women arrived at the Curves, Katherine saw that her timing was perfect; the drift had melted just enough that she could determine where it had lain. As she suspected, the snow line coincided with a line of kobresia that was dying or already dead.

The last night that Jean and Katherine spent at the Rock Cabin was so clear that the women could see the lights of Estes Park and even Denver. Hanging over Deer Mountain was a full moon, bisected by a band of clouds. The lower part of the moon was silver and the upper part gold.

The next day the women made their final trip down. Hidden Valley Ski Area was holding a snow carnival, and when Katherine came to an obstacle course for downhill skiers she put on her snowshoes and "flew through the course" with a speed and agility that amazed Jean, even though she knew

Katherine had run the course the previous year. It was a good conclusion to Katherine's life at the Rock Cabin.

In 1979 Katherine earned her doctorate in botany and published her dissertation about kobresia in "Ecological Monographs." Friends, playing on her surname, dubbed her "Dr. Ding-a-ling." Her major professor, Larry Bliss, believes that Katherine did an excellent piece of research that will "stand the test of time and future studies." He says that she was the first person to live and work "in a severe alpine environment in winter in order to learn what the plants were doing" and that she presented the "best and most interesting" seminar for her PH.D. dissertation of the nearly three dozen student seminars he'd overseen.[40] In the appendix to her thesis Katherine paid tribute to Emily:

Emily wisely dealt with the problems she faced by taking a 10 day break in March. Thus at the end of the three month period, I became heavily dependent on her to make almost all decisions.

Despite the often unpleasant surroundings, my drive to achieve certain goals was almost always strong enough to keep me working. I was motivated both by curiosity and by a desire to prove that I could work under any conditions. This probably was necessary to accomplish research objectives. On the other hand, such a high level of motivation clouded my judgment, and I tended to put field work ahead of both comfort and safety. If I knew that 20 min. more work would give me some data I wanted, I let my toes get frost-bitten. Emily, with somewhat less at stake in the research, was not motivated to work this way. Her reluctance often helped to balance my fanaticism.

Emily and I shared many jokes and many prayers, and our friendship was warm. Both of us developed in self-confidence and in faith in God.[41]

For the first few years after their stay at the Rock Cabin, Emily and Katherine were wary of each other, although they did go on a backpacking trip together in the summer of 1972. However, after Emily finally showed Katherine her diary, the women had a candid discussion about what had happened on Trail Ridge. They cleared the air completely, allowing an extraordinarily intense bond to form. In 1976 Emily married Tom Fose. They now have two children, Auburn and Mike, and live in Denver.

Katherine continued at the University of Alberta on a postdoctoral fellowship, studying plants in another severe environment, King Christian Island in the High Arctic. She lived in a trailer in which she was able to rig up a shower. It was easy living compared with that at the Rock Cabin, although she had several too-close encounters with polar bears.

In 1975 Katherine accepted a teaching position at the University of Nevada in Las Vegas. She told Joyce Gellhorn (Greene) that at least Nevada "had no polar bears," but she didn't tolerate heat well.[42] Friends feel that she gradually began to gain confidence on her own but that her marriage to Richard Hunter, a botanist who works at the nearby Nevada test site, increased her self-esteem tenfold and marked the beginning of an extremely happy time of her life. Emily thinks that although Katherine remained a "very intense, driven person," she became driven by a "desire to accomplish, rather than by a desire to prove."

Katherine went through a difficult pregnancy and gave birth to a son, Elijah Daniel, nicknamed "Lije." When the baby was five months old, Katherine was diagnosed as having embryonal cell cancer of the ovaries. She died in May 1984 at the age of thirty-nine.

In the mid-1970s Rocky Mountain National Park authorities tore down the Rock Cabins.

6

The Modern Recreationists

Until the 1930s, Colorado's mountaineering women climbed exclusively in the United States and mostly in Colorado. Elizabeth (Betsy) Strong Cowles Partridge, who lived in Colorado Springs for virtually her entire adult life, was the first Colorado woman to climb mountains all over the world.

By the time Betsy Cowles took up climbing in the mid-1930s, she had several female examples to follow. One was Eleanor Davis Ehrman, whose technical climbing was done in psychological isolation compared with that of all the Colorado female climbers who followed her. But Eleanor was probably aware of the mountaineering exploits of two American women, Fannie Workman Bullock and Annie Peck, who made well-publicized climbs in the late 1800s and early 1900s. However, Fannie and Annie for the most part were conquering glaciated peaks in India and South America over twenty thousand feet high, which, though they presented worthy problems, bore little relation to the sheer rock faces that Eleanor was negotiating. In short, they were concentrating on ice and snow, adhering to climbing traditions established on Mont Blanc in 1786. Thus Eleanor climbed without any female mentor, although she must have served as a mentor to the few female friends that she initiated. Clearly, Albert Ellingwood's abiding confidence in her abilities was crucial to her success as a climber. But he was working with a pupil who had the "right stuff," not the least of which was her training as an athlete in a topnotch, innovative women's school.

Another example for Betsy Cowles was the remarkable Miriam O'Brien Underhill, who preceded Betsy by several years. Miriam's background fit to a tee the profile of most early American female climbers: she was born in the East (New Hampshire), educated in the East (Bryn Mawr and Johns Hopkins), learned to climb in Europe (the Alps), and began her serious mountain climbing with male guides. However, by the late 1920s she was leading hair-raising routes manless, very untypical of early American female climbers. Miriam O'Brien Underhill is often referred to as the outstanding American female climber of her generation.

And Betsy Cowles greatly benefited from her membership in the American Alpine Club. In its early days, the AAC had simply ignored climbing in the Rocky Mountains. None of its eighty-three original members were from Colorado, and the vast majority lived in East Coast states, with a scattering from the West Coast. Frederick Chapin, a Bostonian who climbed Colorado mountains in the 1880s, gave an explanation that was valid for many decades. "It is probably true that Americans are more familiar with the Alps than with the Rocky Mountains," he wrote, "for the high valleys of Switzerland are so easy of access, and the distances are so small, that one can cross many glacier passes and ascend important peaks with much less trouble than he can visit such an out-of-the-way place as Estes Park and climb the mountains which surround it."[1] But the AAC was a significant factor in Betsy's climbing achievements, for through the AAC she met climbers and mountains all over the world.

ELIZABETH STRONG COWLES PARTRIDGE

When she arrived in Colorado Springs at the age of twenty-one, Betsy Cowles was merely an attractive, poised, cultured, and charming bride. She gave not the slightest indication that she would one day become Colorado's first female mountaineer of international stature. Born on April 2, 1902, in New Britain, Connecticut, and a graduate of Vassar, she married Alfred Cowles III, scion of a Chicago publishing family. Alfred (known as Bob) brought Betsy to Colorado Springs, where he had already settled to avoid a family tendency toward tuberculosis.

Bob was ten years older than Betsy, "very handsome, good looking, a rather heavyset, large man," and, in the words of one friend, "stuffy."[2] The Cowleses adopted a daughter, now Ann Cowles Walsh of Durango, Colorado, and a son, Richard Livingston Cowles, now of San Diego. Bob was an ardent golfer. Though Betsy played very well, her heart was not in it. Bob was also an avid cardplayer. Betsy was neither skilled nor enthusiastic. Nevertheless, for years she dutifully played golf and cards with Bob's friends. One evening, after a particularly disastrous game of bridge, Betsy's partners began their usual analysis of her plays, pointing out mistakes. Suddenly, Betsy picked up the two decks of cards, flung them at the ceiling, and stalked out. Perhaps her father, John Henry Strong, sensed her dissatisfaction. At any rate, in 1933 he persuaded Betsy to go mountain climbing with him in Switzerland. Before the trip, he came to Colorado to instruct her in the rudiments of mountain travel.

John Strong was a retired Baptist minister living in Larchmont, New York. At the age of fifty-seven he'd taken up mountain climbing, contrary to his physician's advice that he avoid all exercise because of a bad heart. He had joined the American Alpine Club and had begun climbing vigorously and often: at the age of eighty-three he climbed the Jungfrau in Switzerland. (Incidentally, John Strong was following a British tradition; as the mountaineering historian Francis Keenlyside has noted, during the Golden Age of mountaineering—the middle decades of the 1800s, when first ascents were common—the typical climber was a "don, barrister or clergyman.") In Colorado, John Strong took his daughter up two high but easy peaks, Mount Sheridan and Mount Sherman near Fairplay, an experience that Betsy enjoyed. Next they made a first ascent of Mount Oxford, a walk-up mountain near Leadville that had caught their attention because a recent survey had elevated it to the status of a fourteener. Father and daughter then knocked off Pikes Peak and Longs, very possibly staying overnight at the Boulderfield Hotel, before sailing to Europe for Betsy's "introduction to Alpine climbing with the best of all possible mountaineering fathers as a companion."[3]

Her first roped climb was on the Dent du Midi. The guide, young Fabian Mathay, wasn't nearly as powerful-looking as she had hoped he'd be. After all, she wrote, she "had no idea what he might be called upon to do to keep me on the mountain next day." However, Betsy did find it reassuring that "everything about him had a look of honorable wear and tear." It made her feel "a little ashamed of the obvious newness" of her own mountaineering equipment. By the time she scrambled over the last boulder to the top of her first climb, "a tremendous sense of achievement" swept over her, and she looked forward to her second Swiss summit, the first on "really high class rock." It was to be a traverse (a climb angling across the terrain) of the Petite Dent de Veisivi. But as Betsy firmly pointed out, "First it should be clearly understood that there is nothing PETITE about this DENT."

Their guide Antoine, Betsy, and her father began the ascent in the dark. Antoine led, carrying a lantern and walking with a "solid yet supple style." At 5:00 A.M. he discarded the lantern and stepped up the pace. "There was altitude to be gained and we gained it without sugar coating." After reaching the top of the col, where the route steepened alarmingly, they roped up. "I soon found that a precipice is worse if you try to ignore it than when you face the fact that it is there," Betsy later wrote. "Next I discovered that one cannot negotiate difficult rock and have enough energy left to worry about abysses. Ten minutes on the ridge and I was completely occupied with the work at hand. And such work! It was just one first class brand of excitement after another."

Betsy learned to edge herself around great bulges of rock, to worm her way up a chimney and to "assimilate" a gendarme (a rock tooth protruding on a ridge). She also learned to regard mountain climbing as fun. Thereafter, Antoine, Betsy, and her father celebrated the top of each mountain by singing "Giene Patrioque" in three-part harmony, "puffing a little the while."[4] By the end of her stay Betsy had climbed the Pigne d'Arolla, the Tête Blanche, a traverse of the Untergabelhorn, the Zinal Rothorn, the Riffelhorn, and finally the Matterhorn by the standard route, the Z'Mutt Ridge.

After her introduction to roped climbing in Switzerland, Betsy spent the next few climbing seasons in Colorado and Europe, the Tetons of Wyoming, and the Canadian Rockies. In 1936 she attended the Swiss Bergschule (mountain school), primarily to learn ice and snow techniques. Her instructor, Kaspar Grass, was a "grand person . . . [with] a sixth, seventh and eighth sense about mountains." She described his climb of the Morteratsch Glacier:

Poised midway on the ice wall, making vicious accurate one-handed blows with his axe, he looked like some kind of demon on the rampage. It appeared to be simple enough: a sideways cut made the floor of the step, followed by three blows at the back and a quick scoop with the flat end of the axe to clear away debris. It was a joy to climb up Kaspar's steps: they were roomy without being enormous and had a fine inward slant that made one feel secure on the most vertical pitch.

But to make ones like his was harder than it looked. One blow and I gave up trying to swing my axe single-handed; even with two I nearly tore my arms from their sockets. Up and up in my estimation went every iceman in the world, for ice, I discovered, is one of the hardest and toughest materials in existence. Then too it turned out to be strangely difficult to hit the place where one was aiming. I seemed either to make a huge bucket of a step in about eighty strokes or a mere chip of a step with ten. First I made them fully three feet apart and exactly in a vertical line so that it became a major problem in equilibrium to get from one to the other, and then so close together that they tended to merge alarmingly. As you can imagine from all this, it was some time before I achieved a presentable staircase with a series of neat niches (made with the flat end of the axe) for handholds at the side.[5]

The Bergschule ended after a three-day trip around the massif of the highest peak in the region, the Piz Bernina. "As I waved goodbye to my schoolmates," Betsy wrote, "I don't know that I felt ready to graduate by any means. But who ever graduates in mountaineering? Or would want to?"[6]

Bob Cowles was extremely tolerant of his wife's new enthusiasm, even though her European mountain climbing trips included trans-Atlantic voyages that added several weeks to their separation. But because of an "affair of the heart" in the 1930s, he and Betsy were divorced. As Betsy's sister put it, "Part of Betsy's magic was that she was frequently—though not lightly—in love."[7]

It was later written that when Betsy took up mountaineering it came as a great surprise to her and all who knew her; she had never shown any "previous interest or aptitude for athletics of any kind." By 1939 she had become such a dedicated climber that she wrote her friend, Paul Pedzoldt, a well-known Wyoming climber who later founded the National Outdoor Leadership School, "I have just about decided to make mountaineering my calling."[8] She was by then a card-carrying member of the American Alpine Club, the Colorado Mountain Club, the Suisses Des Femmes Alpinistes, and the Ladies Alpine Club (of Britain). When Betsy embarked on her "calling" she was thirty-one. By the time she'd tapered off, nearly twenty years later, she had compiled an impressive mountain vita.

Bob Ormes has said that though many people called Betsy a great climber, he would describe her as a "good climber with tremendous endurance."[9] Whatever the adjectives, Betsy most certainly left her mark. She was the first woman to climb the East Ridge of the Grand Teton and the North Ridge of the Grand Teton; she was probably the first woman to climb Buck Mountain in the Tetons; and she was a member of the second party to climb the North Ridge of Mount Moran, also in the Tetons. In the Santa Marta Range of northern Colombia, she organized and was a member of the party that made first ascents of La Reina (over eighteen thousand feet high), Pico Ujueta—both named by the party—and De Brette Peak. And in 1950 she was a member of the first party of Westerners to trek into the Everest area of Nepal.

In short, Betsy was the first of what is today a common species of Colorado mountaineers who use the state's mountains primarily as a training ground for ascents elsewhere. This is not to say that Betsy didn't have strong bonds with the Colorado mountains—she climbed them over and over again—but only that she loved mountains all over the world as well.

During the 1940s and 1950s Betsy was extremely active in the American Alpine Club, serving as a councilor and a member of the House and Hospitality committees and the Editorial Board. In 1947 she was the only female AAC officer who was also a vice-president. During her climbing years and afterward, she was acquainted, in many different ways, with most of the world's mountain "greats." Once, for example, she met the daughter of the renowned English climber Edward Whymper, whose name is forever associated with the first successful ascent and tragic descent of the Matterhorn. She discussed alpine poetry and the psychology of climbing groups with the famed English poet-climber Geoffrey Winthrop Young. And she corresponded with the likes of Willi Unsoeld (Tom Hornbein's partner on the pioneer ascent of the West Ridge of Everest), Sir Edmund Hillary (who, with the Sherpa Tenzing Bhutia, made the first ascent of Everest), Bradford Washburn (who mapped, climbed, and photographed Mount McKinley), Maurice Herzog (member of the first team to climb the Himalayan mountain, Annapurna), and Bill Tilman (well-known Himalayan climber, sailor, and writer).

Betsy climbed with the best American male climbers of her time and with several of the topnotch females, a limited group that included Elizabeth Knowlton and Polly Merrick. Colorado climbers knew her well. She was the fifth—or sixth—woman to climb all the fourteeners. (She and

Dorothy Teague Swartz climbed their final fourteener on the same day in August 1949.) Although Betsy belonged to the Colorado Mountain Club, she usually climbed with friends rather than as part of an official CMC group. One of her favorite climbing companions was Harry Standley of Colorado Springs, a professional photographer who undoubtedly taught her a great deal about composing and printing black-and-white photographs.

Between her mountain climbing trips, Betsy was a strong and active supporter of the Colorado Springs Symphony, the National Association for the Advancement of Colored People, the League of Women Voters, the Women's Education Society of Colorado College, and the Colorado Springs Fine Arts Center. And always she evangelized the joys of mountain climbing, mostly to Colorado audiences. Betsy presented slide shows for the public, for the CMC, and for the Fountain Valley School in Colorado Springs, inspiring dozens of kids to take up mountain climbing. She taught climbing to CMC Pikes Peak Juniors.

She served as a mentor to many a young woman who hesitated on the brink of a rappel. Betsy had firm ideas about how to introduce women and children to roped climbing, a refreshing viewpoint in a sport that was then so dominated by men. "The importance of this sense-of-success cannot be overemphasized," she wrote. "It is the sine qua non. Remember it especially in relation to the second commandment: *Don't ever let her get scared* . . . [and] never dream of undertaking anything at all difficult until she's entirely at home with simple chimneys, slabs and ledges and you're dead certain she's enjoying herself. That's the vital thing to watch for: is she having a good time?"[10]

Although Betsy fully accepted the fact that one sometimes had to "wear the hairshirt" while climbing, she had strict standards about how a woman should look while she wore it. "I have a white tailored Nylon blouse, easily washed and fresh looking," she wrote, "that should be nice for fancy with a bright sweater, don't you think. . . . I've never been one to feel that the rough life became more and more delightful the worse you look."[11] She always carried lipstick. When camping out, even on a climbing trip, she relaxed by reading the *Oxford Book of English Verse*, Shakespeare's tragedies, or the Bible.

Betsy lived all of her adult life in Colorado Springs, except for a period during World War II when she and her children moved to New York City.

Even then she couldn't bear to be away from the Colorado mountains for too long and persuaded her thirteen-year-old daughter and two female friends to take a thousand-mile bike ride around the state.

After the war, when Betsy was back in the Springs, she served as an unofficial hostess for visiting mountaineers. She threw parties to which she invited all her climbing friends, rich and poor, famous and obscure. The hors d'oeuvres were ample and the whiskey was expensive and smooth, a far cry from young climbers' usual evenings of cheap beer. And Betsy was good to her climbing friends in other ways. Bradford Washburn credited Betsy with bringing him and Othmar Gurther together; the two then collaborated on a relief map of Mount McKinley (Denali) in Alaska, the highest mountain in North America. Dee Molenaar said that Betsy was "definitely instrumental" in the success of his application to join the 1953 American expedition to the world's second-highest mountain, K2.[12] (He met Betsy when he was the civilian adviser to the army's Mountain and Cold Weather Training Command in Colorado Springs.) And Bob Ormes, an English professor at Colorado College at the time, is grateful to Betsy for giving him the money to hire a guide for the Matterhorn, an expense his salary wouldn't allow.

Betsy kept detailed diaries of her climbs and trips. They formed the basis for her many articles, most of which appeared in the publications of mountaineering clubs and in Colorado Springs newspapers. Although she never hesitated to admit that she was tired or clumsy or scared, the dominant flavor of her accounts was joyousness and a great sense of fun. Often, she edited out the illness and the endless rainy days that her diaries mentioned.

Betsy usually illustrated her articles with black-and-white photographs. She had been forced into taking pictures after her father had lost his Leica in a Yosemite stream and had insisted that she become the photographer on their outings. She once said that she much preferred photographing mountains to photographing people, but in fact she was extremely good at both, as her pictures, particularly those of her 1950 trip to Nepal, indicate. Over one hundred of her black-and-white prints are housed at the American Heritage Center of the University of Wyoming in Laramie. They are a stunning survey of mountaineering in the 1930s and 1940s and in some cases represent the first views that Westerners had of remote parts of the world. For example, until Betsy visited the Santa Martas, Colombia had banned all photos—period. But with the help of John D. Rockefeller, Jr., and his son Nelson, Betsy obtained special permission to take pictures. And her 1950 trek in Nepal was a photographic coup, since her party was the first group of Westerners to receive permission to scout out the approaches to Everest from within Nepal's borders. Before 1950, Nepal was closed and climbers had to approach Everest from Tibet. After the Chinese invasion, however, Tibet became off limits to Westerners and Nepal opened up.

In 1958, when Betsy was nearly fifty-six years old, she married General Earle E. Partridge (known as Pat), who was head of the North American Air Defense Command in Colorado Springs. Betsy confided to her friend Eleanor Davis Ehrman that she was marrying a "wonderful man and he likes mountains, too, and that's just the frosting on the cake!"[13] Her father, John Strong, then ninety-three years old, performed the wedding ceremony.

Betsy taught her new husband the basics of rock-climbing, and, as a surprise for him, earned her pilot's license. They climbed, trekked, and flew all over the world until Betsy's death in 1974 of cancer. Betsy's friends established a memorial fund, which was used to purchase an oil painting, *In the Colorado Rockies* by Henry Arthur Elkins. It now hangs in the Colorado Springs Fine Arts Center. Betsy's personal library of mountaineering books found its way to the Special Collections Rare Books Room of Norlin Library at the University of Colorado, Boulder. It includes fine old volumes printed in Europe as well as contemporary books, many of which were inscribed by the authors or given as gifts to Betsy by well-known mountaineers. Betsy had already donated her complete set of the British *Alpine Journal*, going back to 1873, to the Colorado Mountain Club headquarters in Denver.

Although none of Betsy's noteworthy climbs were in Colorado, she showed Coloradans that mountaineering on a global scale was entirely feasible and a lot of fun. While it is true that she lived in a time when climbers were "fewer, perhaps more amateur, less expert and specialized than now," Betsy Strong Cowles Partridge was a standout in that era.[14] Her mountaineering attitudes blew fresh air into the sport as practiced by Coloradans.

RUTH EWALD GAY

Ruth Ewald was thirteen years old when she guided her first party up Longs Peak, for pay, in 1947. She had learned her mountain skills from Paul Nesbit, a teacher from Colorado Springs who spent his summers leading nature walks and guiding parties up Longs Peak, and from junior nature programs run by Rocky Mountain National Park. Although Ruth's first trip was so traumatic that she made up her mind never to guide again, she changed her mind a few years later and became a guide for the Estes Park YMCA hikes. As part of her job she led parties up Longs Peak, and currently she holds the women's record for the most ascents of that peak—seventy-two. She enrolled at Colorado State University, majoring in forestry recreation. During her college summers she became Rocky Mountain National Park's first female seasonal ranger to dress in an official uniform and meet the public. Today Ruth studies rain forests as a plant ecologist in the Botany Department of the University of Hawaii.

INESTINE ROBERTS

Inestine Roberts took up climbing Colorado peaks after she moved to Colorado Springs in the late 1930s. At the age of sixty-eight she joined the Pikes Peak Group of the CMC and began leading official club hikes. When in her eighties, she boasted that she'd never had a sick day in bed since the birth of her seventh child, and she continued her usual chores, such as climbing a high ladder to saw off the broken limb of her maple tree.

The locals knew her as the oldest female climber of Pikes Peak. At the age of eighty-five she was still able to ascend Colorado's most famous mountain, although it took her three days to do so. On August 11, 1957, Inestine, who by then weighed only eighty-five pounds, struggled to the top for the fourteenth time. People at the Summit House tried to dissuade her from retracing her steps and offered her a ride down. (Pikes Peak is America's most civilized fourteener; a nonhiker can ascend it in the comfort of either a cog railroad or an automobile.) However, Inestine firmly declined because she was in charge of a garden club table and wanted to gather alpine flowers for an upcoming exhibit.

She started walking, slowly, down the rocky trail. When night came, she huddled beside a boulder on the lee side. The next day she continued looking for tundra flowers, cheerfully assuring a concerned hiker that she was quite all right. Then Inestine wandered off the trail, still above timberline, looking for new flowers. Later, searchers found her on the tundra, dead from a heart attack. She was nearly eighty-eight years old.

Between 1935 and 1970 the skier Marjorie Perry had no female counterpart in Colorado. However, in June 1946 two women from Jackson Hole,

Wyoming, pulled off a whopping first; Marianne Stevenson Magnuson and Betty Wollsey skied down the Dinwoody Glacier of Gannett Peak, Wyoming's highest mountain, becoming the first skiers ever in the Wind River Range. Their account suggests that they had acquired ski mountaineering expertise in Europe.

There may have been Colorado women with comparable skiing experience, but if so, they apparently directed their skills to the emerging sport of downhill skiing. Gradually, women from the Front Range began driving to ski areas, midweek, by the carload. However, it was only a question of time before old-fashioned skiing, now called "cross-country" or "touring," enjoyed a revival. In 1972 a group of Boulder women who had met through the CMC began cross-country skiing on weekdays, manless, probably the first women in Colorado to do so. Now known as the Wednesday Ladies, they've skied and hiked together for seventeen years and have logged more than eight thousand miles. Many comparable groups have sprung up, such as the High Country Hikers of Colorado Springs and the Trail Marms from Denver. In one sense they represent a new trend. In another sense, however, they've simply reinvented the Fraser Ladies Hiking Club of 1915.

These women are symbolic of the dramatic changes that have occurred in how Colorado outdoor women relate to the mountains. Today the state has dozens—perhaps hundreds—of proficient female mountaineers, although only a few are described here in detail: Jean Ruwitch, who with Louise Shepherd climbed the Diamond "free"; Coral Bowman, who founded the first rock-climbing school for women in Colorado, if not in the country; and Gudy Gaskill, whose unique contribution is not as a fine mountaineer (which she is), but rather as the sustaining force behind the 470-mile Colorado Trail. Julia Archibald Holmes would be incredulous of these women. And, no doubt, envious of their options.

It wasn't until the mid-1970s that Colorado women began climbing hair-raising rock routes on their own terms, a change that is beautifully illustrated by the female climbing history of Longs Peak. Of course one has to recognize that the concept of what is "hair-raising" has evolved considerably over the years, for men as well as women. Still, when Addie Alexander made the first documented female ascent of Longs in 1871, she inaugurated a modus operandi that persisted for the next hundred years. Men led; women followed. As the prevailing high-standard routes became more demanding, the pattern was reinforced. Until the 1960s there were few rock-climbers—period—and only a small number were female. Probably the percentages were not much different from those recorded by Paul Nesbit in his 1946 book *Longs Peak: Its Story and a Guide for Climbing It*, in which he noted that of the more than three hundred recorded East Face ascents of Longs, only twenty-two (7 percent) were made by women.

Longs Peak climbing standards escalated dramatically in 1960, when a smooth, overhanging section of the East Face known as the Diamond was climbed for the first time by two California men, Bob Kamps and David Rearick. However, it wasn't until 1975 that an all-female party climbed it. Their route was D-7, and they used direct aid.

Some climbing definitions are in order. *Direct aid* refers to climbing in which the climber uses devices other than the rock itself to ascend. *Direct aid* contrasts with *free climbing*, in which the climber depends only on the rock itself, using the depressions and nubbins and cracks and chimneys of the rock for footholds and handholds. In both methods the climber is attached to a rope that is threaded through a piece of protection (an anchor, such as a chock, nut, piton, or friend) usually wedged into a crack in the rock. As the leader climbs, the second climber on the rope pays out the rope, or belays, in such a way that the second climber can stop the leader's fall. A leader who does fall will fall below his or her piece of protection only as far as he or she has climbed above it—assuming that the protection stays in place and that the belayer is competent. Therefore, of the members of the party, the leader risks falling the farthest. Finally, *third classing* is climbing without using any kind of protection.

MOLLY HIGGINS, STEPHANIE ATWOOD, AND LAURIE MANSON

When Laurie Manson, Stephanie Atwood, and Molly Higgins used direct aid on their route up the East Face, D-7, they were climbing the Diamond in the only style to which it was accustomed. Ironically, the day they chose to try for their Diamond "first" turned out to be the same day that two men had chosen for attempting another first—a free climb of D-7. When Wayne Goss and Jim Logan arrived at the horizontal ledge known as Broadway, the women were already there, bivouacking before an early start. American climbing etiquette was very clear: since the women were there first, they had the right to be first on the route. Aside from the aesthetic pleasure, being first is also far less dangerous because one doesn't risk being hit by rocks dislodged by climbers above. Jim and Wayne knew that three people using direct aid would be much slower than two who were free-climbing. Finally, after much discussion, the women let Wayne Goss and Jim Logan go ahead. As it turned out, both parties achieved their firsts that day.

JEAN RUWITCH GORESLINE AND LOUISE SHEPHERD

Five years later, in 1980, the team of Jean Ruwitch and Louise Shepherd attempted to be the first all-female party to climb the Diamond free. Louise was a twenty-two-year-old Australian woman who was very good, although she'd been climbing for only two years. Jean was a thirty-year-old native Coloradan who had been climbing for fifteen years.

Their decision to free-climb the Diamond was not part of a master plan to do a first but was more of a question: "What shall we climb next weekend—how about trying the Grand Traverse?" It had evolved from Jean's first physical contact with the Diamond the previous week. She and a friend, Richard, had decided to try the Grand Traverse, a route neither had climbed before. Jean had led the first pitch, or distance between two belay stances, and unwittingly stopped short. This put Richard too low, and when he led the second pitch, a traverse, he pulled off a huge block of rock and fell.

He hadn't put in any protection and was only on Jean's belay, which jerked her violently. Hearing him groan, she shouted, "Richard! Richard!" Finally, after an endless silence, he said he was okay, that he just wanted to rest for a while. Jean, however, insisted that they rappel down. Louise Shepherd met them at the bottom. By then it was obvious that Richard, far from being okay, had injured an ankle and smashed his tailbone. Jean and Louise walked on either side, supporting him, until they reached the Chasm Lake Shelter. A ranger radioed for a horse to be brought up, much to Richard's relief.

The accident did not intimidate Jean or Louise. The next Monday, August 11, 1980, they hiked in the five miles to the base of Longs Peak to give the Grand Traverse their best shot and spent the night under overhanging rocks. "It was my passion for rock climbing which had led me from my home in South Australia to the famed Rocky Mountains in Colorado," Louise later wrote. "There are few female climbers in Australia so the experience of climbing with another woman was new and exciting. A kind of equality exists between two women which is sometimes lacking in a male-female partnership."[15]

The alarm went off at 5:30 A.M. The women wriggled out of their sleeping bags, fully dressed, and crawled out from under their night's shelter, a huge boulder. Their water was frozen. "In the east, the grey dawn slowly obliterated the lights of Denver sprawled over the Great Plains of Colorado," Louise wrote. "Up here in the thin air of the Rocky Mountains, Jean and I gulped our hot tea and started packing our gear. . . . The sky was clear as we crossed the moraine to a steep frozen snowfield. Completely inexperienced on ice, I inched my way up, gripped with panic every time my feet slipped. Jean climbed with an ease of familiarity which I envied."

At the top of the snowfield, between the ice and rock, was a gap two meters wide. Louise had to psych herself up in order to cross it and reach the base of the North Chimney, "a notoriously dangerous gully [that is] a natural funnel for any loose rocks and debris accidentally dislodged." As she later wrote, "Unroped, we carefully worked our way up the steep sides of the gully and an hour later scrambled safely onto the broad ledge below the main face."

The day was beautiful. Although several other climbers followed them, Jean and Louise were first in line for what is officially called the Grand Traverse. Climbers, however, call it the Casual Route because after Charlie Fowler had third-classed it solo and was asked how it was, he replied, "Oh, casual."

"The most difficult part now lay ahead," Louise recalled. "Glowing orange from the morning sun, the East Face rose sheer before us. Yesterday, on the gruelling approach march, I was eager to challenge this strikingly symmetrical face. Now I felt oppressed by its enormity. Fears and doubts crowded my mind. I busied myself by uncoiling the rope. Jean tied herself to one end and I, the other. We would remain roped together for the next 350 metres."

The Grand Traverse is actually a combination of routes. It begins on D-1 (by which the Diamond was first climbed), traverses over to the Yellow Wall, gains altitude again on the lefthand side of the Diamond, and then traverses onto Table Ledge. It consists of eight pitches: the crux pitch—the most difficult pitch of the climb—is the seventh. Jean and Louise customarily alternated leads and also arranged each climb so that they would take turns leading the crux pitch. Today it was Jean's turn. She would lead the first, third, fifth, and seventh pitches.

She started up, just as she had the week before. This time, however, she knew that she had to climb all the way up to "the purple sling," the beginning of the real traverse. Jean moved easily, although she was well aware that the route was difficult to protect. When she reached a small ledge about 120 feet above Louise, she securely anchored herself in (attached herself to the rock by means of a device at the end of her rope) and pulled the rope up taut. Then Louise began climbing, removing the nuts that Jean had placed. When Louise came to what she'd heard was the most dangerous part of the climb, Jean gave her a look of encouragement. As Louise writes:

The rock formed holds but no cracks in which to place [nuts]. I kept going. Ten metres above Jean I found a tiny fissure into which I poked the smallest [nut] I had with me. Clipping in the rope, I looked around uncertainly. A line of holds led up and left to a deep crack. Trying to stay calm, I concentrated on those holds. . . . Some tense moments . . . then I reached the crack and slotted in a large [nut].

"No more rope!" shouted Jean from below.

Having no ledge to stand on, I had to tie myself closely to the [nuts] in the crack and hang there, a human fly suspended on a vast wall of rock. The straps of my harness were digging painfully into my flesh by the time Jean reached me.

The clear day held as they made their way up. Jean wore French rock-climbing shoes called "E.B.'s," long pants, and a turtleneck over a polypropylene shirt. In the morning, when sun fell on the rock face, she stripped down to the polypro. Neither woman wore gloves.

The route was vertical to slightly overhanging. Both Jean and Louise had climbed on rock faces in Yosemite National Park that dwarfed the East Face of Longs. But climbing the East Face of Longs is grueling because it entails a long walk in to the base and because the entire climb takes place above 12,000 feet. The weather is another major factor; often storms sneak up on climbers from their blind side, the west.

Although Jean and Louise had rain gear, they were not prepared to spend the night suspended in hammocks attached to the cliff by nuts and slings. Had the weather turned bad, they would have rappelled down. Fortunately, the weather stayed good and they made steady progress. In midafternoon they came to the crux pitch, which was rated 5.10. (At that time a rating of 5.11 would have indicated the highest degree of severity in a free climb.) Jean, who was leading, remembers that it had one "real difficult move": a gap in handholds forced her to pull up on a tiny nubbin of rock. One pitch later, they were off the wall. They coiled the rope and scrambled over the last two hundred feet of broken rock to the summit. "Panting from exertion and dizzy from the effects of high altitude, we threw down our gear and hugged each other exultantly. We'd made it." It was four o'clock.

Although Louise claimed to have been bothered by the altitude on Longs, the highest mountain she'd ever climbed, Jean was impressed by her friend's performance. For Jean, the climb was "fun," full of "big holds" and "nice dihedrals" (a dihedral being a "corner" where two rock faces meet). On top, Jean and Louise asked a man, who'd hiked up by the Keyhole route, to snap their picture. Then they guzzled water and tore into their sandwiches. Finally satisfied, they "lingered awhile, gazing down on the surrounding peaks and plains stretching for miles in every direction." Since the late afternoon sky was darkening, they reluctantly put on their packs and descended by the steep Cable Route, now minus the cables. Jean recalls that it made her nervous.

In retrospect, Louise remembers her free ascent of the Diamond as technically easier than other climbs she had made but also as very challenging because of the "alpine experience." This experience of climbing in thin air did not make her a convert. A half-dozen years later she wrote that the part of climbing that appeals to her most is "the unique amalgamation of physical, mental and psychological stresses." She went on to say that these stresses are even more pronounced in alpine climbing, where "survival and the stoicism to endure physical misery become an integral part. . . . For those reasons alpine climbing repulses me; I prefer fun in the sun!"[16]

Climbing continues to be the focus of Louise's life. She supports herself in "relatively unskilled, or semi-skilled jobs in cities (such as laboratory technician, shop assistant), sometimes . . . in climbing-related fields (such as climbing instructing, technical advisor and participant in film-making, writing articles, photography, slide-shows, etc.) and sometimes . . . by unemployment benefits." Jean calls Louise "the best woman climber I've ever climbed with."[17] The Ruwitch-Shepherd free ascent of the Diamond was one not only for the record books but, more important for the participants, it was a splendid day of joy. There was no foreshadowing of what would happen the next year.

When Jean climbed the Diamond, she was very good and getting better. As a kid she'd been a tomboy. Her father had often taken her downhill skiing and had sometimes let her cut classes, as long as she kept her grades up. She'd enjoyed high school gymnastics, although she wasn't particularly skilled at it. At the age of fifteen she'd taken a rock-climbing course sponsored by the Boulder branch of the Colorado Mountain Club and Rocky Mountain Rescue. "I think I was a natural," she later said. "I just loved rock climbing. It seemed like so much fun to me." She picked out an instructor, Evans Winner, who looked older and more experienced and who taught her a lot. For six years Jean climbed intensely and was soon capable of following on an extremely difficult pitch, rated 5.10, although she never led one that hard during those years. Then she burned out and quit climbing, cold turkey. A few years later she picked it up again and followed a climber on a tricky route in Eldorado Springs rated 5.9. It was easy for her.

She married Tom Ruwitch, a fine climber, who told her that no one really knew what climbing was all about unless he or she was doing some leading. "In many ways, he was right," Jean concedes. She began leading, probably, by her own admission, "very unsafely at first," since she wasn't very good at placing protection—chocks or nuts. "I would get really fed up fiddling around trying to find the right nut. So I would just make the move anyway. Luckily I never fell."

Gradually she became competent at leading, although she found that each spring she had to get used to it again. "Every year you just go through this terrifying stage where you don't want to let go to make a move. You don't feel comfortable with just three points [hands and feet] on the rock. Then, after a while, you feel comfortable."

Jean became better and better. Her partners were some of the best climbers around, both male and female. Since she'd learned much of her rock-climbing in Eldorado Canyon, near Boulder, she was best at face-climbing, which mostly involves using tiny handholds and footholds. She contrasted herself with a Yosemite-weaned climbing friend, Molly Higgins, who was especially good at cracks. Jean didn't care if her partners were male or female but was put off by ones who were competitive. "I've never been competitive except with myself. I've just always tried to do the best I could with what I knew." She was not so driven that she couldn't back off if the climb wasn't fun.

In Yosemite, for example, she and Beth Bennett, a climbing friend, warmed up on an extremely demanding climb, the South Face of Washington's Column. Then they tackled the Nose, which was even more difficult. The Nose was so big—three thousand feet—that climbers had to sleep out on the face for a couple of nights. It was the biggest wall Jean had attempted. On the first day she and Beth climbed up to Sickle Ledge where they spent the night. She recalls sleeping next to a pile of excrement that was eight inches high. "It was so disgusting—and the cracks were just filled with garbage—cans, orange peels, pop cans—you name it, it was there."

We started up and got into the Stoveleg Cracks. I had to climb up 70 feet without any protection because if you put protection in below where the pendulum point is, then it screws up your second [climber]. The crack was a 5.8 or a 5.9 but I really didn't like the idea of climbing it without any protection. I used to love my protection. So I put in my two #3 friends and I just ended up [direct] aiding the crack.

Then Beth had a hard time following the pendulum. At one point it sounded like there were tears in her voice. So I said, "Beth, do you want to go down?" And she said, "YES!" So we both rappelled down and that put my desire to do a big wall out of my mind.

Jean spent the summers of 1978 and 1979 as Grand Teton National Park's second female climbing ranger. In addition to her physical ability on rock, Jean could tell a dirty joke as well as the men. "And," she says, "it turned out I could do more pull-ups than one of the guys—so that impressed them." In fact, Jean could do five sets of ten and even, at her peak, fifteen pull-ups at one stretch, although "the last two were sort of poor."

The year after Jean and Louise free-climbed the Diamond, Jean was moving particularly well on rock. Boulder, Colorado, is on the edge of winter, so it often has sunny days in December and January. Avid climbers like Jean can take to the rocks between snowfalls. Since the rock-climbing season begins in March, it's possible for a climber to be in top form by May. In May 1981 Jean was in the top climbing form of her life. However, her marriage was disintegrating, so she headed to California to climb and to think things out. There, while she was climbing the East Buttress of the Middle Cathedral in Yosemite, two other climbers passed her. Several pitches above her, they dislodged a rock, which hit her a glancing blow. When Jean finally regained consciousness seventeen days later, she couldn't talk, her right side was paralyzed, her left middle finger had been amputated, and, equally traumatic, her long hair had been shaved. Over the next two years she had two operations on her head and three on her hand and underwent "every kind of therapy imaginable." Today she can't use her right hand nearly so well as her left. Brushing her teeth is hard ("I just use both hands"); shuffling a deck of cards is almost impossible. By and large, however, she has made an amazing recovery.

During her long period of recovery, Jean decided to finish climbing the fourteen thousand-foot mountains of Colorado. Although some of the fourteeners have exposed (scary and steep) sections, all the easiest routes are traditionally third-classed. Her father accompanied her on many of them, the last of which, Handies Peak, she climbed on August 8, 1983. Jean has also resumed cross-country skiing. Although she can no longer do parallel turns on her three-pin bindings, she has been able to relearn how to make linked telemark turns. She also swims and runs and has completed a half-marathon. On her good days she can do four pullups.

Jean sued the climbers who had passed her and caused her climbing accident in Yosemite; she was awarded an out-of-court settlement generous enough to enable her to finish her degree at the University of Colorado, majoring in kinesiology. She found that it was almost as easy to type with nine fingers as with ten. In the fall of 1986 she enrolled at the University of Southern California; two years later she graduated with a master's degree in physical therapy. She has since remarried, lives in Eldorado Springs, and is working with patients who have traumatic brain injury.

For the first few years after her climbing accident Jean "really resented" the climbers responsible for taking away her prime climbing years. "But," she says, "there's nothing I can do about it and it doesn't pay to be bitter." Climbing is no longer the same for her. Jean finds that a pitch rated 5.6 is really hard for her now, and terrifying. She has a lot of fear to work through but isn't sure that she even wants to work through it. "The accident changed my life, basically," she says. "When I was in the hospital I had lots of time to think about what I wanted to be when I grew up. . . . There *is* life after climbing."

CORAL BOWMAN WILBER

Jean Ruwitch Goresline and Coral Bowman Wilber are contemporaries, although they never climbed together. (Jean regarded Coral as a much better climber than she.) Like Betsy Cowles, Coral Bowman looked feminine while "wearing the hairshirt." Often when she prearranged, by phone, a meeting at Eldorado Canyon with a climbing client, no one would approach her. As she explains, "I didn't look like what they thought a person who climbed hard was supposed to look like."[18] She is five feet five and weighed 102 pounds during her most intense climbing period. Anyone who has old-fashioned ideas about female climbers would guffaw at the notion that Coral was once one of the most skilled female climbers on two continents.

Coral, born in 1949, was raised in Lincoln, Nebraska. As a kid she wasn't athletic, although she was something of a tomboy. She feels that being the middle of three girls, only eleven months older than her little sister, contributed to the "little bit of competitive instinct that got bred in there." Since her father was a professor at the University of Nebraska and had summers off, Coral and her family often visited national parks and hiked in the New Hampshire mountains. Heights never bothered her.

She attended the University of Nebraska for three years and then quit to go to Canada with a group of friends. A few years later, while earning an elementary school teaching degree at the University of Colorado, she learned to kayak and cross-country ski and became head seamstress for an outdoor equipment company called Clan Robertson. Its owner, Brian Robertson, was a Scottish climber of note who ran the Colorado Alpine School. He took Coral out bouldering on Flagstaff Mountain. (*Bouldering* is climbing up boulders or small outcroppings. It allows one to practice maneuvers that are often extremely hard technically in relative safety, since the boulders are such a short distance off the ground.) It was Coral's first experience with "what rocks were about," and she loved it. They went climbing often.

In retrospect, Coral thinks that Brian was a "pretty good teacher" and describes the arrangement as the "*de rigueur* climbing experience" for a woman at that time. "It was the female learning from the male—the sort of sink-or-swim approach," she says. "Right away I was taken on climbs that were fairly difficult and I was scared. But I was with someone who said, 'You're going to climb or else.'"

Coral's first real climb was Wind Ridge in Eldorado Canyon, a few miles south of Boulder and one of the most famous climbing centers in the United States. Then she tackled the Bastille Crack. Much later, after she had learned how to climb, Coral repeated Wind Ridge and the Bastille Crack and wondered how she'd survived her initial climbs. She speculates that a lot of fear was mixed with the desire—and not much technique. "The more Brian would yell, in one sense, the more determined I would get, too," she comments.

In the 1970s, when Coral was beginning to climb, there were still very few female climbers in Colorado; all of them, with one brilliant exception, were climbing on about the same level as Coral. As a result, since she sought out people who would not only lead but also teach her how to lead, she climbed exclusively with men. One day when Coral was still a neophyte struggling up a pitch in Eldorado Springs, she noticed a group of climbers to her right, easing their way up a wall that she regarded as impossible. She was shocked when she realized that one of the climbers with short-cropped hair was a woman. Later Coral found out that she had witnessed Diane Hunter—the brilliant exception—free-climbing the first pitch of Wide Country, an astonishing event because it was one of the few Eldorado pitches that had the maximum rating of that era, 5.11. The day was a revelation for Coral; before she'd watched Diane climbing, Coral had unconsciously assumed that she could never climb as well as men because her muscles would never be big enough.

In a very remote way Coral came to regard Diane as an inspiration, and even as a mentor. After Coral earned her teaching degree, she flew to Australia to fulfill a long-standing dream. Soon after, she learned that Diane Hunter had plunged to her death while third-classing a relatively easy descent of the Cathedral Spires in Rocky Mountain National Park. Coral taped a photograph of Diane on her wall.

She joined some Australian climbing clubs, figuring it would be a good way to find partners. It was. A month after her arrival she met Ann Bevan, an Aussie of the same age and climbing ability. There were other serious female climbers in the area, and Coral and Ann regarded two in particular, who were "pushing the limits of female ascents," as inspiring. Coral and Ann developed a routine of searching through a guidebook to the local rocks, deciding on a goal, and setting off. They had an understanding that if neither of them could get up it, they would give up the climb rather than enlist the aid of a more experienced climber. This was a radical switch from Coral's previous climbs. In Eldorado Canyon she had climbed with "guys" who were better climbers than she and who achieved their goal virtually all the time. But in the process, the guy would have led and Coral would have followed.

Coral taught elementary school for a few years and, at the age of twenty-six, joined a group of "the first climbing bums of Australia," marrying one of them. They worked as little as possible, climbed as much as possible, slept in tents, and lived on unemployment checks. Most of their waking moments were spent on the crags along the southeast coast of Australia, between Brisbane and Melbourne. This climbing differed from climbing the high walls of Eldorado Springs in that the crags were generally much shorter—two or three hundred feet as opposed to five or seven hundred feet. It eliminated "dealing with elements" and left only the challenge of "getting up trickier sections of rock." For the next couple of years Coral pursued the sport "pretty relentlessly" and basically for herself. She very rarely climbed with a partner of lesser ability. Her "driving desire" was to climb with people of her ability or better.

Sometimes people asked her if she had fun while climbing so whole-heartedly, and she thought it a very strange question. "That wasn't how I looked at it," she says. "It was really like my work, in a certain sense. Somehow I had to be doing something, and the way that I put some value into it was to think of it as 'This is my work.' My underlying assumption here was that work wasn't much fun, either." Her single-mindedness began paying off. Coral increased the levels at which she was climbing, and after she'd achieved the next level she didn't back off by "enjoying climbing." She and her husband followed the climbing seasons of Australia and the United States, living in a great long summer of warm rocks. During this time Coral returned to Eldorado Canyon and discovered that she was now climbing as well as Diane Hunter had been at the height of her career. However, unlike Diane, Coral often preferred climbing with a female partner who was within her ability range to climbing with men. Thus she "was making a statement that 'Women are doing these things.'" It was very important to her to climb with women "so no one could say 'A man led the hard pitch.'"

During the summer of 1977 Coral, Sue Giller, and Beth Bennett decided to tackle C'est La Vie, a route in Eldorado Springs that includes a steep and slightly overhanging dihedral. Although no woman had ever led the route before, Coral was sure she was up to it; it involved stemming (placing hands and feet on opposite walls), a technique she enjoyed, and jamming a hand into a tight crack, for which her small fingers would be a definite advantage.

After a series of pitches, the women reached the crux pitch, rated 5.11.

Coral had heard conflicting opinions about which kind of boot was best for the dihedral, so she wore one kind and carried another kind in her pack. In the end she wore a stiff boot on one foot because "there was a bulge about the size of a dime that you had to stand on and a stiff boot lets you keep your weight on it a little easier. And I wore a soft boot on the other foot." After putting in her protection, Coral went for it, moving confidently and well. "It fell together and I was really pleased." Beth and Sue joined her and they all descended. There they chatted with a friend who had been photographing them while arguing with male spectators who didn't believe that it was a woman who was leading C'est La Vie.

In 1978 Coral decided to attempt a roof route (a *roof* is a rock ceiling) called Guenese. Although she was tired from bouldering the night before, she started up with Sue Giller. It was a very demanding route, with a crux rated 5.11.

You went up this sort of tricky steep wall, and had to make some moves to the left with not very good protection, and after you'd done that part, then you went out diagonally about ten feet on this roof. But it was supposed to be easier—the roof is about 5.9. You're sort of hanging upside down but there are some big holds. I was trying to find a place to go out and I looked down at Sue—who was miles below me—and she said, "I don't think you're in the right place." So I traversed back and launched out right.

It takes some real arm strength and you hook your feet on the holds too. I knew the types of techniques to be used for this, but I thought I remembered somebody telling me about there being a bolt or something and I couldn't locate it. [A *bolt* is a piece of protection that is installed more or less permanently.] I had one last move to make but I kept thinking that without the bolt, if I fell I'd cut back and smash into the wall. So I reversed my moves—I was scared, you know, and I was furious that I'd done the crux move and was just dinking around. So I said to myself, "Well, damn it, if everybody does this, I'm just going to do it, too." So I went out under the roof again and made the move successfully and went further up a few feet until I could belay Sue.

Coral later found out that the bolt she had been searching for was missing and that very likely she and Sue had been the only ones to make the climb until it was replaced. Reflecting on the experience later, Coral wondered if it had been arrogance or stupidity or determination that had driven her to do a route she thought "everyone was doing."

To keep her superb climbing technique honed, she climbed frequently and bouldered or buildered (climbed buildings). She did not do exercises other than those that strengthened her arms. "When you're on a vertical wall, you need a lot of finger strength because the holds are often very sharp but very small," she says. "Technically you can keep your balance on a wall if you have small holds. As soon as the climb starts to get overhanging, the holds tend to get bigger. Your feet help some, but you really have to hold on with your arms." When Coral was a fledgling climber she could not do one pull-up. Now she could do fourteen or fifteen at a stretch, which gave her an edge on many of the difficult climbs that she was routinely doing and, in fact, often leading. Her forte was the "short, hard burst," a climb of high intensity that lasted anywhere from one hour to five or six hours. After such a climb she would go home, eat dinner, and boulder for several hours. "The climbing took a lot of mental stamina and the bouldering a lot of physical stamina."

By 1978 Coral was acknowledged as one of the best female rock-climbers in the United States. For the first time she and her husband were so nearly on the same ability level that some days she could boulder up pitches that he couldn't. They were finding it increasingly hard to handle the competition and tension that was developing between them. Although they didn't talk much about climbing when they were together, it was the focus of their lives. Yet each one was beginning to want something more from life as well, and they were moving in different directions. Eventually they were divorced. Coral says that she is enormously indebted to her former husband for "the expertise I gained by participating with him in climbing."

By this time Coral had achieved several first ascents in Australia and was the first woman to have led a number of climbs in Eldorado that had previously been led only by males. However, she was coming to realize that being "on the top of the pyramid" was not the pure pleasure she had imagined it would be. Although she didn't articulate her vague dissatisfactions, she was aware that they were there. And then, on a fall day in 1978, Coral and Sue Giller began a climb of the Naked Edge in Eldorado Canyon. It was a scorcher, so they took lots of water. When they had climbed far above the ground, they began hauling up, on a separate rope, the pack that contained the water bottles. To their annoyance, the rope became stuck on a rock flake, which meant that one of them had to descend to free it. Sue climbed down to where Coral was setting up a rappel; Coral clipped in (attached the rope to an anchor using a carabiner, or metal ring) and began the rappel by backing off a sloping ramp. In a flash of horror she realized that her rappel rope had come unclipped from the anchor and that she was beginning a free fall to the ground, three hundred feet below. Her adrenalin surged.

I fell about twenty feet free and during that fall I saw all my friends and family in a large group. And I thought how stupid it was that I was falling and that I didn't want to die. That's when I saw the jammed haul rope come within reach and I knew I had a chance, albeit a slim one.

I grabbed that rope—and still thought I was not going to make it because it burned my hands instantly. I slid on that rope for about thirty feet and then I stopped myself. I was hyperalert—I didn't believe that I could hold myself. It all happened so very fast. Somehow hanging on the rope by one hand, I managed to unclip from the useless rappel rope, clip into the haul rope that was still anchored back up at the belay, and rappel down to the top pitch of the Edge. I clipped out and hollered, "Sue, help me!" I felt like a helpless little bird up high in its nest. I was shaking and stunned. We managed to do the traverse and rappel off the route, though my hands were pretty useless by this point.

Coral's hands received second-degree burns. Three weeks later she taped her hands and was able to climb again, or as she puts it, "to get back on the horse." Although she continued to climb for another year, the accident forced her finally to begin paying attention to the "messages" she'd been ignoring. Then one day she quit climbing. For six months she "sort of switched life-styles," enlarging her circle of friends to include ones she met from women's groups. Some of them asked her to take them climbing, which she did.

In 1981, a few months after Jean Ruwitch's accident, Coral started the Great Herizons Climbing School. Her intent was to create a rock-climbing school for women in an environment that was more conducive to their learning than was the one in which she had learned. Mostly, though, Coral wanted to share what she knew with other women. Before, she had not wanted to climb with lesser climbers because she'd been afraid it would slow her "pursuit of getting to the top of climbing."

From the beginning Great Herizons did well, although—as Coral points out—most climbing schools are not very lucrative. (It supported a modest life-style during the climbing season; Coral picked up entry-level jobs to support herself during the rest of the year, once even selling lingerie.) Slowly, Coral developed teaching methods. She hired both female and male instructors, although she found there were many more males than females to choose from. Instructors had to be capable of leading at least a 5.9 pitch and experienced in communicating with people, preferably as teachers—the subject was unimportant. Coral discovered that it was much easier to locate hotshot climbers than it was to find good climbing teachers. "In teaching," Coral explains, "you're often out for eight hours belaying people up and down the same little piece of rock, or showing them how to do rappels and dealing with their fears and anxieties. So teaching is not really about climbing for yourself, but rather about assisting others."

Great Herizons stressed safety. Coral felt strongly that women especially needed to learn the basics so they could be responsible for themselves in a climbing party of men. She had often seen "the guy tying his girlfriend into a rope and then off they'd go. She didn't even know how to tie a knot and she was leaving the ground!" Most of Coral's weekend clients were locals who were just sampling the sport. In such a class the students spent the morning on the ground learning about ropes, knots, belaying, and rappelling. In the afternoon they did thirty- or forty-foot climbs, selected so that an instructor could climb to a student at any time if the student started "losing it." The climber was always belayed by another student. Coral observes that in teaching it's necessary "to decide how hard to help push someone through something that is always dealing with fear." She explains: "Climbing is about fear; that's a big piece of why people do it. You don't get over the fear in climbing; if you like it you're probably somebody who learns how to manage the fear at a comfortable enough level."

After a year Coral expanded classes at Great Herizons to include men. From the school's first day, men had made inquiries about it, and Coral had eventually decided that some men might want to learn climbing in an environment less intimidating than that of most other climbing schools. Also, it made financial sense to include men: potential male clients far outnumbered female ones. Coral felt that both men and women benefited from mixed classes. In a beginners' class, for example, a man who pulled himself up by his arms learned something about technique by watching a woman who climbed the same pitch using her feet. The reverse was also true. Coral felt it was good for women to see that arm strength is an asset in climbing; as a result, they might work to build up their own arm muscles.

She gave students the option of climbing a short route blindfolded, to wean them away from the "very typical" notion that when they were climbing, "what they were doing was looking for handholds."

When you hear someone in trouble, they say, "I can't see where to go. There's nothing for me to hang onto." Meanwhile they do have two feet which are usually flailing and they aren't looking down to move their feet and they've gotten very stretched out because they're trying to stretch for those handholds. They lose their feet and, of course, it really isn't possible to climb without your feet. When they're blindfolded, they can't see where they're going so of course there's no "I can't see the handholds." . . . Quite often that person would climb it *better* with his eyes blindfolded.

Running Great Herizons was hard work. After a full day of instructing, Coral had to hustle clients, return their calls, keep accurate accounts, and arrange for instructors. On her day off she often didn't feel like climbing, and she found that it was difficult, if not impossible, to keep her body and mind fine-tuned for maximum climbs. As a result, for the first time in her life she began to have fun on climbs, taking pleasure in her contact with the rocks and enjoying the presence of clients on an easy climb.

By this time the proportion of women to men at climbing centers such as Eldorado Springs had changed from that seen when Coral had first climbed, and she applauded the change. All-female teams had become a common sight. The days in which each climbing area had its own hotshot female climber, "a prima donna supported by males," were gone. Now, good women climbers from all parts of the country were frequently friends who climbed together. The old myth that "men climb with strength and women climb with finesse" had finally been laid to rest. "Most of the people—men *and* women—who are top climbers," Coral observes, "basically have professional athletes' physiques. It takes a very well developed upper and lower body. The women climbers are very strong in the upper body and the men have great footwork. Climbing has a lot to do with the strength-to-weight ratio—how strong you are compared to your body weight, plus the mental factor."

In 1983 Bob Godfrey, a climber, writer, and photographer, filmed Coral on Longs Peak climbing sequences for a proposed movie about Isabella Bird, a project that was the brainchild of the director Victress Hitchcock. Coral wore a burgundy Victorian suit and hat, high boots, and long underwear to cut the sharp September wind. The intent was to simulate

Isabella's historic climb by photographing dramatic mountain scenery with distant shots of Isabella slipping while Jim hauled her up. As it turned out, Coral didn't have to fake slipping. Her smooth-soled boots had no grip. She had no control and found it "scary" to slip on the rocks and snow. Coral was so moved by the experience of portraying Isabella that she regards it as one of the highlights of her climbing career.

In 1983 Coral married Scott Wilber, an entrepreneur from Boulder who does not rock-climb. After a pregnancy, in the spring of 1985 she decided to cease operating Great Herizons. (In 1987 Mag Hastey and Tracy Bascomb reopened it.) Coral now has a son and daughter and "is absorbed" in her family. She has given up hard climbing, saying, "I no longer have the reason that I had before to climb at an intense level or to put that kind of time into climbing."

Jean Ruwitch Goresline and Coral Bowman Wilber were Colorado manifestations of an international trend that had started in the 1970s: women were gaining the confidence and ability to climb difficult, big mountains on their own. For example Grace Hoeman, a physician from Anchorage, Alaska, led the first successful all-female party to the top of Mount McKinley in 1970. An all-female party conquered an eight thousand-meter peak, Gasherbrum II, in Kashmir, for the first time in 1977. One year later a team of women put two members on top of Annapurna, 26,540 feet high. (Incidentally one of the women on Annapurna, Vera Komarkova, was from Boulder, Colorado.) As yet no all-female team has climbed Mount Everest, although seven women—including two Americans, Stacy Allison and Peggy Luce (first and second, respectively)—have made successful ascents of the world's highest mountain.

GUDRUN GASKILL

Gudrun Gaskill, six feet tall, white-haired, and lean, is the quintessential mountain woman: she is a skilled climber, hiker, river-runner, and cross-country and downhill skier. In recent years, however, she has become something else as well. Gudy is the Supermom of the Colorado Trail, a 470-mile path through some of America's most beautiful country.

The Colorado Trail was linked in the fall of 1987, completed and dedicated in the summer of 1988, and will be refined in the coming years. A blend of existing trails, logging and mining roads, and brand new trails, it zigzags across the Continental Divide twelve times and wends its way through high peaks and deep valleys. Most of the new trail is gentle, having been designed for families with small children and for non-macho folks. Much of the route lies close enough to towns that trail users can come out of the hills once in a while to restock their supplies. Gudy, the trail's chief architect, says that because the trail is meant to educate its users, it deliberately skirts the edges of wilderness areas, already "too popular" in her view.[19] It passes through three ghost towns, three mining towns, manmade environmental disasters, and reforested burns, as well as picture-postcard vistas. Over two thousand volunteers, from every state and from several foreign countries, sweated to build the trail, but it is no exaggeration to say that without Gudy, the project would have died years ago.

Gudy's involvement began in 1973 when, as head of the Colorado Mountain Club's Huts and Trails Committee, she was asked to serve on the advisory committee for something called the Colorado Trail. She said yes, and found out that the trail was an idea concocted during a lunch conversation between Bill Lucas, then head of the USDA Forest Service, Rocky Mountain Region, and Merrill Hastings, then publisher of the *Colorado Magazine*. The idea of a long trail appealed to her. "Here in Colorado there's hardly a trail anymore that's nicely maintained," she observes. "Nobody's concentrating on anything specific. Most of our trails are destination trails to a lake or pass so you come back on the same trail you went up on."

By the end of its first year, the advisory committee had set up bylaws and rules to create a Colorado Mountain Trail Foundation; Gudy was elected to its board. The committee had also begun to recruit volunteers to inventory a twenty-five-mile-wide corridor in an effort to gather enough data to select the best route for the Colorado Trail. Gudy helped teach seniors from Arvada and East high schools how to make winter inventories of possible routes, which was extremely important because the trail was to be used for skiing as well as for hiking and horseback riding. First, Gudy had to teach the kids how to cross-country ski. Then she and Chuck McConnell, the Forest Service's regional director of recreation, took them to a hut and taught them how to build snow caves for shelter, and how to dig a snow pit, a useful technique in judging avalanche danger. Each group of kids went out for a week or two as part of their senior seminar program. They gathered information on potential routes from Bailey to Breckenridge and on over Vail Pass. During two winters students from Western State College in Gunnison covered the country from Marshall Pass down Fooses Creek and back over to Leadville.

Merrill Hastings published two lengthy articles about the proposed trail in the *Colorado Magazine*, which Gudy believes "got the project off the ground." Then the Gates Foundation presented a $100,000-grant to the Colorado Trail Foundation. It seemed the Colorado Trail would be completed in short order, but that was not the case. The money vanished in executive directors' salaries and telephone bills, with very little trail to show for it. Gudy was responsible for the few miles of trail that were actually constructed. The Gates Foundation did not renew its grant the following year, and dissension and resignations began unraveling the Trail Foundation. It looked as though the Colorado Trail was heading into the sunset.

Meanwhile, Gudy helped sponsor a trail-building seminar in Monument, near Colorado Springs. The instructor, a retiree who'd built trails all his life, explained to his audience that there were two different ways to build a trail. The first was for each worker to use the same tool all day, jumping from a completed section to the next section requiring his specialty. The second method was for workers to switch tools and jobs, simply trading a pulaski (axe-pick) for a rock bar when necessary. Using information she learned in the seminar, Gudy experimented and by trial and error learned how to build trails. She came to prefer the "trade-off" method, finding it less boring than "jumping."

For several years she recruited members of the Colorado Mountain Club to help build trails, including a couple of miles of the Colorado Trail. Individuals donated money for food, which was the primary expense. Gradually, Gudy became more and more involved. In addition to recruiting builders, arranging for the care and feeding of the volunteers, and often running the trail crew camp herself, she conferred with the district rangers of the seven national forests that the trail was to cross. Together they worked out the details of the final routes, such as the types of bridges that needed to be built and the logistics of the trail construction. Gudy, who became the official spokesperson for the Colorado Trail, gave interviews, launched publicity, presented slide shows, solicited donations, wrote grant proposals for major funding, arranged for a Colorado Trail guide to be written, and all the while continued to direct the trail crew program.

In 1985 an article in a national publication moved several thousand people from all over the country to apply to work on the trail, although the foundation could use only 150 people, the number necessary for the summer's game plan. The trail grew an unprecedented number of miles— twelve. The following summer, in 1986, twenty-six miles were built, and during the summer of 1987 over forty miles were added. Gudy wrote personal thank-you notes to all those who worked on the trail and made sure that the names of the thousands of applicants were entered on her computer. She continued to supervise most of the volunteer trail crews. By now she was a veteran boss.

The very first thing we do with a new crew is to allow them to walk on the part of the trail that has been built the week before, if there is one. Then we come back to camp and pick up the tools, and talk about every single one. We give a hands-on demonstration about how the tools are used and carried safely so that we don't have any problems. Then we talk about how we will actually build the trail—using the "jump" method or "trading-off" method.

The trail crew was presented with a flagged route. The job of the first person was to "pull a line," which means to etch a physical line through the duff on the forest floor, removing a few tree branches to create a trail that, though raw, is unambiguous. The line-puller was followed by two or three people who removed offending trees in the middle of the trail or across it. "You can't get stumps out. It takes forever." After the loggers came two or three workers whose job was to "pull the tread," that is, to build up a three-foot-wide trail, using rocks or soil if the trail sloped. (Horses require a trail at least three feet wide.)

The crew members at the end of the line specialized in trimming tree branches, removing rocks with a pry bar, filling in holes, and grooming the trail—raking and smoothing it. The routine wasn't always routine. Sometimes an ad hoc crew was formed to deal with a special problem, such as stubborn tree roots. Often the entire crew pitched in to build a bridge or to cart rocks for a stream crossing. "Three people can be working on one deep gully the whole day." Above tree line, the crew built five-foot cairns to mark the trail, making it visible in the clouds or a blizzard. A work crew completed an average of one mile of new trail in a week, and for a bargain price. Gudy estimates that in recent years a mountain trail suitable for horses that is built by hired labor costs an average of eleven thousand to twelve thousand dollars a mile in Colorado. However, that same mile built by volunteer labor cost only five hundred dollars, and most of that sum was spent on food. To be sure, the work was rigorous, especially for out-of-staters, who gasped in the high altitudes. But it was also fun for motivated men and women. According to one poll, most workers came because they wanted to "give something back" to the outdoors.

All the volunteers paid their own way to the construction site, arriving on Saturday. Sunday and Wednesday were rest days or, for those who preferred, hiking days. If Gudy was in charge, she led crew members up hard peaks, often fourteeners, on their days off. "They love it," she commented at the time. "It practically kills some of them, but they love it." Sometimes the Forest Service hosted a "thank you" barbecue. By the second night people knew each other's names and were on comfortable terms with each other. Often there was at least one guitar player to strum and sing after supper. Usually a "fantastic camaraderie" had formed by the week's end.

During the first few years of Colorado Trail construction, when all the volunteers were from Colorado, an overwhelming number of workers were women; sometimes, in fact, there was only one man on an entire crew. After Gudy began advertising nationally, however, slightly more men than women signed up. About a quarter of the volunteers were between twenty-five and thirty years old. Very few were under twenty—the minimum age was sixteen—and not many were between forty and fifty. However, a lot were between fifty and sixty, and some were in their seventies. Gudy found that in-state people who were in their sixties signed up confidently, whereas slightly younger out-of-state volunteers hesitated and wondered if they were too old. "Grandpa Mauthe (Al Mauthe) is seventy-five or seventy-six," she says. "He's strong as an ox and out-skis anybody that I know. He goes skiing four days a week because it's free for him. He goes wind surfing and swims every single morning. When he gets on a pulaski, the chips just fly. I can't believe what he does." Gudy soon quit checking the age given on the applications.

Although the trail took about two years longer to complete than Gudy had hoped, she has seen it through. It represents an extraordinary achievement and the tangible evidence of Gudy's enchantment with Colorado's mountains. Gudy first came to Colorado in the 1930s with her German father, Paul Timmerhaus, her Norwegian mother, Elsa, her brother, Klaus, and her twin sister, Ingy. Paul worked as a summer ranger in Rocky

Mountain National Park, and "since there was nothing else to do," the family hiked. At the age of sixteen, Gudy and her sister graduated from high school in Chicago as salutatorian and valedictorian, respectively, and enrolled at Western State College in Gunnison, Colorado. (The college had advertised a lighted ski course on the campus, but the "course" turned out to be on a hill behind the campus, with a light that didn't work and a rope tow that didn't operate.) At about the same time, Gudy's parents sold their house in Chicago and bought a small ski lodge near the Winter Park Ski Area in Colorado.

The Timmerhauses knew very little about managing a ski resort and only slightly more about skiing. Their only skiing experience was down hills in Illinois forest preserves; they had used wide leather bindings over the instep, supplemented with strips of inner tubes that Paul had added to help keep the skis on. But by spending college breaks at her parents' ski lodge, Gudy soon learned how to ski. Mastering the rope tow, however, was another matter. Even Gudy, young and strong though she was, had so much trouble gripping the tow that she invented a system whereby she tied a monkey wrench to her wrist and clamped the wrench onto the rope. This worked well until one day when Gudy was tired and on the last run. As she reached the top of the tow she began to unclamp the wrench but found that she didn't have the strength to release it. In desperation she flipped the wrench as hard as she could—and snapped the rope in two. Skiers fell off the entire length of the rope tow, but Gudy was saved from being pulled into the tow mechanism.

Often Gudy skied the slopes with a friend who worked at her parents' lodge; they regarded themselves as "hot stuff." One day, while carving arabesques in the snow, they misjudged and collided. The girl's ski pole punctured Gudy's chin, going in underneath and emerging out the top. Frantically they phoned the only physician in the county, Doc Susie, who was out on a call some thirty-five miles away in Grand Lake. Susie agreed to meet them at the town of Granby, midway between Winter Park and Grand Lake. When they arrived at Granby, however, there was no sign of Doc, so they continued toward Grand Lake. The road was badly rutted because of the construction of Shadow Mountain Reservoir, but they managed to lurch along, growing more distraught with each mile. By now Gudy had lost so much blood that she thought she might bleed to death. Finally they met up with Doc Susie, who stopped right then and there and built a little fire by the side of the road. After sterilizing her instruments, she sutured Gudy's chin, without using any anesthetic. Eventually, the wound healed just fine.

Gudy learned how to cross-country ski on the track at the Western State College campus. At that time neither the diagonal stride nor the more modern "skating" techniques were used in American cross-country. Racers simply ran as fast as they could on their old army skis, which were shaved down. Gudy recalls that she and her friends even removed the paint on their skis so they could go a little faster. When a national nordic ski competition was held at Winter Park, for men only, Gudy tucked all her hair inside a ski cap and entered, assuming the judges wouldn't know that "Gudrun" was a female name. She was almost to the finish line when somebody yelled: "Gudy, Gudy! What are you doing in that race—you can't be in that race!" She came in third.

During her college summers of 1945 and 1946, Gudy worked at Longs Peak Inn. Her boss was Enos Mills's widow, Esther, then in her late fifties, whom Gudy found to be "an austere person."

I can still see the set of her mouth—I don't know that she ever smiled. Bonnie Patterson and I did all the waiting of tables and making of beds that first summer. And Joe was the cook and his wife did the laundry. We were the only hired help, since there wasn't anybody there because of gas rationing during World War II. I mean, maybe Mrs. Mills would have one or two guests a week and those people had gas because they were connected with the army.

The hired help was forbidden to talk to the guests except when waiting tables. However, when Mrs. Mills took her afternoon nap, Bonnie and Gudy would sneak down to the library on the main floor, select a book, and climb back to their rooms. There was so little work to do that Bonnie and Gudy alternated taking days off, and sometimes Joe's wife covered for them in case a guest dropped in. On her days off, Gudy hiked. She preferred Twin Sisters, Longs Peak by the Cable or Keyhole Route, or a two-day trip to Grand Lake and back, which was somewhat complicated without a car. Gudy would hitchhike to Bear Lake and hike twenty miles over the Divide to visit her parents at their vacation cabin in Grand Lake. After staying the night, she would try to hitch a ride back over Trail Ridge Road. If she couldn't snag one, she hiked back over the Divide to Bear Lake by moonlight. Over the course of two summers Gudy climbed Longs Peak thirty-two times. Sometimes, inspired by thunderstorms, she wrote poetry on the summit.

When Gudy was a freshman at Western State she read an advertisement on the school bulletin board: "Have jeep, will travel. Looking for mountaineers." Gudy signed up the first weekend, the only girl among five "cigar-smoking males." She discovered that the writer of the ad, Dave Gaskill, was a student in the German class she taught. Dave later said that Gudy's German class was the only college course he took in which he didn't learn much and still received an A.

Dave and Gudy made many winter and summer climbs together, skied up quite a few fourteeners, and became some of the earliest river rafters on the Colorado. In 1948 they were married and immediately moved to Kansas, where they began operating a sheep camp. With their summers free, they started the "Smoke Gets in Your Eyes" Traveling Camp for Boys. It was quite successful. The Gaskills recruited youngsters between the ages of twelve and fourteen from the Boy Scouts and from church camps in Missouri and Kansas, and set up headquarters at the Timberhaus Ski Lodge in Winter Park. Friends acted as counselors. For ninety dollars a boy could explore jeep roads and climb fourteeners for two weeks, all expenses paid. Most of the kids were quite taken with the program; Gudy and Dave had many repeats. If a camper passed certain criteria, he would be inducted into a secret organization that permitted him to sign "KFK" after his name on a peak register. Today, some forty years later, Gudy and Dave still find an occasional "KFK" at the top of a peak. Dave has kept track of the campers, most of whom are now parents and even grandparents, and he reports that many are in professions related to the outdoors.

Eventually blizzards wiped out the sheep business, and the Gaskills took off for Albuquerque, Los Angeles, and finally the Denver area. Along the way they had children, Dave became a geologist for the U.S. Geological Survey, and Gudy acquired a master's degree in community recreation and a doctorate in education. (Dave and Gudy have three daughters, one of whom is adopted, and two sons.)

The Gaskills joined the Colorado Mountain Club, and for the next fifteen years Gudy sponsored the CMC Juniors. She'd already had a lot of practice with her own kids, since Dave's job took him away for months at a time and Gudy "wasn't about to stay home." Mostly she led the CMC Juniors up fourteeners, "just about every other weekend," which resulted in her climbing all of Colorado's fifty-four peaks over fourteen thousand feet. "I never would have done it on my own," she says. Gudy learned technical climbing from a CMC-sponsored school and climbed two highly respectable routes, the Ellingwood Ridge of Crestone Needle and Stettners Ledges on Longs Peak. In 1977 she became the first female president of the Colorado Mountain Club, founded in 1912. Through the years she has also led CMC trips for adults, such as multinight ski trips hut-hopping near Aspen and tours to New Zealand and the huts of Europe.

Although Gudy is still refining the Colorado Trail, its completion has given her a freedom she's not had for many years—to travel, ski, run rivers with Dave, hike midweek with her female friends, to play tennis and the cello again, to paint and pot, to go on an archeological dig. And to walk the Colorado Trail from beginning to end, experiencing it as a continuity rather than as bits and pieces. It's a trip she anticipated for fifteen years.

Epilogue

The mountain women described in this book are but a sampling. They have been selected somewhat arbitrarily, although I have emphasized pre-1950 subjects, including just enough contemporary ones to indicate trends. (Happily, Colorado mountain women are today no novelty; there are hundreds.) Deciding who should be included in—and excluded from—the book was painful. In the end I had to select women who fit into logical chapters and who represented a balanced diversity. Had space permitted, I would have included nearly a score of others.

First and foremost, I would have included the Colorado female conservationists and preservationists who came after Virginia Donaghe McClurg, Lucy Peabody, and the Colorado Cliff Dwellings Association (the creators of Mesa Verde National Park in 1906). For in my opinion these female watchdogs have benefited Colorado's mountainous country more than has any other group of women.

Mary King (Mrs. John D.) Sherman, for example, persuaded the General Federation of Women's Clubs to endorse the formation of Rocky Mountain National Park, which was established in 1915. (Her husband, John Sherman, was one of Katherine Garetson's neighbors. The Shermans were friends with Enos Mills.) Some years before the dedication, Mary King Sherman had lived in a cabin in Tahosa Valley while recuperating from a lengthy illness. When she was finally well enough to struggle to the top of Longs Peak with her son, she was so grateful to be healthy again that she vowed to devote the rest of her life to conserving scenes of great beauty. Mary Sherman later became known as "The National Park Lady."

In 1930 Frank Spencer, a history professor at Adams State College in Alamosa, Colorado, spoke to the members of a chapter of P.E.O. (a national organization of college women) to which his wife belonged. He proposed that the nearby sand dunes, which abut the Crestone Peaks in the San Luis Valley and are some of the largest inland dunes in the world, receive some kind of permanent protection. His wife, Elizabeth Spencer, and other women, such as Jean Corlett and Myrtle Woods, organized a drive to bring this about. In 1932, largely through the efforts of P.E.O. chapters in Alamosa, Monte Vista, and Del Norte, President Herbert Hoover signed the proclamation that created the Great Sand Dunes National Monument.

Many years later, **Bettie Willard** and **Estella Leopold**, backed by the Sierra Club and the Colorado Mountain Club, respectively, led the fight to preserve some of the most remarkable fossil beds in the world, situated thirty-five miles west of Colorado Springs. Bettie, a plant ecologist who had earned her doctorate at the University of Colorado, was on the staff of the Thorne Ecological Foundation. Estella was a research paleontologist with the U.S. Geological Survey in Denver; she had studied the fossil beds extensively. (Her father was the famous conservationist Aldo Leopold.) For three years, allied with the Colorado Open Space Council, the women battled it out with indifferent politicians and developers. But finally, in August 1969, the six-thousand-acre Florissant Fossil Beds National Monument became a reality. Bettie and Estella were jointly awarded the Colorado Wildlife Federation's "Conservationist of the Year" award.

Bettie Willard's part in preserving the Florissant Fossil Lake Beds is but one of dozens of her accomplishments. Her studies of how people affect tundra, conducted on Trail Ridge Road in Rocky Mountain National Park, have influenced the administration of public lands throughout the country. Bettie was not included in the chapter about botanists because her influence goes so far beyond that and because at least half a book would be needed to do her justice. She is a writer, a teacher, a researcher, a superb organizer, and a catalyst for sweeping national and international changes.

There are several other contemporary Colorado women who have played a major part in protecting the state's mountain country. One is **Elizabeth Nitze Paepcke**, who first came to Colorado in 1917. She and her family stayed at Longs Peak Inn, where, influenced by Enos Mills, she became "interested in mountain climbing and the study of the ecology of the Estes Park surroundings."[1] Many years later she and her husband, Walter, became known for preserving the Victorian charm of Aspen, Colorado, and for making the city a cultural center. In 1966 Elizabeth gave Aspen nearly thirty acres of tranquil, undeveloped land close to the city's center and worth millions of dollars. She also established the Aspen Center for Environmental Studies (ACES).

Muriel MacGregor, an Estes Park resident with a law degree, who died in 1970, willed that her mountain ranch of nearly two thousand acres be used for charitable and educational purposes. Thirteen years later, after acrimonious lawsuits, her desire was finally realized. The Department of the Interior paid four million dollars for a conservation easement to the property, which by that time had been reduced to twelve hundred acres because of heirs' claims, lawyers' fees, and taxes. The MacGregor Ranch is now within the boundaries of Rocky Mountain National Park, although it is managed by its own board of directors.

And finally there is **Forrest Ketchin**, who painstakingly drew a map that color-coded degrees of human abuse in drainages of the Indian Peaks Wilderness, west of Boulder. Her map was a significant influence in the Forest Service's decision in the 1980s to restrict camping and fires in the wilderness, especially on the too-popular east side of the Divide.

The conservationists are only some of the women omitted from this book. There are others. **Martha Maxwell** came to Colorado Territory in 1860, a few years after Julia Archibald Holmes climbed Pikes Peak. Martha, who had attended Oberlin College, and her husband, James, eventually settled in Boulder with their only child, Mabel, and Martha's half-sister, Mary Dartt. Caught in an unhappy marriage, Martha devoted much of her energy to taxidermy, often leaving her husband and daughter to fend for themselves. Martha frequently camped in the mountains, sometimes alone, to shoot specimens. In the process she carefully observed the habits and surroundings of birds and animals and became a first-rate naturalist. She displayed her mounted creatures innovatively, "sculpturing" them into lively postures and simulating their natural habitats in backgrounds that she fabricated. At the American Centennial Exhibition of 1876 she represented Colorado, assembling a huge display of Colorado birds and animals in their natural surroundings. Martha answered endless questions from the public, which was highly intrigued by this tiny, feminine "Diana," dressed in a hunting costume.

After the Exhibition, James begged Martha to come home to Boulder. She never did, choosing to live in the Boston area. Although she found barely enough work to support herself, Martha happily studied college chemistry and biology and became active in the Women's Congress. However, she neglected her health and died at the age of fifty in 1881. (The specific cause of death was an ovarian tumor.) None of her mounted specimens have survived, but a variety of owl, now known as *Otus asio maxwelliae*, is named for her.

In 1870 **Helen Henderson Chain** came to Denver as the young bride of J. A. (James Albert) Chain, a partner in the Chain and Hardy stationers and bookstore. Helen, who had acquired an interest in art at a seminary in Jacksonville, Indiana, began taking painting lessons from a Mr. Porter in Denver. Evidently she learned quickly, for a few years later, after Porter's death, she succeeded him as a painting instructor. In 1876 her oil of Longs Peak was sent to the American Centennial Exhibition in Philadelphia. She regularly exhibited her own work and that of her pupils. In 1878 the renowned painter Thomas Moran praised a sketch she had made of Sierra Blanca viewed from La Veta Mountain. Helen not only painted mountains but also climbed them. Her ascents included several fourteeners: Torreys Peak, Mount Lincoln, Longs Peak, and Pikes Peak. She was the first woman to paint the Mount of the Holy Cross and probably the first woman to climb it.

Although J. A.'s health was poor, he and Helen took camping trips throughout Colorado. In 1885, or possibly earlier, Helen visited the cliff dwellings of Mesa Verde for the first time. The Chains traveled so much— to Yellowstone, the Grand Canyon, Yosemite, Mexico, and Europe—that relatives nicknamed Helen "Trot." In 1892 she and J. A. embarked on a trip around the world. Their ship was wrecked in the China Sea and they drowned.

Helen's paintings are housed in the basement of the Colorado Historical Society, the Healy House in Leadville, and the University of Colorado Law School. Two exquisite watercolors, one depicting the Mount of the Holy Cross, hang in the MacGregor Ranch museum in Estes Park. But most of Helen Chain's paintings are forgotten, whereas those of her pupil Charles Partridge Adams are well known.

In 1882 **Anne Ellis**, then five or six years old, and her family arrived in

Bonanza, ten thousand feet above sea level, near the San Luis Valley. There Anne grew up poor, but she was powerfully touched by the beauty of the mountains and by the humor and poignancy of life in a gold-mining town. Although she never went beyond the fifth reader in school, she came to love books and learning. Anne married when she was seventeen, was widowed, married again, and was widowed a second time. A friend described her as a "wild spirit compelled by circumstances to knuckle down. . . . Her eyes looked out with a humorous and faintly satiric gleam."[2] To support herself and her two children, she took in sewing and spent summers cooking at mountain camps for miners, sheepshearers, a haying crew, and a government telephone-construction gang. Then, much to the surprise of Anne and all who knew her, she ran for Saguache County Treasurer and won. (Saguache County is in the mountains of western Colorado.)

Shortly after she began a third term, Anne contracted asthma and was forced to quit work. While trying to recover her health in New Mexico sanitariums, she began writing a book about her life in Bonanza. Anne's recall was so good, and her language so vivid, that a Harvard professor called *The Life of an Ordinary Woman* (1929) one of the most expressive human documents about western life that he had ever read. She wrote two more autobiographical books, *Plain Anne Ellis* (1931) and *Sunshine Preferred* (1934). Throughout her books and letters she talked about the beauty of the mountains and their wildflowers, and how they restored her.

In 1938, when Anne was in her early sixties, she received an honorary master of letters degree from the University of Colorado. A few months later she died in Denver and was buried in Bonanza. Her attitude about life was summed up in *Sunshine Preferred*. "It may be a helluva life," she wrote. "Still, it's the best one we know and I'm damned if I'll let it down me. I may tremble at life, I may shake my fist and thumb my nose at it, still, at the same time, I waft it a kiss."[3]

Muriel Sibell Wolle grew up in Brooklyn and was educated at what is now the Parsons School of Design in New York City. In 1926 she arrived at the University of Colorado campus in Boulder to instruct in the newly formed art department. A few weeks later, on a bus trip to the mining towns of Central City and Black Hawk, Muriel had her first look at mine dumps, decaying and abandoned buildings, and weathered headframes. She discovered that the mountains were strewn with such remnants, and she vowed to paint and draw them all.

Muriel was a city person, timid about camping out, and had no talent for climbing over rough country. Yet she felt such a sense of urgency to immortalize Colorado's ghost towns before they disappeared that she became fearless in her quests to track them down. She hired drivers to jeep her up abandoned roads, she forded rushing streams, and she tramped through bogs and boulder fields to follow leads about old settlements. Muriel developed a shorthand technique: she made hundreds of quick sketches on her trips and then, at her leisure, completed the lithographic crayon drawing of the sketches, sometimes at a party with good friends and often many years after she'd visited the site.

In 1949 Muriel published *Stampede to Timberline*, thanks largely to the encouragement of her husband, Francis Wolle, an English professor at the University of Colorado. The book, which describes Colorado's mining towns, has become a classic and is still in print. Later Muriel wrote *The Bonanza Trail* (1953), which describes mining camps throughout the entire West; *Montana Pay Dirt* (1963); and *Timberline Tailings* (1977), which contains new information on Colorado ghost towns and was published posthumously. She died in 1976 at the age of seventy-eight. The fine arts building on the University of Colorado Boulder campus is named for her.

In 1938 two writers from Colorado Springs, **Belle Turnbull** and **Helen Rich**, made a permanent move across the Divide to Breckenridge in the isolated, high-mountain county of Summit. They settled into a primitive log cabin, which lacked running water, electricity, and telephone, in order to concentrate on writing while living in the mountains they loved so well. Helen, who was forty-four, took a job as a caseworker in the county welfare department. Belle, who was fifty-six, apparently had sufficient outside income that she didn't have to work.

Fifteen years earlier Belle, a member of the Colorado Mountain Club, had written "Mountain-Mad," which described her intense—and inexplicable—love of the mountains.

Mountains cast spells on me—
Why, because of the way
Earth-heaps lie, should I be
Choked by joy mysteriously;
Stilled or drunken-gay?

Why should a brown hill-trail
Tug at my feet to go?

Why should a boggy swale
Tune my heart to a nameless tale
Mountain marshes know?

Timberline, and the trees
Wind-whipped, and the sand between—
Why am I mad for these?
What dim thirst do they appease?
What filmed sense brush clean?[4]

Their house on French Street looked out on the Tenmile Range, a view that suited Belle and Helen. They delighted in the physical rigors of their new life. Belle commented that a Vassar education hadn't taught her how to "deal with frozen water pipes, or how to break trail through a 14-inch fall of snow with webs [snowshoes], or how to get rid of packrats, or how to hang a haunch of venison or how to cut up a jab of firewood for a Franklin Stove." Helen found woodchopping therapeutic. "The beauty of the thing about living where I do," she wrote, "is that I've got a woodpile when I come home from a day's work with nerves all frayed out. I go to work on the woodpile, saw wood, then split it into kindling if necessary; then I'm ready to go to work on the typewriter."[5]

After the move to Summit County, Helen wrote two published novels, *The Spring Begins* (1947) and *The Willowbender* (1950), as well as an unpublished novel about a local legendary dancehall girl named Silverheels. Belle received the Harriet Monroe prize, selected by *Poetry* magazine, a few months after her move to Summit County in 1938. (Dylan Thomas was one of a dozen other poets to receive the award.) She also published a "novel in verse," *The Goldboat* (1940); a prose novel, *The Far Side of the Hill* (1953); and two volumes of poetry, of which the better known is *The Ten Mile Range* (1957). Belle and Helen used Summit County—its mountains, mines and people—for their subject matter. Although all their books are now out of print, they are well worth reading because of their high literary quality and historical interest. The women wrote about the West as they observed it, minus the romance and myths that their contemporaries so often described. Belle died in 1970, at the age of 88, and Helen a year later.

In 1911, when they were small children, **Alice** and **Helen Dickerson** moved "up the Buckhorn," west of Fort Collins, with their parents, who proved up on the last homestead in the canyon. The sisters have lived there ever since. Although they've added a few modern conveniences, such as propane lamps, their way of living has stayed much the same for nearly eighty years. The sisters still cook on a wood range and use water piped from a spring on the hill behind their house.

Through the years they've earned cash with a variety of jobs, such as boarding work crews or cooking for fishing resorts on the Poudre River. They once gathered alpine plants for a California nursery. Another summer they collected lodgepole pinecones, which they sold to the Forest Service for seeds. The Dickersons kept dairy cows for many years and became well known for the cream and sweet butter they sold in town. Helen ran a summer roadside stand in which she sold her own homemade goods, such as pine-needle baskets, fudge, divinity, chocolate-covered candy bars (which she called "mountain maids"), and clocks carved like wooden lace. During the Great Depression, Alice learned how to run a trapline, earning enough money to buy a car. She gave up trapping long ago, however, and objects to killing any animals (except an occasional "pest"), on principle. In recent years she banded birds, without pay, until the required paperwork got to be too much. Now Alice no longer drives a car. Friends, neighbors, and Forest Service rangers deliver mail and groceries and help out with fencing and cutting firewood. To show their appreciation, Helen and Alice give away vegetables from their garden or bread hot from the oven and spread with the wild-berry jam they make.

There were yet other women in the mountains quietly "doing their thing." In 1909, for example, **Olga Schaaf Little**, born in Germany, took her first packtrain of burros up to the Ruby Mine on Junction Creek in the rugged La Plata Mountains of southwest Colorado. (For many high-mountain mines, packtrains were the only means of taking equipment and supplies to the local mines and carrying ore back down.) A Durango liveryman who was short on men and knew that Olga was skilled with horses persuaded her to try packing, often a difficult and dangerous job, by telling her how high the pay was compared with the wages for women's jobs. Despite her initial skepticism, Olga became a good packer, never uttering a cussword and never mistreating her animals. For thirty years she packed into the high mines of the La Platas, winter and summer. She always followed the advice given her when she was quite young: to trust her animals and never force them to go where they balked.

Vena Apgar (Snyder), the mother of three children, chauffeured passengers up the Big Thompson Canyon. Her husband, who hauled freight in a Stanley Steamer truck for the Loveland–Estes Park Auto Stage Company, was responsible for her unusual job. After the birth of their first son, he'd asked Vena if she wanted a baby carriage or a Stanley Steamer. When she chose the latter, he taught her how to drive her new car on narrow mountain roads and how to manage the intricacies of the boiler. From 1913 to 1925 Vena drove a Stanley Steamer for the stage company. She was so skilled that the local celebrity "Lord" Jack Ogilvy of the *Denver Post* staff always requested her as his driver.

In 1919 **Helen Dowe**, an artist, became the first female fire lookout for the U.S. Forest Service. She served on the Devil's Head station in the Pike National Forest, near Colorado Springs, for two years, from May to October, until her marriage to a surveyor, John Burgess.

Augusta Mengedoht, reputedly a concert violinist from Omaha, Nebraska, broke her back while riding a horse on the desert, probably in the early 1930s. Although doctors told her she'd never walk again, she was convinced she'd recover her health if she moved to Colorado. Augusta was right. In 1935, having spent several summers managing the dining rooms for local resorts, she purchased the Fawnbrook Inn in Allenspark, a mountain settlement fifteen miles south of Estes Park. In the course of repairing her building, she became the first female licensed plumber in the state. Augusta also acted as head cook and, when time permitted, as a trail guide for horseback parties. In 1946 she sold the inn (still a thriving restaurant today) and helped build her "dream house" on what is now the Skinner Road near Allenspark. Eventually, when she could no longer shovel snow because of back troubles, she sold her house. In 1977, at the age of eighty-four, Augusta died in a nursing home in Longmont, Colorado.

But what do they add up to—these female climbers, skiers, writers, artists, botanists, conservationists, packers, physicians, taxidermists, innkeepers, chauffeurs, trail builders, homesteaders? What ties such a disparate bunch together? Their most obvious commonality is that they were white Anglos. If comparable minority women existed, they were omitted from written records. However, I suspect that comparable minority mountain women did not exist in Colorado, for this was a land in which white, Anglo men were in control. And, as Patricia Limerick has pointed out in her book *The Legacy of Conquest*, from the beginning, racism has been prevalent in western states such as Colorado. It seems very unlikely that a woman could have been Hispanic, black, Oriental, or a non-Anglo white *and* conspicuously unconventional in the mountains, where she was often by herself. It was tough enough for a white, Anglo female.

Another thread that binds the subjects of this book together is that they were from backgrounds in which education was valued. In many cases they grew up in affluence, but I suspect this is not important in and of itself; the key is that their families valued education for daughters—an attitude unusual for the times—and that they supported their daughters' educations, usually financially but always emotionally. Martha Maxwell attended Oberlin College, the first coeducational institution of higher learning in the United States, opened in 1833. Dr. Susan Anderson graduated from the University of Michigan, one of the first institutions to admit women to medical school. Hazel Schmoll was the first woman to earn a doctorate in botany from the University of Chicago, one of the first major universities that were coeducational from the beginning. Other subjects in this book graduated from the very first colleges for women in the United States, founded in the 1800s, that offered the same curricula as men's schools. The "Seven Sister" colleges—Mount Holyoke, Smith, Vassar, Bryn Mawr, and Wellesley, Barnard, and Radcliffe—became known for their excellence at the same time they were criticized for producing unfeminine graduates. For women, higher education went hand in hand with membership in sororities or student government organizations, which proved to be training grounds for effective leadership in postcollegiate activities.

Basically, the early Colorado mountain women were not so different from their educated sisters in other parts of the country. In both the West and the East, educated women were suffragists, ardent members of women's organizations, intellects, and fearless originals. (And the adventurous Englishwomen Isabella Bird and Rose Pender, though unusual, were by no means unique among their educated, Victorian countrywomen.) The difference between the subjects of this book and their nonmountain counterparts is more of degree than of kind. Still, encounters with mountains put extraordinary demands on body and mind. The terrain was steep and often a wild tangle of nature. The air was short on oxygen, the weather cruel. Distances were sweeping; loneliness, or at least isolation, was endemic. Entering the Colorado high country, women left behind a predictable support system, exchanging it for a self-reliance that almost none had been adequately prepared for. This is true even today, although to a lesser extent.

The Colorado mountains forced women, as well as men, to rapidly establish their priorities, to separate social niceties from practical ways of coping. Ultimately, the experience produced women—and men—as lofty as the mountains they touched.

Glossary

Anchor A means of attaching the climber's rope to the rock.

Arete A steep ridge.

Belay To manage a rope in such a way that one climber can check a fall of another climber.

Bolt An artificial anchor placed in a drilled hole.

Bouldering Climbing boulders or small rock outcroppings.

Carabiner A metal "safety pin" through which a rope may be inserted, usually to an anchor.

Chimney A crack in the rock wide enough for a climber.

Clip in To attach the climber's rope to an anchor, usually by means of a carabiner.

Crack A crack in the rock too narrow for a climber.

Crampons Metal spikes attached to boots for walking on ice or hard snow.

Crux Pitch The most difficult pitch of a climb and the one that determines the climb's numerical rating of difficulty.

Dihedral A "corner" where two rock faces meet, approximately at a right angle.

Direct aid Devices, other than the rock itself, used to assist in climbing.

Exposed Long and steep enough that a fall will be fatal.

Face A relatively smooth expanse of rock.

Fourteener A mountain over 14,000 feet in elevation. Of the sixty-seven peaks in the contiguous United States over 14,000 feet, fifty-four are in Colorado, of which the highest is Elbert at 14,433. Only 14,495-foot Mount Whitney in California is higher.

Free climbing Climbing in which only the rock itself is used for handholds and footholds, in contrast to *direct-aid* climbing.

Leader	The climber who goes first.
Move	A climber's single maneuver on rock, comparable to a single step on a horizontal surface.
Pitch	The distance between two belay stances, often the length of the rope between climbers.
Pulaski	A combination axe-pick used in constructing trails.
Protection	An anchor, such as a piton, chock, nut, or friend.
Rappel	A quick means of a controlled descent by sliding down a rope.
Sling	A short length of rope used for attaching a carabiner and rope to an anchor.
Technical climb	A climb on ice, snow, or rock which is rated Class 5 or above. (Class 1 is hiking on trails; Class 2, hiking and bushwhacking; Class 3, scrambling in which rope may or may not be used; Class 4, climbing where some protection is occasionally used. Class 5 are the most severe free climbs and require the use of protection. Class 6 are direct-aid climbs.)
Telemark turn	A type of ski touring turn first developed in Telemark, Norway, once described as a cross between a ballroom dance step and a curtsy.
Third-classing	Free climbing without using any rope or protection.
Three-pin binding	A means of attaching a ski boot to a cross-country ski that allows free movement of the heel, thus requiring much skill in executing downhill turns.
Traverse	A climb that contours or angles across the terrain.
Wall	An enormous face of rock.

CHAPTER I

Sources
and
Notes

Sources

I found that Francis Keenlyside, *Peaks and Pioneers: The Story of Mountaineering* (London: Paul Elek, 1975), was extremely useful in learning about the early history of mountaineering in Europe. For early Colorado mountaineering history, I relied on William M. Bueler, *Roof of the Rockies: A History of Mountaineering in Colorado* (Boulder: Pruett Publishing Co., 1974) and Bob Godfrey and Dudley Chelton, *Climb!* (Boulder: Alpine House Publishing, 1977).

Agnes Wright Spring, *A Bloomer Girl on Pike's Peak 1858* (Denver: Denver Public Library, 1949), provided virtually all the background for the biography of Julia Archibald Holmes, supplemented by sources I have cited.

Although most of my information about Addie Alexander came from Colorado newspapers, I also consulted James Willard and Colin Goodykoontz, *Colorado Colonization 1866–1872* (Boulder: N.p., 1926).

I relied heavily on Giraud Chester, *Embattled Maiden* (New York: G. P. Putnam's Sons, 1951), to chronicle Anna Dickinson's life. In addition I used Anna Dickinson's own book, *A Ragged Register (of People, Places and Opinions)* (New York: Harper and Brothers, 1879); Franklin Rhoda, *Summits to Reach: Report on the Topography of the San Juan County* ed. Mike Foster (Boulder: Pruett Publishing Co., 1984); various newspapers (all cited); and a copy of a letter from James T. Gardiner.

Source material about Isabella Bird came primarily from her book *A Lady's Life in the Rocky Mountains* (1879; reprint, Norman: University of Oklahoma Press, 1960), from transcripts of her unedited letters to

Henrietta Bird, from Anna M. Stoddart, *The Life of Isabella Bird (Mrs. Bishop)* (London: N.p., 1907) in the collection of P. C. Gottlieb, and from the first edition of Enos A. Mills, *The Story of Estes Park and a Guide Book* (Estes Park: N.p., 1905). I also found the following books very helpful: Dorothy Middleton, *Victorian Lady Travellers* (New York: E. P. Dutton and Co., 1965), and Mabel Downer Durning, *Historical Reminiscing in the Allenspark Mountain Area* (Longmont: N.p., 1975).

All the material about Rose Pender came from a book she wrote, *A Lady's Experiences in the Wild West in 1883* (1888; reprint, Lincoln: University of Nebraska Press, 1978). Information about the Signal Service came from James H. Smith, "A Winter on Pike's Peak," *Youth's Companion*, March 10, 1887.

Elkanah J. Lamb, *Miscellaneous Meditations* (Denver: Publishers' Press Room and Bindery Co., [ca. 1913]), was my primary source in writing about Carrie Welton. Also consulted were John L. Jerome Hart, *Fourteen Thousand Feet* (Denver: Colorado Mountain Club, 1925), and a photocopy of selected pages from Joseph Anderson, ed., *The Town and City of Waterbury, Connecticut, from the Aboriginal Period to the Year Eighteen Hundred and Ninety-Five*, vol. 3 (New Haven: Price and Lee Co., 1896), supplied by the Connecticut Historical Society. As always, Louisa Ward Arps and Elinor Eppich Kingery, *High Country Names* (Denver: Colorado Mountain Club, 1966), was invaluable.

Frederick H. Chapin, *Mountaineering in Colorado: The Peaks about Estes* (Boston: Appalachian Mountain Club, 1889; reprint, Lincoln: University of Nebraska Press, 1987), provided estimates about the number of people climbing Longs Peak in the late 1800s.

Information about Victoria Broughm was derived mostly from Joe Mills, *A Mountain Boyhood* (New York: J. H. Sears and Co., 1926; reprint, Lincoln: University of Nebraska Press, 1988), and from Enos Mills, *Wild Life on the Rockies* (Boston and New York: Houghton Mifflin, 1909; reprint, Lincoln: University of Nebraska Press, 1988). However, a few details came from Enos A. Mills, *Early Estes Park*, 5th ed. (Estes Park: Robert H. and Enda Kiley, 1980).

Notes

1. *The Journals of Zebulon M. Pike with Letters and Related Documents*, ed. Donald Jackson (Norman: University of Oklahoma Press, 1966), 1:345.

2. W. Anderson, in *Outing* 15, no.4 (January 1890): 265.

3. J. A. Archibald [Julia Archibald Holmes], "A Journey to Pikes Peak and New Mexico," *Sibyl* 3, no.18 (March 15, 1859): 521–31. Unless otherwise noted, the following quotations concerning Julia Archibald Holmes are from this source.

4. Julia Archibald Holmes, letter to Jane B. Archibald, "From the Rocky Mountains—Mrs. Holmes Ascends Pike's Peak," *Lawrence Republican*, October 7, 1858).

5. William N. Byers in *Rocky Mountain News*, September 28, 1864, as cited in William M. Bueler, *Roof of the Rockies*, 32.

6. *Boulder County News*, August 26, 1871.

7. "A Trip in the Mountains and up Long's Peak," *Greeley Colorado Sun*, August 14, 1873.

8. *Rocky Mountain News*, August 9, 1873.

9. *Boulder County News*, June 21, 1873; *Georgetown Miner*, as cited in *Rocky Mountain News*, November 17, 1969.

10. Giraud Chester, *Embattled Maiden*, 114; Anna Dickinson, *A Ragged Register (Of People, Places and Opinions)*, 260.

11. *Rocky Mountain News*, September 6, 1873.

12. James T. Gardiner, transcript of letter written to his mother from Middle Boulder, September 10, 1873, John L. Jerome Hart Papers, Department of Special Collections, University of Colorado Libraries, Boulder.

13. *Rocky Mountain News*, September 21, 1873.

14. Ibid.; *Boulder County News*, September 19, 1873.

15. *Boulder County News*, September 26, 1873.

16. Isabella Bird, *A Lady's Life in the Rocky Mountains*. Unless otherwise noted, the following quotations concerning Isabella Bird are from this source, pp.72–207.

17. In Enos A. Mills, *The Story of Estes Park and a Guide Book*. The following quotations of Platt Rogers are from this source, pp.18–25.

18. Anna M. Stoddart, *The Life of Isabella Bird (Mrs. Bishop)*.

19. Isabella Bird, transcript of Letter 4 to Henrietta Bird, November 18–20, 1873, Department of Western History, Denver Public Library.

20. Rose Pender, *A Lady's Experiences in the Wild West in 1883*. Unless otherwise noted, the following quotations concerning Rose Pender are from this source, pp.56–61.

21. Elkanah J. Lamb, *Miscellaneous Meditations*. Unless otherwise noted, the following quotations concerning Carrie Welton are from this source, pp.72–89.

22. Enos A. Mills, *Wild Life on the Rockies*. Unless otherwise noted, the following quotations concerning Victoria Broughm are from this source, pp.138–40.

23. Joe Mills, *A Mountain Boyhood*. The following quotations are from this source, pp.212–14.

CHAPTER 2

Sources

Information about the Ladies Hiking Club of Fraser is derived from a citation in Robert C. Black III, *Island in the Rockies: The Pioneer Era of Grand County, Colorado*, 2d ed. (Granby, Colo.: Grand County Pioneer Society, 1978).

Most of the information about the Burnell sisters is from Enos A. Mills, *The Adventures of a Nature Guide* (Garden City, N.Y.: Doubleday, Page and Co., 1923), and from Hildegarde Hawthorne and Esther Burnell Mills, *Enos Mills of the Rockies* (Boston: Houghton Mifflin Co., 1935). Other sources were "Cabin Holds Legacy of Enos Mills," *Longmont Daily Times Call*, June 6, 7, 1981; corrections to a draft of this manuscript by Enda Mills Kiley, September 22, 1986; a taped interview of Enda Mills Kiley, June 28, 1974, in the Estes Park Library, Estes Park; a taped interview of Mrs. O. L. (Crete) Dever by the author, April 1985; a taped interview of Patience Kemp by the author, January 17, 1986; and a taped interview, "The Thirties in Estes Park: A Museum Program," in the Estes Park Library.

The quoted material about the Pifer sisters came from a 1979 taped interview of Anne Pifer Austill by Lulabeth Melton and from a 1985 video of Anne Pifer Austill taped by Jack Melton and Lulabeth Melton; both sources are in the Dorsey Museum at the YMCA of the Rockies in Estes Park. Other sources were letters from Anne Pifer Austill to the author; a brochure about Anne Austill titled "World Reports Personalized"; Mary Howarth, "Anne Pifer Austill Recalls Estes Park Area of 1920s," in *Estes Park Trail Gazette*; Kent Dannen and Donna Dannen, *Rocky Mountain National Park Hiking Trails, Including Indian Peaks,* 4th rev. ed. (Charlotte, N.C.: East Woods Press, 1983); and Jack R. Melton and Lulabeth Melton, *YMCA of the Rockies: 1907–1982* (Estes Park: YMCA of the Rockies, 1982).

Most of the information about Eleanor Davis Ehrman was derived from two taped interviews: one made by Elinor Eppich Kingery and Eleanor Vincent, November 3, 1983, located at the Colorado Historical Society, Denver, and one made by the author, May 14, 1985. In addition, Robert Ormes provided many details in a taped interview with the author, May 13, 1985. Also consulted were Jane Koerner, "Peaking at History: Eleanor Davis—Colorado's Greatest Woman Mountaineer," *Colorado Springs Magazine*, May 1983; J.L.J.H. [John L. Jerome Hart], "Albert R. Ellingwood, 1888–1934," *American Alpine Journal* (1935); and William M. Bueler, *Roof of the Rockies: A History of Mountaineering in Colorado* (Boulder: Pruett Publishing Co., 1974).

A taped interview of Eleanor Bliss, March 23, 1985, was my major source for the biography of Marjorie Perry. I am indebted to Eleanor Bliss for permission to quote from her unpublished manuscript, "Crossing the Rockies Astride in 1926," and for her corrections to drafts of this manuscript. Marjorie Perry also provided material through her article, "When Skiers Were a Curiosity," *Trail and Timberline*, no.558 (January 1950). And her nephew, Bob Perry, and his wife, Ruth, supplied invaluable details through letters and conversations, as well as excellent photographs of

Marjorie. Other sources were Carol McMurrough, "Marjorie Perry: Woman of the West," *Denver Post*, May 4, 1969; Lief Hovelsen, *The Flying Norseman* (Ishpeming, Mich.: National Ski Hall of Fame Press, 1983); "Marjorie Perry, Obituary," *Denver Post*, August 4, 1969; and Edward T. Bollinger, *Rails That Climb* (Golden: Colorado Railroad Museum, 1979).

My main sources for writing about Harriet Vaille Bouck were a taped interview of Harriet Bouck Irving by the author, February 4, 1986, and letters from, as well as a phone conversation with, Polly Bouck. I also relied on Harriet Vaille, "Arapaho Hunting Grounds Revisited," *Trail and Timberline*, no.558 (June 1965); M. P., "End of the Trail: Harriet Vaille Bouck," *Trail and Timberline*, no.519 (March 1962); Louisa Ward Arps and Elinor Eppich Kingery, *High Country Names* (Denver: Colorado Mountain Club, 1966); "Colorado Geographic Board," *Trail*, November 1914; Oliver W. Toll, *Arapaho Names and Trails* (N.p.: Privately printed, 1962); and scrapbooks and clippings, "Colorado Mountain Club," Box 144, Colorado Historical Society.

Many of the details and quotations about Agnes Vaille's climb of Longs Peak came from a little-known and apparently unpublished manuscript written by Charles Edwin Hewes, one of the original owners of the Hewes-Kirkwood Lodge (now the Rocky Ridge Music Center). The first part of the manuscript is Hewes's recording of Walter Kiener's account of his climb of the East Face with Agnes Vaille, as Hewes remembered the account two days after their conversation on December 29, 1931. The second part of the manuscript consists of some personal notes by Hewes about Walter Kiener and Agnes Vaille. Thanks to

Gayle Waldrop and Everett Long, I became aware of the existence of this manuscript. Thanks to Robert Bauer, I was put in touch with Ken and Laurie Houde, who had discovered the manuscript in the back of a drawer of a secondhand file cabinet they had purchased in 1983. I am deeply indebted to the Houdes for granting me permission to quote from the Hewes-Kiener manuscript.

Elinor Eppich Kingery was extraordinarily helpful in providing material about Agnes Vaille. She permitted me to read her unpublished manuscript and other material she had written, located in the Colorado Historical Society Archives. She also wrote me letters and patiently corrected several drafts of my manuscript. And again, Harriet Bouck Irving and Polly Bouck gave me much assistance.

Other sources were Barbara J. Euser, ed., *A Climber's Climber: On the Trail with Carl Blaurock* (Colorado: Cordiellera Press, 1984); William L. Myatt, "The Colorado Mountain Club," *Colorado Magazine*, October 1962; Stephen H. Hart, "The Bishop: A Rock Climb in Platte Canon," *Trail and Timberline*, no.143 (September 1930); Carl A. Blaurock, "Tragedy on Longs Peak," Denver Westerners' *Roundup*, September–October 1981; articles about Agnes Vaille's death, in January 1925 issues of the *Rocky Mountain News* and the *Estes Park Trail* and the February 1925 issue of *Trail and Timberline*; "Notes by the Editor," *Trail and Timberline*, no.77 (February 1925); the John L. Jerome Hart Scrapbook, located in the Department of Special Collections, University of Colorado Libraries, Boulder; the obituary of Walter Kiener, in the *Estes Park Trail*, March 31, 1961, loaned by Lillie Asmus; and a report by C. C. Way, Rocky Mountain National Park File #143 (March 9, 1920), located in the Archives, Rocky Mountain National Park Headquarters, Estes Park.

Information on the two Dorothy Colliers came primarily from Dorothy Ellen Collier Bullivant's letters to the author and her corrections to drafts of the manuscript. Other sources were Merrill J. Mattes, "The Boulderfield Hotel: A Distant Summer in the Shadow of Longs Peak," *Colorado Heritage* 1 (Spring 1986); conversations with Everett Long; and Paul Nesbit, *Longs Peak: Its Story and a Climbing Guide*, 7th ed. (Colorado Springs: Paul Nesbit, 1969).

Notes

1. "A Great Walking Club," *Outing* 9, no.4 (January 1887): 381.

2. J. A. Shepard, acting superintendent, Rocky Mountain National Park File #143 (December 6, 1920), 3, Archives, Rocky Mountain National Park Headquarters, Estes Park.

3. Enos A. Mills, *The Story of Estes Park and a Guide Book*, (Estes Park: N.p., 1905), 93–95.

4. Patience Kemp, taped interview with the author, January 17, 1986.

5. "Rocky Mountain National Park Annual Reports, 1915–1930" (1917), Archives, Rocky Mountain National Park Headquarters; Mrs. O. L. (Crete) Dever, taped interview with the author, April 1985.

6. F. O. Way, superintendent, "Monthly Report March, 1918" (1917), Archives, Rocky Mountain National Park Headquarters.

7. Anne Pifer Austill, video tape by Jack Melton and Lulabeth Melton, Summer 1985, Dorsey Museum, YMCA of the Rockies, Estes Park. The following quotations concerning Anne and Isabel Pifer are from this source.

8. Eleanor Davis Ehrman, taped interview with Elinor Eppich Kingery and Eleanor Vincent, November 3, 1983, Colorado Historical Society, Denver.

9. Eleanor Davis Ehrman, taped interview with the author May 14, 1985. Unless otherwise noted, the following quotations of Eleanor Davis Ehrman are from this source.

10. Robert Ormes, taped interview with the author, May 13, 1985.

11. Ibid.

12. Albert R. Ellingwood, "Climbing in the Sangre de Cristo," *Trail and Timberline*, no.4 (June 1925). Unless otherwise noted, the following quotations concerning the climb are from this source, pp. 2, 4.

13. Jane Koerner, "Peaking at History: Eleanor Davis—Colorado's Greatest Woman Mountaineer."

14. Albert R. Ellingwood, "The Eastern Arete of the Crestone Needle," *Trail and Timberline*, no.81 (June 1925), 6, 8, 9.

15. Robert Ormes, letter to the author, November 3, 1988.

16. Carol McMurrough, "Marjorie Perry: Woman of the West," *Denver Post*, May 4, 1969.

17. Ibid.

18. Eleanor J. Bliss, "Crossing the Rockies Astride in 1926," unpublished manuscript, Collection of Eleanor J. Bliss. The following quotations concerning the trip are from this source.

19. Marjorie Perry, "When Skiers Were a Curiosity." The following quotations concerning the ski trip are from this source.

20. Harriet Vaille Bouck, "Arapaho Hunting Grounds Revisited."

21. Ibid.

22. Harriet Bouck Irving, taped interview with the author, February 4, 1986.

23. Polly Bouck, letter to the author, November 1986, Department of Special Collections, University of Colorado Libraries, Boulder; Irving, taped interview.

24. Bouck, letter to the author.

25. Ibid.

26. Bouck, letter to the author; Barbara J. Euser, ed., *A Climber's Climber: On the Trail with Carl Blaurock*, 5; "Agnes Wolcott Vaille," *Trail and Timberline*, no.77 (February 1925), 2.

27. Bouck, letter to the author.

28. "Agnes," *Trail and Timberline*, 2, 3; "Agnes Vaille Dies in Storm After Climbing Longs Peak," *Rocky Mountain News*, January 13, 1925.

29. Bouck, letter to the author.

30. Charles Edwin Hewes–Walter Kiener, Unpublished manuscript, [1931], Collection of Ken and Laurie Houde. Unless otherwise noted, the following quotations concerning Walter Kiener and his climbs with Agnes come from this source.

31. Elinor Eppich Kingery, comments on a note sent to Louisa Arps accompanying the manuscript of Jack Moomaw's *Recollections of a Rocky Mountain Ranger* (which he published in 1963), Colorado Historical Society.

32. Euser, *Climber's Climber*, 58.

33. "Notes by the Editor," *Trail and Timberline*, no.77 (February 1925), 9.

34. Agnes W. Vaille, Christmas card to Gayle Waldrop, December 1924, Collection of Gayle Waldrop.

35. Elinor Eppich Kingery, unpublished manuscript, November 20, 1963, Colorado Historical Society. The following quotations of Elinor Eppich Kingery are from this source.

36. Bouck, letter to the author.

37. Dorothy Ellen Collier Bullivant (Mrs. George), letter to the author, October 23, 1986. Unless otherwise noted, the

following quotations concerning the Colliers are from this source.

38. Merrill J. Mattes, "The Boulderfield Hotel, A Distant Summer in the Shadow of Longs Peak," 37.

CHAPTER 3

Sources

Most of the information about Virginia Donaghe McClurg came from letters, newspaper clippings, and scrapbooks in the Colorado College Library and in the Pioneers' Museum, both of which are located in Colorado Springs, and from the Archives, Mesa Verde National Park Headquarters, Mancos. The master's thesis of Patricia E. Hoben, "The Establishment of Mesa Verde as a National Park" (University of Oklahoma, 1966), presented invaluable background. I am especially grateful to Robert Ormes, whom I interviewed on May 13, 1985, for providing a rare, firsthand impression of Virginia McClurg, and to his father and mother, Manley Dayton and Virginia R. Ormes, whose *Book of Colorado Springs* (Colorado Springs: Dentan Printing Company, 1933), provided details I did not find elsewhere.

Information about early explorations of Mesa Verde came from a file in the Carnegie Historical Library of Boulder, including Jesse L. Nusbaum's 1926 paper, "Re-Excavation of Step House Cave," reprinted in 1981 by the Mesa Verde National Park Museum Association. I also consulted William H. Jackson and William M. Holmes, *Mesa Verde and the Four Corners Hayden Survey, 1874–1876* (Ouray, Colo.: Bear Creek Publishing Co., 1981), and perused F. H. Chapin, *The Land of the Cliff Dwellers* (Boston: W. B. Clarke and Co., 1892).

Other sources were Maurine S. Fletcher,

ed., *The Wetherills of the Mesa Verde: Autobiography of Benjamin Alfred Wetherill* (Lincoln: University of Nebraska Press, 1987), and Selim Hobart Peabody, comp., *The Peabody (Paybody, Pabody, Pabodie) Genealogy*, ed. Charles Henry Pope (Boston: Charles H. Pope, Publisher, 1909), thanks to Nancy Peabody McCaffrey.

Notes

1. Robert Ormes, taped interview with the author, May 13, 1985.

2. Mrs. Gilbert [Virginia] McClurg, "Two Annual Addresses by the Regent of the Colorado Cliff Dwellings Association" (Pueblo, 1903, and Denver, 1904), Virginia McClurg Papers, Colorado College Library, Colorado Springs.

3. Ibid. (1903); *Mancos (Colo.) Times*, October 13, 1899.

4. "Colorado Cliff Dwellings Association," 9, n.d., Irving Howbert Papers, Colorado College Library; *Denver Times*, May 2, 1900.

5. *Rocky Mountain News*, October 29, 1899.

6. *Denver Republican*, September 10, 1901.

7. Virginia McClurg, "The Story," Virginia McClurg Papers, Colorado College Library.

8. Virginia McClurg, "Theodore Roosevelt Appreciated Mesa Verde Cliff Dwellings and Associations," Virginia McClurg Papers, Colorado College Library; McClurg, "Two Annual Addresses" (1904).

9. "Colorado Cliff Dwellings Association," 3.

10. McClurg, "Two Annual Addresses" (1904).

11. Ibid. (1903, 1904).

12. "Make It a National Park," *Denver Post*, February 23, 1906.

13. Virginia McClurg, "Regent of the Colorado Cliff Dwellings Association Replies to an Editorial Attack," *Rocky Mountain News*, March 11, 1906.

14. Virginia McClurg, letter to Mrs. Decker, November 20, 1906, Virginia McClurg Collection, Colorado Springs Pioneers' Museum.

15. Ibid.

16. Jesse Nusbaum, "Comments for the Regional Director, Region Three," July 26, 1946, copy in Archives, Mesa Verde National Park Headquarters, Mancos.

17. Cited in a letter from Dr. J. L. Nusbaum to Don Watson, July 14, 1954, Archives, Mesa Verde National Park Headquarters.

18. "The Mystery of America—Ancient Cliff Dwellings Phantom Cliff Canon, Manitou, Colorado," Brochure, Virginia McClurg Collection, Colorado Pioneers' Springs Museum.

19. As quoted in Gilbert McClurg, Preface to *Poems by Virginia Donaghe McClurg* (Colorado Springs: Colorado College, 1933), vii, viii.

CHAPTER 4

Sources

My most valuable sources for the biography of "Doc" Susie Anderson were taped interviews of Glenn and Dianne Wilson, February 3, 1986; Mrs. Minnie Cole and Mrs. Hazel Briggs, April 17, 1986; Ruth and Ralph Phillips, January 16, 1986; and Dick Mulligan, January 16, 1986, all by the author. Also used were Leo Zuckerman, "81 Year Old Doc Susie Is Fraser's Only Physician," *Rocky Mountain News*, December 14, 1951; Cale Kenney, "Dr. Susan Anderson: The Story of the Gutsy Little Lady Who Doctored the Railroad Men, Lumberjacks and Ranchers of the Fraser Valley," *Alpenglow*, vol. 51, located in the Grand County Historical Association Museum Archives, Hot Sulphur Springs, Colorado; a letter to the author from Roger Brady, Susan Anderson's nephew, May 5, 1986; Mary Reed Stratton, Scrapbook and Miscellaneous Papers, 1939, Archives, Denver Medical Library, Denver; Idealia D. Baumgarten, "Pioneer Personalities," January 5, 1950 (Grand County Historical Association Museum archives); letters from Morris M. Long to the author, January 28 and March 4, 1986; a letter from Kerry Murphy to the author, February 11, 1986; a letter from Frank Carlson to the author, May 1886; Margery Frank, "Dr. Anderson Makes Her Calls," *Pic Magazine*, May 11, 1943, located in the Grand County Association Historical Museum Archives; and a conversation with Paul Gilbert, January 17, 1986.

The following books were also very useful: Edward T. Bollinger and Frederick Bauer, *The Moffat Road* (Chicago: Swallow Press, 1962); Edward T. Bollinger, *Rails that Climb*, ed. William C. Jones (Golden: Colorado Railroad Museum, 1979); and Robert C. Black III, *Island in the Rockies: The Pioneer Era of Grand County*, 2d ed. (Granby, Colo.: Grand County Pioneer Society 1969). Finally, I am grateful to the University of Michigan Alumni Association in Ann Arbor for sending me a copy of "'Doc Susie' Passes Away," July 1960, Clipping 16822; a copy of "June Meeting," *Regents Proceedings*, University of Michigan, 1897; and a copy of Eugene Foster, "'Doc Susie' Slows Down a Little at 81," *Washington Post*, August 17, 1952.

I learned about women homesteading in Colorado from Nell Brown Propst, *Those Strenuous Dames of the Colorado Prairie* (Boulder: Pruett Publishing Co., 1982);

from Margaret Duncan Brown, *Shepherdess of Elk River Valley*, ed. Paul E. Daugherty (Denver: Golden Bell Press, 1982); from a taped interview of Patience Cairns Kemp by the author, January 17, 1986; from a book by Patience's mother, Mary Lyons Cairns, *Grand Lake in the Olden Days* (N.p.: privately published, 1971); and from Feral Atkins's file in the Archives, Rocky Mountain National Park Headquarters, Estes Park.

Most of the material for the biography of Katherine Garetson came from her unpublished manuscript, "Katherine of Big Owl," Estes Park Library, Estes Park. I also received information from two taped interviews located in the Estes Park Library: one of McClelland G. Dings, made by Mel Busch, September 14, 1981, and one of Glen and Cleo Tallman, January 20, 1984. In addition, I used details from Elizabeth G. Dings's letters to the author, February 13, 1986, and October 31, 1986, and assorted issues of the *Estes Park Trail* from the 1920s.

Notes

1. Leo Zuckerman, "81 Year Old Doc Susie Is Fraser's Only Physician"; Dianne and Glenn Wilson, taped interview with the author, February 3, 1986.

2. Zuckerman, "81 Year Old Doc Susie."

3. Cale Kenney, "Dr. Susan Anderson: The Story of the Gutsy Little Lady Who Doctored the Railroad Men, Lumberjacks and Ranchers of the Fraser Valley"; Zuckerman, "81 Year Old Doc Susie."

4. Zuckerman, "81 Year Old Doc Susie."

5. Eugene Foster, "'Doc Susie' Slows Down a Little at 81"; Zuckerman, "81 Year Old Doc Susie."

6. Morris M. Long, letter to the author, March 4, 1986.

7. Idealia D. Baumgarten, "Pioneer Personalities"; Zuckerman, "81 Year Old Doc Susie."

8. Foster, "'Doc Susie' Slows Down."

9. Dianne and Glenn Wilson, taped interview.

10. Mary Reed Stratton, comp., "Outline Histories of Women Physicians of Colorado"; Dianne and Glenn Wilson, taped interview.

11. Ruth and Ralph Phillips, taped interview with the author, January 16, 1986.

12. Dobells was a solution used to irrigate wounds and throats. It was an aqueous solution consisting of sodium bicarbonate, borax, and phenol, a topical anesthetic in glycerine. (Information from Seymour Wheelock, M.D., conveyed by Anne Klenk, May 28, 1986.)

13. Ruth and Ralph Phillips, taped interview.

14. Baumgarten, "Pioneer Personalities."

15. Ruth and Ralph Phillips, taped interview.

16. Dianne and Glenn Wilson, taped interview; Kerry Murphy, response to questionnaire from the author, February 11, 1986.

17. Ruth and Ralph Phillips, taped interview.

18. Murphy, response to questionnaire; Dianne and Glenn Wilson, taped interview.

19. Kenney, "Dr. Susan Anderson."

20. Ruth and Ralph Phillips, taped interview. Frank Carlson, whose father owned the pool hall in question, wrote a letter to the author (May 1986) in which he stated: "I did not hear of this game, but it is very possible that it occurred. One of the preachers took up some money for a church

bell and got in one of the poker games in town and lost the money. The fellows heard about it and bought a bell for the church."

21. Minnie Cole and Hazel Briggs, taped interview with the author, April 17, 1986.

22. Dianne and Glenn Wilson, taped interview.

23. This and the following quotes concerning Katherine Garetson are from her unpublished 125-page manuscript "Katherine of Big Owl," in the Estes Park Library, Estes Park. This endearing account is based on her diaries.

24. Glen and Cleo Tallman, taped interview, January 20, 1984, Estes Park Library, Estes Park.

25. Rose Kingsley, *South by West or Winter in the Rocky Mountains and Spring in Mexico*, ed. Charles Kingsley (London: W. Isbister and Co., 1874), 99.

CHAPTER 5

Sources

Comments about early female botanists came from Nancy G. Slack, "Nineteenth-Century American Women Botanists: Wives, Widows, and Work," in Prim G. Abir-Am and Corinda Outraum, eds., *Uneasy Careers and Intimate Lives: Women in Science, 1789–1979* (New Brunswick: Rutgers University Press, 1987).

In writing the biography of Alice Eastwood, my primary sources were Alice Eastwood's memoirs, located in Special Collections, California Academy of Sciences, San Francisco, and Carol Green Wilson, *Alice Eastwood's Wonderland: The Adventures of a Botanist* (San Francisco: California Academy of Sciences, 1955). However, I also relied on an article in the *Denver Post*, November 25, 1942; Alice Eastwood,

"Penstemon Moffatii," *Zoe: A Biological Journal* 2, no. 3 (October 1891); Joseph Ewan, *Rocky Mountain Naturalists* (Denver: University of Denver Press, 1950); Katharine Bruderlein Crisp, "Obituary of Alice Eastwood," *Green Thumb*, May, 1954; Susanna Bryant Dakin, *A Tribute to Alice Eastwood* (San Francisco: California Academy of Sciences, 1954); a conversation with Henry Evans, April 19, 1987; and William A. Weber, ed., *Theodore D. A. Cockerell Letters from West Cliff, Colorado, 1887–1889* (Boulder: Colorado Associated University Press, 1976).

In writing about Hazel Schmoll, I leaned heavily on her "Autobiography" (1950) and her papers and clippings, all in the Hazel Schmoll Papers in the Western Historical Collections, University of Colorado Libraries, Boulder. In addition, I consulted Jane Cracraft, "At Home in the High Country," *Denver Post*, May 14, 1967; a taped interview of Hazel Schmoll by Rachel Homer, located in the Carnegie Historical Library, Boulder; a taped interview of Hazel Schmoll, located in Norlin Library, University of Colorado, Boulder; a taped interview of Anne Goodnow, November 6, 1986, by the author; and a taped interview of Pieter Hondius, November 17, 1986, by the author.

The following have also been useful: Hazel Schmoll's annual "Greetings from Colorado's Glacier and Indian Peaks Area" (Ward, Colorado), loaned by Anne Goodnow; a conversation with Mary Bows, October 16, 1986; Betty Schmutzler's corrections to a draft of the manuscript, April 8, 1987; Muriel Sibell Wolle, *Stampede to Timberline* (Denver: Sage Books, 1962); and Irene Pettit Mckeehan, *Colorado: Short Studies of Its Past and Present* (N.p., 1927).

My primary source for the biography of Ruth Ashton Nelson was a taped interview of Ruth Nelson by the author, April 24, 1986, aided by Peggy Johnson. Other sources were a taped interview of Tom Blaue by the author, May 20, 1986; a taped interview of Dee Godesiabois by the author, July 11, 1986; Marjorie L. Shepherd, "Ruth Ashton Nelson: The Early Years," *Green Thumb*, Autumn 1978; articles and interviews from the Feral Atkins File in the Archives, Rocky Mountain National Park Headquarters, Estes Park; a taped interview of Ruth Ashton Nelson by Dorothy Huyk, June 28, 1978, from the Collection of Sue Gentle (original in the National Park Service Archives, Harper's Ferry, West Virginia); a taped interview of Alice and Louis Cherbeneau by the author, July 11, 1986; Jane Ramsey, "Ruth Nelson," Roger L. Williams, *Aven Nelson of Wyoming* (Boulder: Colorado Associated University Press, 1984); and a postcard to the author from William A. Weber, December 1986.

I've been able to tell the story of Katherine Bell Hunter only because of Richard Hunter's sympathetic support, which has included helpful additions and corrections to drafts of the manuscript, and because of Emily Dixon Fose's wonderful cooperation, in a taped interview by the author, August 7, 1986. Emily also made corrections to various drafts of the manuscript and showed me around Katherine's sites on Trail Ridge. To Richard and Emily I can only say, again, thank you.

In addition, I relied on a taped interview of Joyce Gellhorn (Greene) by the author, November 26, 1985; a taped interview of Joyce and George Bennett by the author, April 7, 1986; letters from Lawrence C. Bliss, September 24, 1985 and November 18, 1986, and his corrections to

a draft of the manuscript; a taped interview of Dave Stevens by the author, May 2, 1986, and his corrections to a draft of the manuscript; a letter from Bernice Weldon to the author, November 15, 1986; conversations with Jean Weaver, November 10 and 16, 1986; a conversation with Dr. Sam Luce, August 21, 1986; and D. E. Glidden, *Winter Wind Studies in Rocky Mountain National Park* (Estes Park: Rocky Mountain Nature Association, 1982), as well as Glidden, letter to the author, October 18, 1986.

Notes

1. Memoirs of Alice Eastwood, Special Collections, California Academy of Sciences, San Francisco. Unless otherwise noted, the following quotations concerning Alice Eastwood are from this source.

2. William A. Weber, ed., *Theodore D. A. Cockerell Letters From West Cliff, Colorado, 1887–1889*, 179.

3. Alice Eastwood, "The Mariposa Lilies of Colorado," *Zoe: A Biological Journal* 2, no.3 (October 1891): 201–2.

4. Maurine S. Fletcher, ed., *The Wetherills of the Mesa Verde: Autobiography of Benjamin Alfred Wetherill* (Lincoln: University of Nebraska Press, 1987), 202.

5. "The California Academy of Sciences," *Science* 23, no.505 (May 25, 1906): 825.

6. Hazel Schmoll, "Autobiography" (1950), Hazel Schmoll Papers, Western Historical Collections, University of Colorado Libraries, Boulder. Unless otherwise noted, the following quotations concerning Hazel Schmoll are from this source.

7. Hazel Schmoll quoted in Jane Cracraft, "At Home in the High Country."

8. Hazel Schmoll, taped interview with Rachel Homer, August 19, 1977, Carnegie Historical Library, Boulder.

9. Ibid.

10. Hazel Schmoll, "Nature Protection & Conservation Conference" (1923), Hazel Schmoll Papers.

11. Stanley L. Welsh and James A. Erdman, "Annotated Checklist of the Plants of Mesa Verde, Colorado," *Brigham Young University Science Bulletin, Biological Series* 4, no.2 (April 1964).

12. Hazel Schmoll quoted in Cracraft, "At Home."

13. In *Dallas Morning News*, May 3, 1967.

14. Hazel Schmoll, "Greetings From Colorado's Glacier and Indian Peaks Area, 1974–1975."

15. Schmoll, "Greetings, 1967–1968."

16. Mary Bows, conversation with the author, October 16, 1986.

17. Certificate in the possession of Hazel Schmoll.

18. Ruth Ashton Nelson, taped interview with the author, April 24, 1986. Unless otherwise noted, the following quotations concerning Ruth Ashton Nelson are from this source.

19. Letter from Enos Mills to Grace Ashton, August 12 [no year], in Estes Park Historical Museum, Estes Park.

20. Amorita Foster, letter to the author, November 1986. Ruth taught botany classes to Amorita Foster, Peggy Johnson, and Beth Watson, who accompanied her on many of her collecting trips and who became loyal and devoted friends.

21. Tom Blaue, taped interview with the author, May 20, 1986. The following quotations of Tom Blaue are from this source.

22. Beatrice E. Willard, foreword to *Plants of Zion National Park: Wildflowers, Trees, Shrubs and Ferns*, by Ruth Ashton Nelson (Zion National Park: Zion Natural History Association, 1976).

23. Emily Dixon Fose, taped interview with the author, August 7, 1986. The following quotations of Emily Dixon Fose are from this source or from corrections Emily made to drafts of the manuscript.

24. Katherine Bell, note to Emily Dixon, January 22, [1971], Collection of Emily Dixon Fose.

25. Dr. Joyce Gellhorn (Greene), taped interview with the author, November 26, 1985.

26. Katherine L. Bell, "Autecology of *Kobresia bellardii*: Why Winter Snow Accumulation Patterns Affect Local Distributions" (Ph.D. diss., University of Alberta, Edmonton, 1974), Appendix II, 165.

27. Dave Stevens, taped interview with the author, May 2, 1986.

28. Bell, "*Kobresia*," 166.

29. Ibid., 164–66.

30. According to Dave Stevens, Windy Gap actually consists of two gaps separated by a rock outcrop.

31. D. E. Glidden, letter to the author, October 18, 1986; D. E. Glidden, *Winter Wind Studies in Rocky Mountain National Park*, 4.

32. Joyce and George Bennett, taped interview with the author, April 7, 1986.

33. Gellhorn (Greene), taped interview.

34. Ibid.; Dr. Sam Luce, conversation with the author, August 21, 1986.

35. Gellhorn (Greene), taped interview.

36. Richard Hunter, letter to the author, November 2, 1986.

37. Although Emily Dixon Fose recalls these details, Bernice Weldon has no recollection of trying to mop the floor and clean the table. However, in a letter to the author, November 15, 1986, she goes on to say: "Being a rather fussy housekeeper, that seems entirely within reason for me to do."

38. "Katherine had lasting damage to her fingernails and toenails; they were wavy and weak and when under stress they

tended to grow out with holes in them."
(Richard Hunter, additions to draft of
manuscript.)

39. Jean Weaver, conversations with the
author, November 10 and 16, 1986. The
following quotations concerning Katherine
and Jean's April stay at the Rock Cabin are
from this source.

40. Lawrence Bliss, letter to the author,
November 18, 1986. In the 1930s a Dane,
Dr. Sorensen, conducted some nonbotani-
cal research in East Greenland under cold-
stress conditions similar to those that Katherine survived (Lawrence Bliss, letter to
the author, September 24, 1985). According to Richard Hunter's additions to a draft
of the manuscript (October 26, 1986), Katherine and Dr. Sorensen corresponded
briefly.

41. Bell, "*Kobresia*," Appendix II, 167.

42. Gellhorn (Greene), taped interview.

CHAPTER 6

Sources

Elizabeth (Betsy) Strong Cowles Partridge's
published writings were an obvious source
of material for my biography of her, as were
her unpublished journals, scrapbooks, photographs, and correspondence located in
the Archives, American Heritage Center,
University of Wyoming, Laramie. And
thanks to Nora Quinlan and Sonia Jacobs, I
was able to peruse Betsy's large personal library of mountaineering books before it
was sent to the Special Collections Rare
Books Room of Norlin Library at the University of Colorado, Boulder. I also relied
on letters from Betsy's sister, Emilie (Mrs.
Macauley Smith), and from Betsy's husband, General Earle Partridge, as well as
taped interviews by the author with Stanley
W. Boucher, May 1985; Robert Ormes,
May 13, 1985; and Eleanor Davis Ehrman,

May 14, 1985. Other aids were Robert
Ormes, *Farewell to Ormes: A Colorado
Mountain Life in Retrospect* (Colorado
Springs: Robert Ormes, 1984), and Harold
William Tilman, *Nepal Himalaya*
(Cambridge: Cambridge University Press,
1952). To gain some understanding of the
history of female mountaineering in the
United States, I perused all issues of the
*American Alpine Journal, Trail and Tim-
berline*, and *Appalachia*.

Information about Ruth Ewald Gay
came almost entirely from a letter she wrote
the author, April 4, 1987, although a few
details were supplied by Jean Weaver. Paul
Nesbit, "End of the Trail," *Trail and Timberline*, no.446 (October 1957), was the
sole source for the story of Inestine
Roberts, just as Marianne Stevenson Magnuson, "Operation Petticoat," *Ski Magazine*
(March 1947), was the sole source of information about pioneer skiing on the Dinwoody Glacier.

In writing about "midweek women," I
relied on my own experiences; on a taped
interview of Marilyn Ransom by the author, May 13, 1985; and on Jinny Kent's
letters to the author, 1986 and August 12,
1987.

Information about the first all-female
team to climb the Diamond comes from
Bob Godfrey and Dudley Chelton, *Climb!*
(Boulder: Alpine House Publishing, 1977).

Jean Ruwitch Goresline provided most
of the information about herself in a taped
interview by the author, January 14, 1986,
and in corrections to drafts of the manuscript. Other sources were Louise Shepherd, "The Long Way Up," *Outdoors
Backpack* (Australia, ca.1983); a letter from
Louise Shepherd to the author, April 24,
1986; and a conversation between Brad
Johnson and the author, October 1985.

Coral Bowman Wilber provided information about herself in a taped interview by the author, February 11, 1986, and in corrections to a draft of the manuscript.

Most of the information about Gudy Gaskill came from a taped interview by the author, May 11, 1986. I also used Ed Marston, "Gudy Gaskill and Some Friends Build a 480 Mile Trail," *High Country News*, August 4, 1986, and an Associated Press article, "480-Mile-Long Colorado Trail Needs Help on Last 56 Miles," *Boulder Daily Camera*, March 19, 1986.

Notes

1. Frederick H. Chapin, *Mountaineering in Colorado: The Peaks about Estes Park* (Boston: Appalachian Mountain Club, 1889; reprint, Lincoln: University of Nebraska Press, 1987), 43.

2. Eleanor Davis Ehrman, taped interview with the author, May 14, 1985.

3. Francis Keenlyside, *Peaks and Pioneers: The Story of Mountaineering* (London: Paul Elek, 1975), 26; Elizabeth S. Cowles, *Alpine Beginner* (N.p.: Privately printed, ca.1934), Department of Special Collections, University of Colorado Libraries, Boulder. The following quotations concerning Betsy's trip to Europe with her father are from the latter source.

4. Elizabeth Cowles Partridge Scrapbook, Archives, American Heritage Center, University of Wyoming, Laramie.

5. Elizabeth S. Cowles, "Bergschule," *Trail and Timberline*, no.220 (February 1937), 19, 20.

6. Ibid.

7. Emilie Strong Smith (Mrs. Macauley), letter to the author, June 3, 1985.

8. Elizabeth Strong Cowles, caption for photo, "North to Everest," *Vassar Alumnae Magazine* (ca. early 1950s), vol.6, Archives, American Heritage Center; Elizabeth

Strong Cowles, letter to Paul Petzoldt, October 1939, Elizabeth Cowles Partridge Scrapbook.

9. Robert Ormes, taped interview with the author, May 13, 1985.

10. Elizabeth Cowles, "Have You a Mountain Widow in Your Home?" *Sierra Club Bulletin* 34, no.6 (June 1949): 17–21.

11. Elizabeth Cowles, "Round Robin Letter #6" (1950), Archives, American Heritage Center.

12. Dee Molenaar, letter, Folder for the Elizabeth Cowles Partridge Memorial Fund, Colorado Springs Fine Arts Center Library, Colorado Springs.

13. Ehrman, taped interview.

14. Robert Ormes, "End of the Trail, Betsy Partridge," *Trail and Timberline*, no.669 (September 1974), 219.

15. Louise Shepherd, "The Long Way Up." The following quotations concerning the climb made by Jean and Louise are from this source.

16. Louise Shepherd, letter to the author, April 24, 1986.

17. Ibid.; Jean Ruwitch Goresline, taped interview with the author, January 14, 1986. The following quotations concerning Jean Ruwitch Goresline are from this interview.

18. Coral Bowman Wilber, taped interview with the author, February 11, 1986. The following quotations concerning Coral Bowman are from this source.

19. Gudy Gaskill, taped interview with the author, May 11, 1986.

EPILOGUE

Sources

Information about Mary King Sherman came from newspaper articles in the Archives, Rocky Mountain National Park Headquarters, Estes Park; Katherine Garetson's unpublished manuscript, "Katherine of Big Owl," Estes Park Library, Estes Park; and the James Grafton Rogers Collection, Colorado Historical Society, Denver.

The history of the Great Sand Dunes National Monument was derived from newspaper clippings supplied by a Monument park ranger, Brenna Conklin.

These few details about Bettie Willard and Estella Leopold were condensed from lengthy taped interviews of Bettie by the author, January 1, 1986, and March 11, 1986, and from a letter to the author from Estella Leopold, March 28, 1987.

The material about Elizabeth Nitze Paepcke came largely from a taped interview of her by the author, September 16, 1986. In addition, a taped interview of Piet Hondius by the author, November 16, 1986, and taped interviews with Bettie Willard, cited above, supplied more background.

The piece on Muriel MacGregor is a distillation of taped interviews with Orpha Kendall by Jill Boice, Estes Park Library, July 3, 1974; by Lennie Bemiss, Estes Park Library, February 9, 1985; and by the author, April 28, 1986; as well as a taped interview with Ruth McGraw (Mrs. Frank) by the author, November 21, 1986. I also relied on letters, diaries, and newspaper articles in the MacGregor Ranch Archives in Estes Park; Glenn Prosser, *The Saga of Black Canyon* (N.p., 1971); and my own article, "The Saga of MacGregor Ranch," *High Country News*, May 14, 1984.

It was easy to write about Forrest Ketchin, for we have served on the Indian Peaks Working Group Board together, and she supplemented details in a taped interview by the author, July 17, 1986.

In writing about Martha Maxwell, I drew heavily on Mary Dartt, *On the Plains and among the Peaks; or, How Mrs. Maxwell Made Her Natural History Collection* (Philadelphia: Claxton, Remsen and Haffelfinger, 1879 [1878]); Mabel Maxwell Brace, *Thanks to Abigail: A Family Chronicle* (N.p.: Privately printed, 1948); and Maxine Benson, *Martha Maxwell: Rocky Mountain Naturalist* (Lincoln: University of Nebraska Press, 1986).

Information about Helen Henderson Chain came primarily from articles that appeared in the *Rocky Mountain Herald*, the *Denver Daily Times*, the *Denver Daily Tribune*, the *Colorado Transcript* (Golden), the *Denver Republican*, the *Rocky Mountain News*, and the *Colorado Antelope*, between 1876 and 1892. Also extremely helpful was Carla Swan Coleman, "A Brief Biography of Helen Henderson Chain (One of the Giants of Fortnightly)," April 5, 1966, in the Department of Western History, Denver Public Library; the Record of Members, in the Central Presbyterian Church of Denver; and a memorandum by Mrs. Mary H. Bancroft (Helen Chain's niece), November 25, 1922, as well as a letter by Ida Lundbeck (Helen Chain's niece), November 6, 1967, both of which are in the Colorado Historical Society.

Information about Anne Ellis came primarily from her own books, all of which have been reprinted as Bison Books by the University of Nebraska Press: *The Life of an Ordinary Woman* (1980), *Plain Anne Ellis* (1984), and *Sunshine Preferred* (1984). I am especially grateful to Anne Matlack, whom I interviewed several times and who wrote "The Spirit of Anne Ellis," *Colorado Quarterly* (Summer 1955). I am also indebted to Dorothy (Mrs. J.D.A.) Ogilvy, whom I interviewed on March 17, 1986, and to

Agnes Norlin for her letter to me of February 13, 1987. Finally, I drew on only a few of the many treasures in the Anne Ellis Papers, Department of Special Collections, University of Colorado Libraries, Boulder.

Writing about Muriel Sibell Wolle was made easier by the hundreds of clippings, letters, scrapbooks, and photographs housed in the Western Historical Collections, University of Colorado Libraries, Boulder. In addition, I taped interviews with Dorothy Lewis (June 20, 1985) and Victoria Barker (April 30, 1985), who knew Muriel well. And I was fortunate to have had Mrs. Wolle as a professor at the University of Colorado in 1956.

Had it not been for Alex and Marie Warner, I might not have heard about Helen Rich and Belle Turnbull. Information about the women came from the Belle Turnbull Papers and the Helen Rich Papers in the Department of Western History, Denver Public Library. Also useful was Elizabeth M. Safanda and Molly L. Mead, "The Ladies of French Street in Breckenridge," *Colorado Magazine*, Winter–Spring 1979.

Information about Alice and Helen Dickerson came mostly from a taped interview with the delightful sisters, May 19, 1986, and from clippings and a transcript of a taped interview in the Fort Collins Public Library.

All the information about Olga Schaaf Little came from copies of newspaper articles sent to me by the Durango Public Library. The Fort Collins Public Library provided clippings about Vena Apgar Snyder. The USDA Forest Service Regional Headquarters in Denver provided clippings on Helen Dowe. And, finally, I was able to find out about Augusta Mengedoht thanks to the Carnegie Historical Library, Boulder,

which houses the papers of the Allenspark Historical Society.

Information about American women of the 1800s and the early 1900s came from Elaine Kendall, *Peculiar Institutions: An Informal History of the Seven Sisters Colleges* (New York: G. P. Putnam's Sons, 1976); Barbara Miller Solomon, *In the Company of Educated Women: A History of Women and Higher Education in America* (New Haven: Yale University Press, 1985); Valborg Fletty, *Public Service of Women's Organizations* (Menasha, Wis.: George Banta Publishing Co., 1951); Florence Howe, *Myths of Coeducation: Selected Essays, 1964–1983* (Bloomington: Indiana University Press, 1984); Mabel Collins Donnelly, *The American Victorian Woman: The Myth and the Reality* (Westport, Conn.: Greenwood Press, 1986); and Patricia Sexton, *Women in Education* (Bloomington, Ind.: Phi Delta Kappa Educational Foundation, 1976).

Dorothy Middleton, *Victorian Lady Travellers* (New York: E. P. Dutton and Co., 1965), describes American and English women of the late 1800s and early 1900s.

Notes

1. Elizabeth Nitze Paepcke, taped interview with the author, September 16, 1986.

2. Anne Matlack, "The Spirit of Anne Ellis," 62.

3. Anne Ellis, *Sunshine Preferred* (Boston: Houghton, Mifflin, 1934; reprint, Lincoln: University of Nebraska Press, 1984), 54.

4. Belle Turnbull, "Mountain-Mad," in *Voices: A Journal of Verse* (ca. 1922) and *Denver Post*, April 3, [1922?], from Scrapbook, Belle Turnbull Papers, Department of Western History, Denver Public Library.

5. *Colorado Springs Gazette Telegraph*, June 27, 1947.

Index